Economic Growth and Environmental Policy

NEW HORIZONS IN ENVIRONMENTAL ECONOMICS

General Editors: Wallace E. Oates, *Professor of Economics, University of Maryland, USA* and Henk Folmer, *Professor of General Economics, Wageningen University and Professor of Environmental Economics, Tilburg University, The Netherlands*

This important series is designed to make a significant contribution to the development of the principles and practices of environmental economics. It includes both theoretical and empirical work. International in scope, it addresses issues of current and future concern in both East and West and in developed and developing countries.

The main purpose of the series is to create a forum for the publication of high quality work and to show how economic analysis can make a contribution to understanding and resolving the environmental problems confronting the world in the twenty-first century.

Recent titles in the series include:

Economic Growth and Environmental Policy
A Theoretical Approach
Frank Hettich

The Political Economy of Environmental Protectionism
Achim Körber

Principles of Environmental and Resource Economics
A Guide for Students and Decision-Makers
Second Edition
Edited by Henk Folmer and H. Landis. Gabel

Designing International Environmental Agreements
Incentive Compatible Strategies for Cost-Effective Cooperation
Carsten Schmidt

Spatial Environmental and Resource Economics
The Selected Essays of Charles D. Kolstad
Charles D. Kolstad

Economic Theories of International Environmental Cooperation
Carsten Helm

Negotiating Environmental Quality
Policy Implementation in Germany and the United States
Markus A. Lehmann

Game Theory and International Environmental Cooperation
Michael Finus

Sustainable Small-Scale Forestry
Socio-Economic Analysis and Policy
Edited by S.R. Harrison, J.L. Herbohn and K.F. Herbohn

Environmental Economics and Public Policy
Selected Papers of Robert N. Stavins
Robert N. Stavins

International Environmental Externalities and the Double Dividend
Sebastian Killinger

Economic Growth and Environmental Policy

A Theoretical Approach

Frank Hettich

Lecturer and Research Fellow, Department of Economics, Ernst-Moritz-Arndt University of Greifswald, Germany

New Horizons in Environmental Economics

Edward Elgar

Cheltenham, UK • Northampton, MA, USA

Published by
Edward Elgar Publishing Limited
Glensanda House
Montpellier Parade
Cheltenham
Glos GL50 1UA
UK

Edward Elgar Publishing, Inc.
136 West Street
Suite 202
Northampton
Massachusetts 01060
USA

A catalogue record for this book
is available from the British Library

Library of Congress Cataloguing in Publication Data

Hettich, Frank, 1966–
   Economic growth and environmental policy : a theoretical approach /
Frank Hettich.
   — (New horizons in environmental economics)
   1. Economic development—Environmental aspects. 2. Environmental
policy. I. Title. II. Series.

HD75.6 .H48 2000
363.7—dc21

99–087153

ISBN 1 84064 369 2

Printed in the United Kingdom at the University Press, Cambridge

Contents

List of Figures

List of Tables

List of Symbols and Abbreviations

Greek Letters

α	share of physical capital in final good production
β	share of physical capital in human capital accumulation
δ_H, δ_K	depreciation rate of human and physical capital
ε	intertemporal elasticity of substitution of consumption
η_F	influence of foreign pollution in utility
η_l	weight of leisure in utility
η_P	weight of (total) pollution in utility
λ	costate variable: shadow price of physical capital
μ	costate variable: shadow price of human capital
π	profit
ρ	rate of time preference
τ_C	consumption tax rate
τ_H	labor income tax rate
τ_K	capital income tax rate
$\tau_P, \bar{\tau}_P$	pollution tax rate, normalized pollution tax rate
χ	elasticity of P with respect to the arguments of P
ς	weight of human capital externality
ω	degree of homogeneity
$\mathcal{H}$	Hamiltonian

Latin Letters

A	level of the technology in production
B	level of the technology in the education sector
C	consumption
D	stock of pollution
F	foreign assets
g	economy's growth rate in the long term
$G\,(\bar{G})$	government revenue (public good)
$H\,(H_0)$	(initial) stock of human capital
$I_H\,(I_K)$	investment in human (physical) capital
$K\,(K_0)$	(initial) stock of physical capital
$l\,(L)$	leisure (home production)
N	absorption capacity of the environment
P	pollution
$r\,(R)$	interest rate (real marginal product of capital)
r_F	foreign capital interest rate
s	fraction of time devoted to education
t	time index
T	lump-sum transfer
u	fraction of time devoted to production
U	level of utility
v	share of physical capital devoted to production
w	wage rate
x, X	used as wildcards
Y	output
Z	abatement activities

Math Symbols

X_X	partial derivative of X with respect to x $(\partial X/\partial x)$
$\dot{X}$	partial derivative of X with respect to time $(\partial X/\partial t)$
$\hat{X}$	growth rate of X $(\dot{X}/X)$
$*$	indicates the foreign country

Superscripts

x^c	indicates the cooperative solution of x
x^{cps}	indicates the central planner solution of x
x^{nc}	indicates the noncooperative solution of x
x^{opt}	indicates the optimal solution of x
x^{priv}	indicates that x is a private good
x^{pub}	indicates that x is a public good

Preface

This book has mainly been written while I was a member of the long-term research program 'Internationalization of the Economy' (Sonderforschungsbereich 178) at the University of Konstanz. Many contacts with both members and non-members of the research program have contributed to the shape of the present study. I further benefited from a research stay at the Economic Policy Research Unit (EPRU) at the Copenhagen Business School.

I owe sincere thanks to my academic teacher, Bernd Genser, who constantly supported this work with both general advice and detailed comments and who created within his research unit a stimulating and cooperative environment. Lucas Bretschger made a large number of valuable suggestions and shared his expertise on the theory of economic growth with me. I am further grateful to Andreas Haufler for detailed comments and his good advice. I am also indebted to Hans-Jürgen Vosgerau for his successful efforts in creating favorable working conditions in the Sonderforschungsbereich 178.

I have further benefited from helpful discussions and suggestions received from Wolfgang Eggert, Hans Peter Grüner, Christoph John, Sebastian Killinger, Karl-Josef Koch, Søren Bo Nielsen, Jürgen Meckl, Carsten Schmidt, Sjak Smulders, Margarita Steinhart, Peter Birch Sørenson and Minna Selene Svane. The numerical simulation has been made possible by Carlo Perroni, who provided me a first orientation in the field of simulating the transitional dynamics in growth models. I especially thank Engelbert Plassmann for carefully reading and correcting the manuscript. Last but not least, I thank my parents for their invaluable support.

Chapter 1

Introduction

1.1 Motivation

Almost all human activities directly or indirectly affect the ecological system of the earth; this is even true for activities which are necessary to satisfy basic needs. Obviously, the effects on the environment become larger and more significant the more extensive is the activity of every single person, and the larger is the population. Both the population size and the per capita activity are reflected by the growth rate of an economy.

In a market economy, prices must express the scarcity of resources to guarantee an efficient allocation. However, some goods do not have a price although their availability is not unlimited in amount. This is the case for many environmental resources and can be explained by market failures caused by externalities. The non-existence of a price reflecting the scarcity of the environmental resource leads to its excessive use. The resulting environmental degradation possesses many facets and creates problems on local, regional and global levels. For instance, metropolitan areas like Mexico City or Athens may suffer from local environmental problems such as smog, aerosol particles, ground-level ozone and nitrogen oxides. Regional environmental problems include acid rain (caused by sulphur oxide emissions and responsible for '*Waldsterben*'), hazardous toxic or nuclear waste, and pollution of rivers and lakes. But in particular

1

international environmental problems such as global warming are gaining growing attention because of their foreseeable or feared irreversibility.[1] It is expected that the anthropogenic greenhouse effect will have severe effects on agriculture, coastal areas, biodiversity, ecological systems and so on. The public in western European countries is aware of these problems. According to an opinion poll, more than 57 per cent of the European Community's population is 'very concerned' about national and international environmental problems (see OECD 1993, p. 289). Without doubt the present pace of environmental degradation jeopardizes the welfare of current and future generations.[2]

The phenomenon of negative environmental externalities is not new, and nor is the classical proposition to their internalization by means of Pigouvian taxes. However, the application of this approach is complicated because of uncertainty about the extent and the effects of environmental pollution. Furthermore, there is uncertainty about the benefits and the costs of internalization. This is true not only empirically but also theoretically. The bulk of literature on environmental economics uses static models. This simplification may be justified for some problems. However, the dynamic dimension is central for many environmental problems: since pollutants accumulate over time, and many natural resources are exhaustible or become exhaustible through overuse, environmental policy measures inevitably affect several generations. Furthermore, economic growth and environmental quality affect each other mutually. On the one hand, economic growth may increase pollution and exacerbate environmental degradation. However, this trade-off is not necessarily trivial, as emissions per output may change due to structural changes, new resource-saving technologies, and innovation in abatement technologies. On the other hand, the environmental quality may affect the productivity of production processes and hence economic growth. This study addresses these issues by using a dynamic framework, and attempts to shed light on the following questions:

---

[1] Humankind's concern with the quality of the environment is not new. For an overview of the roots of environmentalism in the western world, see Grove (1992). For a recent survey of global environmental problems, see Sandler (1997).

[2] For the costs of environmental pollution see, for instance, Pearce and Warford (1993, Ch. 1).

- What kind of policy can reverse tendencies towards increasing pollution?
- Will a tighter environmental policy or a revenue-neutral environmental tax reform, though increasing welfare, inevitably reduce economic growth?
- Does environmental taxation provide an efficient and permanent source of revenue for government expenditure?
- Does a sustainable development necessarily preclude economic growth? Or equivalently: is environmental degradation a necessary part of the economic process of industrialization?
- How will higher preferences for a clean environment affect optimal growth rates?
- What are the effects of environmental care in the short and medium term, that is, off the balanced growth paths?
- What are the effects of international cooperation on growth, welfare and pollution?
- What are the possibilities for a small open economy to pursue an independent environmental policy?

A natural dynamic framework for answering these questions is provided by modern growth theory. Inspired by the seminal papers of Romer (1986) and Lucas (1988), growth theory is again one of the main interests of economic studies. Apart from the countless papers in journals this is expressed in the monographs of Grossman and Helpman (1991), Barro and Sala-i-Martin (1995) and Aghion and Howitt (1998). The past few years have witnessed a rapid expansion of literature using *endogenous growth models* to explore the growth implications of tax policies. This literature shows that distortions caused by taxes may affect long-term economic growth. If this is true, taxes exert a significant effect on welfare. In this study we focus on the dynamic effects of environmental policy by incorporating pollution and abatement technologies into different endogenous growth models, which take into account consumer preferences, and physical and human capital accumulation. Although our focus is on environmental policy, we also analyse the dynamic effects of non-environmental taxes and show how they can internalize an externality if a pollution tax is not available. Neoclassical growth theory is not appropriate for analysing the above-mentioned questions since it assumes rather than explains long-term economic growth. Furthermore, as Romer (1989, p. 51) states 'it never really mattered what the government did'. By contrast, in endogenous growth models the long-term growth rate is determined by preferences, technologies and fiscal policy.

This study provides a comprehensive analysis of the effects of environmental policy in growth models driven by human capital accumulation. The structure of this study reflects the increasing complexity of the chosen and developed modeling frameworks. For all models to be analysed we derive both the market-driven price path and the socially efficient price path. The positive analysis of this study examines the long-term growth effects of taxes on consumption, pollution, capital income and labor income, their channels, and their influence on relevant macro variables. The normative analysis addresses the question of an optimal taxation scheme to internalize environmental externalities and to provide an efficient level of public abatement activities. The study contributes to the literature both by combining several existing models in a coherent analytical framework and by developing new models. It focuses on the effects of environmental policy in closed and open economies in the short, medium and long terms. In particular, the analyses of open economies and transitional dynamics augment the literature since both issues have been largely neglected in the theory on endogenous growth and environment.

The rationale for investigating open economies is evident as many environmental problems, for instance, acidification or pollution of rivers and lakes, are international rather than national in nature or even possess a global character, for example, the anthropogenic greenhouse effect. Of course we can interpret the whole world as a single closed economy, and analyse the effects of global environmental policy on growth and welfare. However, national governments are presently not willing to install a supranational authority vested with the required competencies to internalize global externalities. Therefore we adopt the framework of a world which consists of two open economies, and analyse the effects of international cooperation in the presence of international externalities. Furthermore, even in the case of a purely national externality, the possibilities of a small open country pursuing an efficient environmental policy may be restricted due to international factor mobility. This study addresses both issues by analysing the strategic interactions between two countries in the presence of international environmental externalities and knowledge spillovers, and by investigating the possibilities for a small open economy with internationally mobile capital to conduct an independent environmental policy.

There are two important and interesting reasons for studying the short and medium term and hence the transitional dynamics of environmental policy. Knowledge of the transition path is necessary to find out the overall losses or gains of utility associated with some policy measure. For instance, a policy measure could be beneficial in the long run but very harmful in the short and medium terms, so that the present value of future welfare is inferior to the 'business-as-usual' scenario. Furthermore, knowledge of the transitional dynamics is necessary to compare unexpected, announced or gradual policy measures. Therefore the adaptation process of the economy in every single period should be known for a founded policy recommendation. To find out how the new balanced growth path is reached in the long run, we simulate numerically the short- and medium-term economic performances along the transition path after a change in environmental policy. For this purpose we calibrate the model so as to capture stylized empirical facts of industrialized countries. The realistic calibration also allows us to quantify the qualitative growth effect in the long run.

In the last few years an academic debate has emerged on the desirability of environmental taxes; this has also attracted attention in the political debate. The study contributes to this topical discussion by studying the effects of an environmental tax reform on pollution and growth. We shall show that there might exist a *double growth dividend* to be reaped by an environmental tax reform.

1.2   Structure of the Study

Chapter 2 serves two purposes. On the one hand it provides a general survey of the existing literature on environmental policy in growing economies. On the other hand it sketches the limits of this study. For that purpose a formal general framework is outlined which is sufficiently flexible to capture all models to be analysed. We start by showing how environmental issues can be incorporated into growth models and how environmental quality may affect preferences and production technologies. After that we briefly review the literature on environmental policy in models of exogenous growth. We then introduce endogenous growth models and develop a general framework for this study. Finally, we present important reasons for studying the adaptation process and review the literature on transitional dynamics in human capital growth models.

Chapter 3 starts with an analysis of environmental policy in the simplest endogenous growth model. This model is also known as the linear growth model, as the production function is linear in the only input factor which is capital. In this base model we first analyse the effects of fiscal policy, ignoring the natural environment. We derive both the market solution and the central planner solution and determine the optimal tax rates. This procedure will be used in all models to be analysed later. We then incorporate the environment and allow for environmental pollution. Pollution is introduced as a side product of economic activity which affects individuals' utility. In the third part we allow in addition for either private or public abatement activities. Again, pollution is a side product of economic activity but can be reduced by spending part of the output on abatement activities. Finally, we depart from the closed economy setup and analyse the strategic interactions between two identical countries in the presence of international environmental externalities and knowledge spillovers.

In Chapter 4, the production technology of Chapter 3 is modeled in more detail. Again we consider an economy with pollution and abatement activities, but in addition introduce an education sector. By using physical and human capitals the first sector produces a perfectly malleable good which can be used for consumption, abatement activities and investment in the physical capital stock. The second sector is an education sector where human capital is accumulated by using time and existing human capital. With this two-sector model – known as the

Uzawa–Lucas model – we overcome an unrealistic shortcoming of the linear model, namely the absence of transitional dynamics. In the first part we analyse the effects of environmental policy in a closed economy along a balanced growth path and derive the optimal tax structure. In the second part we focus on the transitional dynamics triggered by a change in environmental policy. To find out how the new balanced growth path is reached in the long run, we simulate numerically the adaptation process for the realistically calibrated model version in the short and medium terms. We simulate both the optimal adaptation path caused by higher preferences for a clean environment and the transitional dynamics of a decentralized economy after a change in the pollution tax rate. Furthermore we compare the effects of unexpected, announced and gradual policy changes. In the last part we restrict the analysis again to the balanced growth path but open up the economy by allowing international environmental externalities and knowledge spillovers. As in the last part of Chapter 3, we also analyse the strategic interactions between two countries.

Chapter 5 extends the closed two-sector economy version of Chapter 4 by introducing elastic labor supply, but leaves the production technologies unchanged. Thus, households not only decide how much time to devote to working and studying but also decide on the hours spent on leisure. We shall see that this modification changes the results substantially. We derive both the market and the central planner solutions, and calculate the optimal pollution tax rate. We determine the consequences of isolated tax-rate changes and of a revenue-neutral environmental tax reform for economic growth. This is done for two alternative pollution specifications: pollution is modeled either as a side product of physical capital used as a production factor in the final good sector, or as a side product of final good production.

Chapter 6 again extends the closed economy version of Chapter 4. While leisure was incorporated in Chapter 5, Chapter 6 now generalizes the education sector. In contrast to Chapter 4, human capital and physical capital are now used as input factors both in the final good sector and in the education sector. Requiring additional physical capital as an input in the education sector reflects the fact that human capital accumulation requires not only knowledge but also books, computers, school buildings and so on. Again we investigate two sources of pollution, either pollution generated directly by final good production or pollution generated indirectly by using physical capital in final good production. We analyse both a closed economy and a small open economy. The investigation of the small open economy starts out from conventional assumptions of international trade models, thereby simplifying the analysis by an exogenously given world interest rate, but broadening the analysis by assuming perfect international capital mobility.

Chapter 7 summarizes the results of the study. For that purpose we briefly review the models investigated by this study. While the study is structured mainly according to the increasing complexity of modeling the production technologies, the concluding remarks address policy issues by subject: the application of optimal tax instruments; the growth effects of isolated tax changes; the growth effects of a revenue-neutral environmental tax reform; the small open economy; the effects of cooperation in the presence of international spillovers; and the transitional dynamics. In an outlook we then deduce and describe possible routes for further research. Finally we try to answer the questions raised in the introduction and derive policy recommendations.

Chapter 2

Survey of Literature and General Model Setup

The purpose of this chapter is twofold: on the one hand it reviews the state of the literature on environmental economics and growth theory; on the other hand it restricts the scope of this study. For the latter purpose we outline a formal general framework which is sufficiently flexible to capture all analysed models. The general setup allows us to classify the study from a formal point of view. This chapter is structured as follows. In Section 2.1 it is shown how environmental issues can be formally incorporated into growth models and how environmental quality may affect preferences and production processes. Section 2.2 surveys the literature of environmental issues in neoclassical growth models. Section 2.3 first introduces endogenous growth models and shows the importance of human capital (Section 2.3.1). Second, the general model of the study is laid out and explained (Section 2.3.2). Finally, Section 2.4 deals with the short- and medium-term effects of transitional dynamics and illustrates their importance.

2.1   Modeling the Environment

In principle there are two ways whereby the environment can be taken into consideration in theoretic growth models: we can focus either on environmental damage and pollution, or on environmental quality and resource extraction. In the former class of models, environmental pollution is regarded as a side product of the production process. Alternatively, in the second class of models pollution arises from the use of the environment in the production process. Thus, pollution is generated due to the rival use of the natural resource. Hence pollution can be modeled either as an 'output' or as an 'input'.[1] Siebert et al. (1980) show that both modeling approaches are equivalent. In the following we model pollution as an output.

Like Forster (1973), Gradus and Smulders (1993) and Huang and Cai (1994) we distinguish between the pollution-generating activity and abatement activities. Following these contributions, pollution is modeled by a function

$$P = P(K, Z), \quad \text{where } P_K > 0 \text{ and } P_Z < 0. \tag{2.1}$$

The symbols denote pollution (P), the physical capital stock (K) and the abatement activities (Z), where P_K and P_Z represent the partial derivatives of the pollution function with respect to physical capital and abatement, respectively. According to equation (2.1) pollution is an increasing function of the physical capital stock, to capture the polluting consequences of economic activity, but a decreasing function of abatement activities. Thus, given a certain stock of physical capital, pollution can be reduced by raising the level of abatement activities.

Abatement activities can either be rival, excludable and hence a private good, or possess the characteristics of a public good. In the case of private abatement activities (see Smulders and Gradus 1996 or Bovenberg and de Mooij 1997) one can think of some end-of-pipe technology, for example filters to reduce emissions, installed by firms. However, pri-

---

[1] For contributions where pollution is modeled as an output factor, see, for example, van der Ploeg and Withagen (1991), Gradus and Smulders (1993) and Ligthart and van der Ploeg (1994). For pollution as an input factor see, for example, Nielsen et al. (1995) and Bovenberg and de Moiij (1997).

vate abatement activities do not have to be end-of-pipe technologies; also firms may have specific pollution-saving technologies. Thus, private abatement measures enable firms to increase output without causing more pollution. Public abatement activities on the other hand can be interpreted as non-rival knowledge about clean production methods. Since it is irrational from an individual perspective for single economic agents to purchase a non-rival good but to rely on free-riding, the government may be called upon to overcome the inefficiently low level of abatement measures (see Ligthart and van der Ploeg 1994 or Nielsen et al. 1995).[2]

Furthermore, abatement activities can be modeled as a flow or as a stock variable. For the latter, see Musu (1990) and van Ewijk and van Wijnbergen (1995). For instance, catalytic converters in cars usually lose their cleaning capacity over time, hence they have to be replaced periodically to guarantee proper operation. Therefore, abatement through catalysts should rather be modeled as a flow variable. On the other hand certain abatement activities can be seen as specific knowledge capital which accumulates over time and hence should be modeled as a stock variable. However, along a balanced growth path this distinction does not change the qualitative results as long as a growing economy requires a growing abatement stock: depending on the modeling, by definition the flow or stock variable grows at a constant rate along a balanced growth path. In addition, investment in the stock grows at the same rate as the stock. Thus, the flow can be interpreted either as investment in the stock or as the stock itself.

For simplicity, in most models abatement activities are produced according to the same technology as physical capital and private consumption. Thus abatement activities Z are a fraction of the homogeneous output Y which can be used without any frictions for consumption C, or net investment in the physical capital stock I_K.[3] Consequently the flow resource constraint of the economy is given by $Y = C + I_K + Z$.

In equation (2.1) pollution is generated by using the physical capital

---

[2] In Huang and Cai (1994) pollution can be reduced both by private and public abatement measures.

[3] An exception is Bovenberg and Smulders (1996), where abatement measures are produced in a separate sector.

stock. Alternatively, output Y could be responsible for pollution.[4] In principle there is a third possibility: pollution could be a negative function of the use of labor (human capital) in production. However, this specification seems less reasonable and we ignore it in the following.

Just as in the case of abatement, pollution can be modeled either as a flow P or as a stock D.[5] Examples are the level of noise or the stock of greenhouse gases in the atmosphere. In the case of stock externalities we can distinguish additionally between exhaustible resources and renewable resources. In contrast to exhaustible resources (see Dasgupta and Heal 1979 for an extensive discussion) a renewable resource permits a constant level of pollution without spoiling the natural resource as long as the pollution level does not exceed the natural regeneration:[6]

$$\dot{D} = P\left(K, Z\right) - N\left(D\right), \quad \text{where } N_D < 0. \tag{2.2}$$

The pollution flow P increases the pollution stock D, whereas the natural regeneration (that is, the absorption capacity of the environment) N decreases the stock of pollution.[7] The absorption capacity of the natural environment could be assumed to be constant. However, it is more realistic to assume that it is decreasing in the stock of pollution. Thus, the more polluted the environment is, the lower is its regeneration capacity. Obviously, a constant level of pollution is in accordance with sustainable development as long as $N \geq P$. In this study, sustainable development is defined in a narrow sense as a path with a non-declining environmental quality.[8] Hence, the natural regeneration is decisive for

---

[4]For instance, van der Ploeg and Withagen (1991), van Marrewijk et al. (1993) and Ligthart and van der Ploeg (1994) assume that pollution is a function of output and abatement activities.

[5]For pollution as a flow, see for example, Forster (1973), Gruver (1976), Gradus and Smulders (1993), Ligthart and van der Ploeg (1994) and Nielsen et al. (1995). For pollution as a stock, see for example, Keeler et al. (1971), van der Ploeg and Withagen (1991), and Bovenberg and Smulders (1995).

[6]See Smulders (1995) for an equivalent function.

[7]$\dot{D}$ represents the change of the pollution stock over time.

[8]The term sustainable development quite often is not solely restricted to environmental quality but used in a broader sense, including also material issues and intragenerational and intergenerational distributional issues. For instance, the Brundtland report defines sustainable development as 'development that meets the needs of the present without compromising the ability of future generations to meet their own

the determination of the sustainable level of pollution (see Hartwick and Olewiler 1986). Using this definition we must distinguish between the requirement to conserve every single natural resource and the requirement to conserve the ecosystem as a whole. Obviously, the latter is composed of renewable and exhaustible resources. In our view it is plausible to assume the ecosystem as a whole to be a renewable resource. We therefore allow for substitution between exhaustible and other exhaustible or renewable resources and do not require a constant stock of every single resource. Hence the exhaustion of certain natural capital stocks must not be in contrast to a sustainable development.[9]

Just as in the case of abatement, it can be stated that if the accumulated pollution stock rather than the pollution flow determines environmental quality, conclusions in our models do not change qualitatively along a balanced growth path. This is shown formally by Smulders and Gradus (1996).

According to a World Bank (1992, p. 44) study the economy is affected by the environment through amenity, productivity and health channels. These channels are decisive for the consequences of environmental policy on growth welfare and other core variables. First, the amenity effect can be modeled as

$$U = U(C, P, ...), \quad \text{where } U_C > 0, U_P < 0. \tag{2.3}$$

Among other arguments, individuals' utility U is a positive function of consumption C but a negative function of pollution P. Examples of such pollutions are acidification, the earthly ozone concentration, the contamination of drinking water and so on.

Second, the environment can have a productive value. This is supported by the results of applied computable general equilibrium models for industrialized countries, see for instance Ballard and Medema (1993) and Brendemoen and Vennemo (1994). The environmental quality can

---

needs' (WCED 1987, p. 43). See Pezzey (1989) and Bretschger (1998b), who express the content of this definition in economic terms and Smulders (1995) for a survey on environmental sustainabiltiy in endogenous growth models.

[9] For a further discussion about this and alternative sustainabiltiy concepts, see Bretschger and Egli (2000).

affect the production process either directly:

$$Y = Y(P,...), \quad \text{where } Y_P < 0, \tag{2.4}$$

or indirectly via the inputs physical capital K and human capital H:

$$Y = Y[K(P), H(P)], \quad \text{where } Y_K, Y_H > 0 \text{ and } K_P, H_P < 0. \tag{2.5}$$

Equation (2.4) states that a rise in pollution lowers output, *ceteris paribus*. For instance, the agricultural output declines, if the quality of the soil deteriorates. Pollution may also reduce the productivity of the labor force: according to an empirical study by Margulis (1992), ozone concentration beyond certain levels hampers a person's ability to concentrate on any given activity for more than very short periods. In equation (2.5) this is taken into consideration by the term $H(P)$. A higher stock of human capital – equivalent to skilled labor – increases output. However, for instance due to concentration difficulties as a result of pollution, human capital can be modeled as a declining function of pollution. Furthermore, physical capital may be affected by pollution as well. For instance, some human activities are responsible for natural disasters which destroy physical capital. In equation (2.5) this is reflected by the term $K(P)$.

Third, environmental quality may affect the learning ability and hence the human capital accumulation:[10]

$$\dot{H} = h(P,...), \quad \text{where } h_P < 0. \tag{2.6}$$

Again, the empirical study by Margulis (1992) supports this negative relationship. He finds evidence that increased levels of lead in children's blood reduce their intellectual development. He claims that Mexico City's automotive pollution has lowered the IQ of 18-year-old Mexicans in the city on average about 4 points. Furthermore, Mexico City's air pollution causes economic losses due to increased respiratory diseases and increased mortality. Equation (2.6) shows how these relationships could be incorporated into the model. Just as in equation (2.5) there may be indirect effects on human capital accumulation.

---

[10] $\dot{H}$ denotes the change of the human capital stock over time.

Fourth, damages from acid rain on buildings show that pollution may also affect the depreciation rates of the physical capital stock $\delta_K(P)$. The same might apply to the depreciation rate of the human capital stock $\delta_H(P)$. Finally, the environment could be modeled as a life-support system, as in Smulders and Gradus (1996). The authors assume that no life and hence no production and consumption is possible if the environmental quality is below a given critical level.

We have seen that there are many possibilities whereby the environment can be incorporated into theoretic growth models. We conclude this section by selecting the appropriate pollution modeling for our study. The target thereby is on the one hand to capture all important economy-ecology relations, but on the other hand to keep the analyses tractable. We have seen that there are in principle two ways of incorporating the environment into growth models. Pollution can be modeled either as an input or as an output of the production process. Since both approaches are equivalent we specify pollution as an output. It is realistic to assume that pollution affects individuals' utility negatively, see equation (2.3). However, while positive productivity effects of a better environmental quality as described in equations (2.4)–(2.6) are certainly conceivable in specific sectors like agriculture or tourism, it is questionable whether they have a considerable effect on an aggregate production for the whole economy. For that reason and in order to keep the analysis tractable, we shall restrict the formal part of the study solely to the amenity effects of the environment. However, we shall show that it is possible to discuss the existence of positive productivity effects of a better environmental quality without a formal analysis. As we use highly aggregated models in this study, only the production of output, or the use of physical capital or labor (human capital) in production can be the pollution-generating activity. Since labor as the pollution-generating factor seems to be less reasonable, we investigate the remaining two plausible sources of pollution, namely pollution generated by final good production and pollution generated by using physical capital in final good production. We assume abatement activities to be both private and public in nature and to be produced with the same technology as physical capital and consumption. Finally for simplicity, we do not model abatement measures and pollution as stocks. However, as mentioned above, this simplification does not change the qualitative results along a balanced growth path.

2.2 Environmental Policy in Models of Exogenous Growth

The role of natural resources and pollution did not receive much attention in growth theory until the early 1970s. However, partially due to the worldwide recession caused by oil price shocks in the 1970s and as a reaction to the pessimistic report of the Club of Rome on 'The limits to growth' (see Meadows et al. 1972) a large number of publications appeared. One strand of literature dealt with exhaustible resources in neoclassical growth models and investigated conditions under which growth was possible.[11] Another strand worked on renewable resources and abatement measures in the neoclassical theory.[12] Most of these papers assumed a central planner economy while the market-driven path was neglected. Therefore, the issues of externalities and optimal measures for their internalization were generally not taken into account.

In neoclassical growth models, the long-term per capita growth rate is determined solely by the exogenous labor-augmenting (Harrod-neutral) technical progress.[13] Only the exogenous technical progress can avoid decreasing returns to the accumulated capital and hence prevent a stationary economy. In general, preferences, technology, or fiscal policy measures may determine levels of macro variables and social welfare but not the long-term growth rate of the economy. Obviously this applies for environmental policy as well. That is the reason why growth is called exogenous in neoclassical growth models.[14]

---

[11]See, for example, Arrow and Kurz (1970), Anderson (1972), Solow (1974), Stiglitz (1974), Dasgupta and Heal (1974, 1979), Solow and Wan (1976), Dasgupta and Stiglitz (1981) and Krautkrämer (1985).

[12]See for instance d'Arge (1971), Keeler et al. (1971), Forster (1973), Gruver (1976), van der Ploeg and Withagen (1991) and Tahvonen and Kuuluvainen (1991, 1993).

[13]That applies for neoclassical growth models both with an exogenous saving rate based on Solow (1956) and Swan (1956), and with an endogenous saving rate based on Cass (1965) and Koopmans (1965).

[14]For a history of growth theory, see Krelle (1985, Ch. 2) or Barro and Sala-i-

In the theory of neoclassical growth, the labor-augmenting technical progress is assumed to be a public good which is available free of charge to everyone, everywhere. However, this is not consistent with the empirical fact that some countries grow faster than others, even for long periods of time (see Fagerberg 1994, p. 1147). Only the transitional dynamics can explain growth-rate differentials between countries in such a framework. Because of different initial conditions, countries may grow at different rates towards the balanced growth path. During the adaptation process the growth rates of the economy in the standard model depend on the relation between capital and labor: poor economies where capital is relatively scarce grow with a higher per capita growth rate during the adaptation process than rich economies. This is the case since poor countries' return to capital is higher, which leads to a higher capital accumulation (see, for example, Barro and Sala-i-Martin 1995, Chs. 1/2). However, King and Rebelo (1993) point out that the transitional growth in the standard neoclassical model is not able to explain the observed growth rate diversity without resorting to an implausibly high real rate of return to capital in a country's early development. A growth theory which rather assumes than explains long-term economic growth is unsatisfactory – especially when agents' preferences which, for instance, determine the saving rates, technology and fiscal policy, do not affect long-term growth at all. Furthermore, such a theory is not consistent with empirical observations: nor are the growth rates even nearly the same in an international comparison (see, for example, Summers and Heston 1991), nor do they converge to a common level (see, for example, De Long 1988 and Baumol and Wolff 1988).[15]

Unlike neoclassical growth theory, in endogenous growth models not only the transitional dynamics but also the long-term growth rate is determined by preferences and technology – such as the capital share – and fiscal policy. That is the reason why growth is called endogenous. Hence, the theory of endogenous growth is capable of analysing the consequences of fiscal policy on long-term economic growth.

Although it seems plausible that fiscal policy influences economic

---

Martin (1995).

[15]For a comparison of empirical observations with exogenous and endogenous growth theories, see Fagerberg (1994).

growth, the issue is controversial in empirical studies. This is not surprising as empirical studies face several problems. For instance, in a
simple correlation Plosser (1992) found a significant negative correlation between average tax rates on income and profits and average per
capita GDP growth in OECD countries for the period 1960-89. However,
such correlations do not provide solid empirical evidence since there are
many other variables affecting the economic growth rate which should be
controlled when the growth/taxation relationship is under examination.
Easterly and Rebelo (1993) find that the negative correlation between
growth and income taxes in OECD countries disappears once the level of
income is controlled. This implies that the negative growth/taxation correlation simply reflects the fact that average income tax rates tend to be
higher in countries with higher income levels and that rich countries tend
to grow more slowly. But also cross-country studies searching for empirical linkages between long-run economic growth and economic policies
are far from reaching consensus. Again, this should not be regarded as
an empirical proof about the ineffectiveness of fiscal policy on economic
growth since such studies face many problems. Already the selection of
a proxy for the tax policy remains a problem. Proxies commonly used
in cross-country studies are government consumption, total government
spending, and average or marginal tax rates. The difficulty with such
proxies is illustrated by means of the proxy 'tax'. The measurement of
tax rates for macroeconomic models has proven to be a difficult task.
As Frenkel and Razin (1991) argue, the complexity of tax credits, ex-
emptions and deductions that exists in most countries complicates the
construction of effective tax rates useful for macroeconomic modeling.
However, the construction of effective tax rates is necessary for cross-
country studies. Furthermore, the problem mentioned above still applies, namely that besides taxes many other factors determine economic
growth. Therefore in an empirical study the chosen regressor set may not
capture all systematic influences on the dependent variable and results
may be misleading. For that reason, the following empirical results need
to be viewed with appropriate caution. Most cross-country studies show
a negative or insignificant partial relation between the growth rate and

the proxy for the tax policy.[16] Levine and Renelt (1992) show that the studies with significant results are generally very sensitive to regression specifications. By altering the set of explanatory variables, the resulting estimates become insignificant. Jorgenson and Wilcoxen focused on the relationship between environmental regulation and economic growth of the USA over the period 1973–85. They found a significant negative relation. The estimated costs of environmental regulation were a 0.19 per cent decline in the annual growth rate and a 2.59 per cent decline in the level of gross national product (see Jorgenson and Wilcoxen 1990, p. 315).[17]

2.3 Environmental Policy in Models of Endogenous Growth

2.3.1 Endogenous Growth Models

The new research area 'Endogenous Growth Theory' – also called 'New Growth Theory' – was inspired by the seminal papers of Romer (1986) and Lucas (1988).[18] The variety of models which have been developed since than can roughly be characterized by the mechanisms that constitute their engine of growth.[19] Following Xu (1994) we distinguish be-

---

[16]Kormendi and Meguire (1985), Marsden (1986), Fischer (1991), Barro (1991), Engen and Skinner (1992) and Mendoza et al. (1997) show a negative relation between growth and the proxy, while Levine and Renelt (1992) and Easterly and Rebelo (1993) have insignificant results.

[17]For the problems of measuring the impact of environmental regulations see Jaffe et al. (1995).

[18]However, already in the 1960s there were first attempts to explain the long-term growth rate endogenously (see Arrow 1962, Kaldor and Mirrlees 1962, Uzawa 1965, Phelps 1966, Shell 1967 and Hammond and Rodriguez–Clare 1993, p. 392 for further papers in this area). See Solow (1994) for a critical discussion about endogenous growth models.

For a survey of the literature on endogenous growth, see, for example, Sala-i-Martin (1990a, 1990b), Helpman (1992), Klundert and Smulders (1992), Verspagen (1992), Bretschger (1993), Hammond and Rodriguez–Clare (1993), Höfert (1993), or Jones and Manuelli (1997).

[19]Although many endogenous growth models violate the conditions of a neoclassical production function (see Section A.1 in the Appendix on page 223 for the conditions of a neoclassical production function) they are in the tradition of neoclassical growth

tween growth driven by human capital, by innovation (see for example Romer 1990 and Grossman and Helpman 1991), and by infrastructure (see, for example, Barro 1990 and Barro and Sala-i-Martin 1992). This characterization is not totally precise, however, it is useful for the issues addressed in this study.[20] In the following we focus on endogenous growth models driven by human capital.

'All that is required to assure the feasibility of perpetual growth is the existence of a "core" of capital goods that is produced with constant returns to scale technologies and without the direct or indirect use of nonreproducible factors' (Rebelo 1991, p. 502). The present study is restricted to endogenous growth models where the core of capital consists of physical and human capital. The theory of human capital was initially only a branch of labor economics, developed by Becker (1964), which studied the accumulation of marketable human skills by heredity, formal education, on the job training and other methods, and tries to explain how these skills influence earnings and job patterns. Uzawa (1965) and Razin (1972) applied this micro theory to macro models by studying human capital in the neoclassical growth model. Lucas (1988) took up this idea and developed an endogenous growth model driven by human capital accumulation. So, unlike labor economics, we are here interested in human capital purely as an engine of growth. Research suggests that human capital is a very important component of national wealth. For instance, Kendrick (1976) estimates that half of the USA total capital stock in 1969 was human capital, Kroch and Sjoblom (1986) conclude that the value of the stock of schooling in the USA is more than twice the size of household net worth, and Davies and Whalley (1991) suggest after reviewing the literature that the stock of human capital is about three times as large as the stock of physical capital. Furthermore, cross-country analyses support the importance of human capital for growth. Romer (1989), Azariadis and Drazen (1990), Barro (1991), Mankiw et al. (1992) and Levine and Renelt (1992) show a strong positive relationship between the stock of human capital and the rate of growth. In those studies, adults' literacy rates (see Romer 1989 and Azariadis and

---

models. For alternatives to the 'neoclassical approach', see Nelson (1995).

[20] For other possible classifications, see Ramser (1993, p. 120).

Drazen 1990) and school enrollment rates at the primary and secondary levels (see Barro 1991, Levine and Renelt 1992 and Mankiw et al. 1992) are used as a proxy of human capital. Both proxies possess shortcomings. For instance, in many industrialized countries the use of either proxy is not convincing because of the prevailing compulsory school education. Barro and Lee (1993) measure human capital by years of completed schooling for persons over 25. They regard the average years of schooling as a superior measure of human capital available for current production compared with the alternative proxies of school enrollment ratios and adult literacy rates. However, Mulligan and Sala-i-Martin (1995) argue that the average years of schooling might understate the true stock of human capital. They found that the stock of human capital in the United States grew twice as rapidly as the average years of schooling.[21]

2.3.2 General Model of the Study

In this section we present a general model framework which is sufficiently flexible to capture all of the growth models used in this study. First of all, we focus on the case of a closed economy. After that we show the modifications for an open economy.

Closed Economy

The closed economy versions of our growth models are contained by the following equations:

$$\dot{H}_t = H\left(H_t, K_t\right) - \delta_H H_t, \quad \text{where } H_X > 0, H_{XX} \le 0, \tag{2.7}$$

$$\dot{K}_t = Y\left(H_t, K_t\right) - C_t - Z_t - \delta_K K_t, \text{where } Y_X > 0, Y_{XX} \le 0 \tag{2.8}$$

$$P_t = P\left(K_t, Z_t\right), \quad \text{where } P_K > 0, P_Z < 0 \text{ or} \tag{2.9}$$

$$P_t = P\left(Y_t, Z_t\right), \quad \text{where } P_Y > 0, P_Z < 0, \tag{2.10}$$

$$U_t = U\left(C_t, P_t, l_t\right), \quad \text{where } U_C > 0, U_l > 0 \text{ and } U_P < 0. \tag{2.11}$$

---

[21]For a discussion about the measurement of human capital, see Barro and Lee (1993), Behrman and Rosenzweig (1994), Mulligan and Sala-i-Martin (1995, 1997); and Becker (1993) for an empirical and theoretical analysis of education.

The symbols denote human capital (H), physical capital (K), the human capital depreciation rate (δ_H), final output (Y), consumption (C), abatement technologies (Z), the physical capital depreciation rate (δ_K), pollution (P), utility (U) and leisure (l). Note that all variables are time dependent, indicated by the subscript t. A variable with a dot denotes the derivative with respect to time while a variable with a hat stands for its growth rate. The model outlined by equations (2.7)–(2.11) describes a two-sector economy.[22] Equations (2.7) and (2.8) describe the education[23] and the final good sector, respectively, and hence the assumed production processes. Equation (2.7) represents the human capital accumulation constraint. In the most general model version the stock of human capital is produced by physical and human capital. The flow resource constraint of the economy is given by equation (2.8). Final output produced by using human and physical capital can be used for consumption, abatement activities and net investment in the physical capital stock.[24] By assuming a separate education sector we acknowledge the fact that human capital differs substantially from physical capital. In some growth models, human capital is specified as being perfectly substitutable with consumption, in fact, it is just an additional form of capital produced with the same technology: final goods can be used for consumption, human capital accumulation and physical capital accumulation (see first model in Jones et al. 1993). However, this seems to be an inadmissible simplification. A special education sector allows us to produce human capital with different inputs and/or with different capital intensities relative to the production technology for final goods. For instance, in the Uzawa–Lucas model (see Lucas 1988) human capital accumulation requires only human capital as input. King and Rebelo (1990) consider a two-sector model where human capital is produced

---

[22] In this study we analyse deterministic models only. For stochastic models with different assumptions about uncertainty, see Stokey and Lucas (1993, part III).

[23] In the following the terms 'studying' or 'human capital' sector are used as synonyms for the education sector.

[24] Both human and physical capital are assumed to be homogeneous goods. For problems resulting from heterogeneous physical capital goods (Cambridge debate), see for instance Burmeister and Dobell (1970) or Burmeister (1980). For a more micro-founded model, with different types of knowledge, human capital and education, see Rustichini and Schmitz (1991).

using both human and physical capital, however with factor intensities that differ from those for the production of final goods. Following the literature we shall call this model the 'generalized Uzawa–Lucas model'. In principle there are two possibilities for treating the sector producing human capital (2.7). Human capital accumulation can be thought of either as a non-market activity or as a market activity. Whereas the former inputs are not subject to factor income taxation, this is the case for the latter. In most models human capital accumulation is assumed to be a non-market activity.[25] This means that in contrast to the final good production sector, neither the individual time input and hence the individual labor income used in the production nor the implicit capital income earned by the production of *human capital* is usually taxed. However, the income of teachers and workers in the education sector is subject to taxation. Although both specifications are plausible we follow the mainstream and assume human capital accumulation to be a non-market activity.[26] Furthermore, we assume human capital to be a pure private good and thus to be rival and excludable.[27]

Equations (2.9) and (2.10) describe both plausible pollution functions. Pollution is generated either by the physical capital stock or by final output.

Dividing equation (2.8) by K yields

$$\hat{K}_t \equiv \frac{\dot{K}_t}{K_t} = \left(1 - \frac{C_t}{Y_t} - \frac{Z_t}{Y_t}\right) \frac{Y_t}{K_t} - \delta_K. \qquad (2.12)$$

According to equation (2.12), the growth rate of the physical capital stock $\hat{K}$ is determined by the saving rate $(1 - C/Y - Z/Y)$, the output-capital ratio Y/K, and the exogenous physical capital depreciation rate δ_K. To guarantee permanent growth, the product of the saving rate and the output-capital ratio must be larger than the physical capital depreciation rate. It is seen that the consumption-output ratio, the abatement-output ratio, and the output-capital ratio must be constant

---

[25] See, for example, Lucas (1990), Trostel (1993), Jones et al. (1993, 1996), Devereux and Love (1994), or Milesi-Ferretti and Roubini (1998b).

[26] For assuming human capital to be a market sector, see Pecorino (1993) and Stokey and Rebelo (1995).

[27] Unlike Lucas (1988) we ignore the possibility of a spillover from the average stock of human capital to final good production.

for a constant physical capital growth rate. A declining output-capital ratio can only temporarily be compensated by a change in the saving rate. Note that the saving rate can only vary between zero and unity, and the same applies for the consumption-output and abatement-output ratios. The mentioned ratios are constant if

$$\hat{C} = \hat{K} = \hat{Y} = \hat{Z}. \tag{2.13}$$

Equation (2.13) is part of the model's balanced growth path condition.[28] A balanced growth path is characterized as a state where all variables grow at a constant rate. To enable balanced growth paths the pollution functions $P(...)$ must be homogeneous of degree ω since either K and Z or Y and Z grow at a constant rate.[29] For the rest of the study we specify pollution functions either as equation (2.14) or (2.15), which are homogeneous of degree zero ($\omega = 0$):

$$P_t = \left(\frac{K_t}{Z_t}\right)^{\chi}, \text{ or} \tag{2.14}$$

$$P_t = \left(\frac{Y_t}{Z_t}\right)^{\chi}, \tag{2.15}$$

where χ is the exogenous elasticity of P with respect to ratios K/Z or K/Y. Note, that the assumption of a pollution function which is homogeneous of degree zero is crucial for the results. If the pollution function is homogeneous of $\omega > 0$, pollution growth is positive for positive output growth. Hence, environmental quality can improve only if the economy slows down and permanent positive economic growth would contradict a sustainable development since pollution rises over time. On the other hand if the pollution function is homogeneous of $\omega < 0$, the level of pollution declines over time for positive economic growth. Assuming a pollution function homogeneous of degree zero implies a constant level of pollution along a balanced growth path. Recall that a constant level

---

[28] The human capital stock grows at the same constant rate as the variables mentioned in condition (2.13). Furthermore, the fractions of time and the physical capital share are constant over time. Neither the fraction of time nor the physical capital share are introduced so far as they depend on the actual model version.

[29] For a non-homogeneous pollution function a balanced growth would not exist.

of pollution is in accordance with sustainable development if the ecosystem is assumed to be a renewable resource and the level of pollution does not exceed its absorption capacity. Hence by choosing the pollution specification we have already decided whether growth in principle is compatible with a sustainable development. However, a constant level of pollution in the presence of economic growth is not an unrealistic assumption, as the following example shows. Countries like Belgium, Denmark, France, Germany, Luxembourg, Sweden, Switzerland and the UK managed to increase their GDP over 23 per cent between 1980 and 1995 but in the same period reduced their CO_2 emissions from energy use (see OECD 1998, p. 17).

Throughout the study we assume identical, atomistic agents with perfect foresight over an infinite time horizon.[30] As lifetime is finite, our specification assumes that economic agents care about their own utility but also about their children's utility (see Barro 1974). Thus we think about the economic agent as being the head of a dynasty. For simplicity we abstain from family size changes. Exogenous population change as used in most models would not change the qualitative results but complicate the analysis.[31] Equation (2.11) describes the preferences of the economic agents. Utility is increasing in consumption and leisure but decreasing in pollution. To ensure the existence of a balanced growth path we must restrict the utility function. To be compatible with positive balanced growth, preferences must be chosen such that households expand their consumption at a constant rate whenever the real interest rate is constant. The necessary conditions imply the following class of admissible utility functions where consumption is multiplicatively sepa-

---

[30] By contrast, in overlapping generation models agents maximize a finite horizon (see Allais 1947, Samuelson 1958 and Diamond 1965).

[31] For endogenous fertility in endogenous growth models, see Barro and Becker (1989) or Becker et al. (1990). The latter is a human capital growth model.

rable from leisure and pollution:[32]

$$U_t = \frac{\left(C_t P_t^{-\eta_P} l_t^{\eta_l}\right)^{1-1/\varepsilon} - 1}{1 - 1/\varepsilon}, \quad \text{for} \quad \varepsilon > 0, \varepsilon \neq 1, \tag{2.16}$$

$$U_t = \ln C_t - \eta_P \ln P_t + \eta_l \ln l_t, \quad \text{for} \quad \varepsilon = 1. \tag{2.17}$$

The parameters η_l and η_P represent the weights of leisure and pollution in utility, respectively, and parameter ε denotes the so-called intertemporal elasticity of substitution.[33] By using l'Hopital's rule it can be proved that equation (2.16) reduces to (2.17) as $\varepsilon \to 1$. Utility is seen to be increasing in consumption and leisure at a decreasing rate, $U_C, U_l > 0$ and $U_{CC}, U_{ll} < 0$, while it is decreasing in pollution $U_P < 0$. Utility is decreasing at an increasing rate $U_{PP} > 0$, at a constant rate $U_{PP} = 0$, or at a decreasing rate $U_{PP} < 0$ for ε larger than, equal to, or smaller than $\eta_P/(1 + \eta_P)$. The function U_t is called the instantaneous utility function.[34] The corresponding lifetime utility is given by the integral of the discounted instantaneous utility over the infinite planning horizon:

$$U_0 = \int_{t=0}^{\infty} U\left(C_t, P_t, l_t\right) e^{-\rho t} dt. \tag{2.18}$$

---

[32] For the necessary conditions on the utility function with the arguments consumption and leisure, see King et al. (1988) and Smulders and Gradus (1996) with the arguments consumption and pollution.

This type of function is commonly used in the literature on endogenous growth. For similar utility functions with the arguments consumption and leisure, see, for example, Lucas (1990), Rebelo (1991) and Jones et al. (1993); and Huang and Cai (1994) Bovenberg and Smulders (1996) and Bovenberg and de Mooij (1997) with the arguments consumption and pollution.

[33] Mathematically this can be expressed by $\varepsilon = -\left(\partial U/\partial C\right)/\left(\partial^2 U/\partial C^2\right) C^{-1}$. For further discussion, see Blanchard and Fischer (1989, p. 40) or Barro and Sala-i-Martin (1995, p. 64).

The term $-1/\varepsilon$ reflects the curvature of the utility function. For example, for $\varepsilon \to \infty$ the utility function becomes a linear curve. It is equal to the elasticity of the marginal utility with respect to consumption.

[34] This type of function is also known as *constant relative risk aversion* (CRRA) utility function and as *constant intertemporal elasticity of substitution* (CIES) utility function (see Blanchard and Fischer 1989, p. 44 and Barro and Sala-i-Martin 1995, p. 65, respectively).

U_0 represents the present value of the future instantaneous utility levels (2.16), and parameter ρ is the rate of time preference, or the subjective discount rate, which is assumed to be strictly positive. The rate of time preference reflects the fact that individuals evaluate today's utility higher than the same utility gain in some future period or the one of their children.[35] As in almost all growth models, the preferences are assumed to be time separable, with a constant intertemporal elasticity of substitution and with a constant rate of time preference.[36] The basic appeal of such preference functions lies in their apparent conformity with some of Kaldor's stylized facts (see Kaldor 1961) of economic development (see Romer 1989, p. 9).

There are different possibilities to model leisure (see Milesi-Ferretti and Roubini 1998b). Leisure could be either modeled as 'raw time', 'quality time', or 'home production'. Raw time is the standard formulation; it is the fraction of time that is spent away from work and study: see, for example, Rebelo (1991) and Mulligan and Sala-i-Martin (1993). Alternatively, following Becker (1965) and Heckman (1976), quality time is defined as raw time times the human capital stock. Finally, leisure could be modeled as home production as in Greenwood and Hercowitz (1991). In that case leisure is a non-market good produced with human and physical capital. In most chapters we do not take into account a leisure-work decision. However, in Chapter 5 we broaden the analysis of Chapter 4 by incorporating leisure as raw time.[37] We shall see that this modification changes the effects of environmental policy on growth substantially.

In the following we show the optimization problem of a central planner for the economy outlined above. We assume the central planner to be a benevolent dictator. A central planner chooses consumption, abatement activities, leisure, and the allocation of human and physical capital between the two sectors in order to maximize the discounted lifetime

---

[35] According to Ramsey (1928, p. 543) it is 'ethically indefensible and arises only from the weakness of the imagination' for the current generation to discount the utility of future generations. For a discussion about the rate of time preference, see Weitzman (1994).

[36] An exception is Zee's model (1997) with an endogenous rate of time preference.

[37] Furthermore, in Section 3.2 we outline a model with home production.

utility (2.18) subject to the human capital accumulation constraint (2.7) and the flow resource constraint of the economy (2.8). Formally the optimization problem reads

$$\max_{C,Z,l...} U_0 = \int_0^\infty U\left(C_t, P_t, l_t\right) e^{-\rho t} dt \qquad (2.19)$$

$$\text{s.t. } \dot{K}_t = Y\left(H_t, K_t\right) - C_t - Z_t - \delta_K K_t,$$

$$\text{s.t. } \dot{H}_t = H\left(H_t, K_t\right) - \delta_H H_t,$$

$$C_t, H_t, K_t, Z_t, l_t \geqslant 0 \forall t, \quad H_0, K_0 \text{ given.}$$

The optimal control problem can be solved by Pontryagin's maximum principle. The current-value Hamiltonian (see Feichtinger and Hartl 1986, p. 18) for this maximization problem is given by[38]

$$\max_{C,Z,l...} \mathcal{H} = U\left(C_t, P_t, l_t\right) + \lambda\left[Y\left(H_t, K_t\right) - C_t - Z_t - \delta_K K_t\right]$$
$$+ \mu\left[H\left(H_t, K_t\right) - \delta_H H_t\right]$$

where λ and μ are the shadow prices of physical and human capital, respectively. This maximization problem cannot be solved without further specifying the production processes, which is done in the next paragraph.

In this study we analyse different endogenous growth models with human capital and we increase complexity step by step. Note that equations (2.7) and (2.8) describe the most general forms of the production processes to be analysed. Table 2.1 surveys different kinds of endogenous growth models with human capital analysed in this study. To study the effects of environmental policy we start in Chapter 3 with the simplest endogenous growth model. As final good production in this model is linear in the only input (capital) it is known as the *linear model*. In the literature this type of model is also called the *Rebelo model*[39] or the *AK*

---

[38] For an application of the deterministic maximum principle for economic models, see Feichtinger and Hartl (1986, Ch. 13), Seierstad and Sydsæter (1987), Beavis and Dobbs (1990), or Chiang (1992, Ch. 8).

[39] The linear growth model was reincarnated by Rebelo (1991) in the late 1980s. According to Rebelo (1991, p. 507) the linear economy resembles models discussed by Knight (1935, 1944) and Hagen (1942). In accordance with Barro and Sala-i-

model, designated according to its production function (A denotes the exogenous level of the technology, see Table 2.1). In the linear model the

Table 2.1: Overview of human capital growth models

ch.	model	production function	resource constraint
3	linear	$Y = AK$	$Y = C + Z + \dot{K} + \delta_K K$
–	one-sector	$Y = f(H, K)$	$Y = C + Z + \dot{K} + \delta_K K$
			$+\dot{H} + \delta_H K$
4/5	Uzawa-Lucas	$Y = f(H, K)$	$Y = C + Z + \dot{K} + \delta_K K$
		$\dot{H} = g(H) - \delta_H H$	
6	generalized	$Y = f(H, K)$	$Y = C + Z + \dot{K} + \delta_K K$
	Uzawa-Lucas	$\dot{H} = g(H, K) - \delta_H H$	

variable K combines human and physical capital into a single argument *capital*. The third row of Table 2.1 outlines a one-sector model with human and physical capital. This model is mentioned but not analysed in this study. Note that in both the linear and the 'one-sector' models, human capital is perfectly substitutable by consumption. However, in the *Uzawa–Lucas model* and the *generalized Uzawa–Lucas model* analysed in Chapters 4, 5 and 6, respectively, for realistic reasons a separate education sector is assumed. Thus in both models human capital is not substitutable with consumption (see rows 4 and 5 in Table 2.1). The studying sector in the Uzawa–Lucas model requires only human capital for the accumulation process, whereas in the generalized Uzawa–Lucas model in addition physical capital is used for human capital accumulation. Chapter 5 extends Chapter 4 by additionally allowing for elastic labor supply.

In Chapters 3–6 we derive both the market solution and the central planner solution. This enables us not only to analyse the effects of tax changes on core variables but also to show the optimal response of increased preferences for a clean environment.[40] Furthermore, the cen-

---

Martin (1995, p. 39) it was Neumann (1937) who first used a production function of the AK type. Furthermore, Solow (1956), Gale and Sutherland (1968) and Benveniste (1976) analysed the dynamic implications of the model.

[40] Formally this is done by increasing the weight factor of pollution in utility η_P.

tral planner solution serves as a benchmark for deriving the optimal tax structure. Since there is only one distortion in the economy, the government can reach a first-best solution by setting the pollution tax equal to the Pigouvian tax. Although the focus is on environmental policy we also investigate flat taxes on consumption, labor income and capital income.[41] We examine the growth effects of all taxes, their channels, and also their influence on all core variables. Furthermore, we examine the ability of non-environmental taxes to internalize the environmental externality in the absence of a pollution tax. We shall see that certain combinations of non-environmental taxes can be alternatively used to internalize the environmental externality. Such solutions depend on whether abatement is assumed to be private or public and whether pollution is a function of output or of the use of physical capital in the final good production. In the models under consideration, the growth implications of taxation depend on whether the real rate of return to capital (both physical and human capital) net of tax is affected by the policy measures. It is important to distinguish between direct and indirect effects. For instance, the direct tax effect of taxes on capital income and pollution will always reduce the real rate of return net of tax and hence economic growth. Due to factor substitution the indirect tax effect works exactly in the opposite direction. However, the strength of the indirect tax effect depends on the specification of the production processes. We consider only tax rates to which the government is fully and credibly committed and ignore the issue of time consistency raised by Kydland and Prescott (1977).[42] Furthermore, we do not discuss the implications of endogenous growth models with tax policy endogenously determined by a political process. In such a case the adoption of a growth affecting tax policy depends on factors such as the status of income or wealth distribution.[43]

---

[41] However, our analysis is restricted to models with human capital accumulation. For the effects of fiscal policy in endogenous growth models driven by innovation and infrastructure but without environment, see Lessat (1994) and Xu (1994). For progressive taxes in an endogenous growth model with human capital accumulation, see Bovenberg and van Ewijk (1997).

[42] See Stokey (1991) for a recent discussion about time consistency

[43] For theoretic models with endogenous tax policy, see Persson and Tabellini (1992, 1994), Perotti (1992), Alesina and Rodrick (1994), Bergström (1997) and

Open Economy

We now review briefly the literature on environmental policy in open endogenously growing economies and show how the closed economy setup must be modified to incorporate international aspects.[44] The analysis of environmental policy in open endogenously growing economies is largely ignored in the literature. Exceptions are van der Ploeg and Ligthart (1994), Elbasha and Roe (1996) and Bretschger (1998a). Elbasha and Roe (1996) find for a small open endogenously growing economy where growth is driven by innovation that long-run growth rises with a country's endowment in primary factors, with the degree of openness and with the degree of market power of patent holders. Furthermore, the effects of environmental policy on growth depend on the intertemporal elasticity of substitution. In a north/south model with two different assumptions on the dislocation of firms from the north to the south Bretschger (1998a) analyses the effects of a tighter environmental policy in the north. By using a model where growth is endogenously driven by innovation he shows that although pollution may rise in the south, the global environmental quality improves. However, the positive environmental effect is accompanied by a lower economic growth rate. Van der Ploeg and Ligthart (1994) analyse the effects of international cooperation on growth and environmental quality in the presence of international environmental externalities, international government spending spillovers, and knowledge spillovers in an endogenous growth model driven by infrastructure. For simplicity they assume two identical countries, implying that international trade and capital flows are absent. This contribution is described in detail in Section 3.5 for the linear model ignoring international government spillovers.[45]

To incorporate international environmental and knowledge spillovers we must modify the analytical framework outlined in equations (2.7)–(2.11). With respect to environmental spillovers we leave the utility

---

Chang (1998) and the anthologies by Cukierman et al. (1992) and Bergström (1997); for an empirical investigation, see Perotti (1996); and for a model which additionally addresses environmental degradation, see Jones and Manuelli (1995).

[44]For a survey on sustainability, growth and the environment in open economies, see Bretschger and Egli (2000).

[45]This simplification does not change the effects of the other spillovers.

function (2.11) unchanged but interpret P now as global pollution which is a function of pollution generated by the home country p and by the foreign country $\overset{*}{p}$. Global pollution is a weighted sum of national and foreign pollution. To model international knowledge spillovers in the linear model where human and physical capital are combined in a single argument (see Section 3.5) we modify the production in the flow resource constraint of the economy (2.8):

$$\dot{K}_t = Y\left(K_t, \overset{*}{K}_t\right) - C_t - Z_t - \delta_K K_t, \quad \text{where } Y_X > 0, Y_{XX} \le 0.$$
$$(2.20)$$

It is seen in equation (2.20) that final output is produced by using the domestic capital stock K and the foreign capital stock $\overset{*}{K}$. The latter is exogenous for the home country and reflects the international knowledge spillover. By contrast, the Uzawa–Lucas model allows us to distinguish between human (knowledge) capital and physical capital. Therefore, to model international knowledge spillover in the Uzawa–Lucas model (see Section 4.4) we change only the human capital accumulation constraint (2.7):

$$\dot{H}_t = H\left(H_t, \overset{*}{H}_t\right) - \delta_H H_t, \quad \text{where } H_X > 0, H_{XX} \le 0. \qquad (2.21)$$

Equation (2.21) states that human capital is produced not only by using domestic human H capital but also by using foreign human capital $\overset{*}{H}$. Again the latter is exogenous for the home country and reflects the international knowledge spillover.

Besides the question of how international cooperation may affect growth, pollution and welfare in the presence of international environmental and knowledge spillovers, we analyse the question whether national environmental policy is still possible in the case of an economy with internationally mobile factors and goods. We can assume either a large or a small open economy. A large country can use its market power to influence world market prices, whereas for a small country the prices of the traded inputs or goods and also the interest rate are determined by the world market and hence are exogenous. In Section 6.3.3 we investigate whether a small open economy can conduct an independent environmental policy. We make the conventional assumptions of international trade models: domestic and foreign capital goods F are perfect substitutes, there is international borrowing and lending, and international trade in capital and consumption goods, but international immobility of labor, that is, human capital. The latter assumption ensures that the small open economy will not specialize over time in either final good production or education.[46] For the analysis in Section 6.3.3 we only have to modify the flow resource constraint of the economy (2.8) to

$$\dot{K}_t + \dot{F}_t = Y\left(H_t, K_t\right) + r_F F_t - C_t - Z_t, \quad \text{where } Y_X > 0, Y_{XX} \leq 0.$$
$$(2.22)$$

According to equation (2.22), final output Y and the foreign interest payments $r_F F$ can be used for consumption, abatement activities and for investments in the domestic and foreign capital stock.

2.4 Transitional Dynamics

To analyse the effects of fiscal policy in endogenous growth models with human capital we must distinguish between their implications in the short and long run.[47] The long-run effects describe the movements of key variables along the balanced growth path. A balanced growth path is characterized as a state where all variables grow at a constant, possibly zero, rate. However, effects in the short and medium term describe changes in variables during the adaptation process caused by the fiscal policy measure.[48] For instance, due to a fiscal policy measure the initial ratio of physical to human capital stocks may not be optimal any longer. This imbalance induces an adaptation process where the new optimal ratio is reached only gradually by investments which increase the relatively scarce capital stock.

---

[46] For a discussion of labor mobility in endogenous growth models with human capital accumulation, see Frenkel and Razin (1996, Ch. 13).

[47] The same applies for shocks, such as exogenous changes in technologies, preferences and the ratio of the capital stocks due to natural disasters or wars.

[48] The basic version of the linear growth model does not possess transitional dynamics. An interesting exception is the model by Zee (1997), which has an endogenous rate of time preference. Likewise, models with international capital mobility do not possess transitional dynamics unless investment costs are included.

In the literature the analysis of transitional dynamics has been largely ignored given the technical difficulties involved in such analysis.[49] However, a small number of contributions have appeared in recent years. Depending on the complexity of the analysed model, the transitional dynamics can be characterized analytically and hence independently of particular parameter values. Caballé and Santos (1993) investigate the transitional dynamics of a central planner Uzawa–Lucas economy. They characterize the necessary and sufficient conditions on technology and preferences that guarantee the existence of balanced growth paths and prove the global convergence of every off-balance path. Furthermore they show how the initial stocks of capital affect the balanced growth path towards which the economy converges. Similarly, Chamley (1993) investigates the effects of taxes in a Uzawa–Lucas model. He allows additionally for externalities that arise in human capital investment and shows that there exist multiple balanced growth paths with different growth rates. Faig (1995) describes graphically the transitional dynamics of a Uzawa–Lucas economy with a public consumption good financed by a lump-sum tax. The transitional processes are caused by technology shocks, government spending shocks and stochastic shocks. He additionally shows how under certain conditions the technology shocks and the government spending shocks can be reinterpreted to explain the effects of taxes on consumption and labor income. In contrast to the neoclassical growth model he finds that the Uzawa–Lucas model realistically predicts that shocks to the final good sector, even if they are permanent, have strong effects on output and employment and weak effects on wages. He also finds that shocks on public consumption have a stronger impact on output when they are transitory rather than permanent. Finally, Ladrón-de-Guevara et al. (1997) analyse the transitional dynamics of Uzawa–Lucas and generalized Uzawa–Lucas models. They show that the transitional dynamics of both models are qualitatively equivalent. Furthermore, they analyse the generalized Uzawa–Lucas model augmented by leisure modeled either as raw or quality time. They show that if leisure is modeled as raw time, there could exist multiple balanced

---

[49]This is even true for neoclassical growth models. For recent contributions, see King and Rebelo (1993) and Chatterjee (1994).

growth paths with differing rates of growth.

The numerical simulation is another possibility for characterizing the transitional dynamics of growth models. Obviously, compared with the analytical method its results are less general since qualitative results may depend on the choice of parameter values. Therefore, to obtain realistic results the model should be calibrated so as to capture empirically stylized facts of an economy. Furthermore, the robustness of the results should be examined by varying certain parameter values in a sensitivity analysis. However, an advantage of numerical simulation is that it yields not only qualitative but also quantitative results. For example, King and Rebelo (1993) argue that even the study of transitional dynamics in neoclassical growth models with intertemporally optimizing agents has remained largely unexplored from a *quantitative* standpoint. This applies, even more so, to endogenous growth models. Mulligan and Sala-i-Martin (1993) show the necessary conditions on technology and preferences that guarantee the existence of balanced growth paths for the Uzawa–Lucas model and the generalized Uzawa–Lucas model. These conditions are not derived analytically but detected by numerous numerical simulation runs with different parameter values. Furthermore, they simulate the adaptation process for different parameter values. Osang and Pereira (1996) study the relationship between different tariffs, growth and welfare for a small open economy with endogenous growth induced by human capital accumulation. In the assumed economy there is trade in consumption and two investment goods. Although all kinds of tariffs reduce welfare in the long run it is shown by means of numerical simulations that the tariff on the technology good is welfare-improving in the short run due to the trade-off between the short-run and long-run effects on capital accumulation. In a generalized Uzawa–Lucas model with leisure modeled as raw time, Devereux and Love (1994) analyse the growth and welfare effects of different taxes in the long run, and also simulate numerically their effects in the short and medium term.[50]

'However, even though in recent years the literature on endogenous growth has also grown at an increasing rate, the dynamics for models with several factors of production are not yet well understood.' (Caballé

---

[50]Other related papers are Perroni (1994) and Grüner and Heer (1994).

and Santos 1993, p. 1043). There are several important and interesting reasons to study the transitional dynamics. Knowledge of the transition path is necessary:

1. to explain historical observations;
2. to examine the model empirically;
3. to figure out which balanced growth path is chosen in case of multiple steady states;
4. to compare the differences of the levels of core variables with the business-as-usual scenario;
5. to show the losses or gains of growth during the adaptation process;
6. to assess the duration of the transition process;
7. to find the overall losses or gains of utility due to a policy measure;
8. to compare welfare effects of unexpected and announced policy measures.

1: Hirshleifer (1987) analyses several historical episodes where an economy suffered great population and/or material losses. In a Uzawa–Lucas economy the former can be interpreted as the stock of human capital tied to labor, the latter corresponds to the stock of physical capital. Analysing the American civil war (1861–65), the revolution in Russia (1918–21), and the cases of Germany and Japan during and after the Second World War led him to conclude: 'the speed and success of recovery in the observed historical instances have been due in large part of the proportionally smaller destruction to population than of material losses'. (Hirshleifer 1987, p. 78). This asymmetry of the transitional paths is just the prediction of the Uzawa–Lucas model. During the adaptation process the growth rate of the economy in the Uzawa–Lucas model depends on whether the economy is endowed in relative terms with a greater amount of physical capital or human capital. If the loss of human capital is relatively larger, then the growth rate will be very low for a long period of time. However, if the loss of physical capital is relatively larger, the growth rate will be large and the economy will recover quickly (see Caballé and Santos 1993, p. 1044 or Mulligan and Sala-i-Martin 1993, p. 761).

2: The empirical implications of transitional paths may be different from those of the balanced growth path. Therefore, the exact prediction of the transitional dynamics is needed to test the models with actual data (see Mulligan and Sala-i-Martin 1993, p. 740).

3: For instance, in the generalized Uzawa–Lucas model with leisure as raw time, there exists a multiplicity of balanced growth paths with differing rates of growth (see Ladrón-de-Guevara et al. 1997). By analysing the transitional dynamics they found that the long-term growth rate is determined by the initial ratio of human and physical capital.[51]

4: The levels of the variables must be known for a proper welfare analysis, see point 7.

5: It may be interesting from a political economy point of view to show the losses or gains of growth during the adaptation process since the GDP growth rate is an important indicator of prosperity and performance in the public debate.

6: If the adaptation process is accompanied by welfare losses over a long time, a government faces intergenerational distribution problems.

7 and 8: Proper assessment of the welfare implications of a fiscal policy measure is the main argument for characterizing the transitional dynamics in this study. Ignoring short- and medium-term effects may lead to wrong policy recommendations. We shall show this by means of two examples: Devereux and Love (1994) investigate the effects of taxes on consumption, labor income and capital income on growth and welfare. By comparing wage taxation with capital taxation in different revenue equivalent tax regimes they find that there is only a tiny difference between both taxes with respect to growth. However, the welfare costs of capital taxation are considerably higher. These higher welfare costs are mainly associated with the transition towards the new balanced growth path. They finally state that ignoring the transitional dynamics leads to a serious underestimation of the welfare costs of capital taxation (see Devereux and Love 1994, p. 511). Furthermore, a policy measure could be beneficial in the long run but very harmful in the short and medium term so that the overall discounted welfare is negative compared to the business-as-usual scenario. Therefore, for a proper welfare analysis of fiscal policy, welfare changes during the adaptation process in every single

---

[51]Becker et al. (1990) also show a multiplicity of balanced growth paths in a human capital model with endogenous fertility. There exists one path with low fertility and high capital stocks and another path with high fertility and low capital stocks.

period must be known.

In this study we analyse not only the implications of fiscal policy along a balanced growth path but also its implications during the transition. We shall analyse the transition process by means of numerical simulations. Analysing the transitional dynamics analytically is mathematically demanding, if not impossible, because of the model's complexity. The models mentioned above ignore environmental pollution. Incorporating the environment complicates the analysis. To my knowledge, Bovenberg and Smulders (1996) is the only contribution which analyses analytically the transitional dynamics of a two-sector human capital model with pollution.[52] Furthermore, existing analytical analyses show that the results from the numerical simulation of the above-mentioned models are robust. But also the numerical simulations are accompanied by difficulties and require a precise understanding of the analysed model. First, the parameters must be chosen to guarantee that growth is possible at all. For instance, the rate of time preference must be smaller than the rate of return to physical capital. Second, the initial ratio between the human and the physical capital stocks must not deviate too much from the ratio along the balanced growth path values. Otherwise the numerical solvers may not be able to find a solution.[53] Third, the variables must be restricted to ensure the existence of a balanced growth path. In nonlinear programming, it is important to help the solver by specifying intervals for the variables as narrow as possible in order to find a feasible solution. Fourth, we must impose terminal conditions to ensure that the finite horizon of the simulations corresponds to the infinite horizon of the theory. The terminal conditions, for instance, pretend that the capital stocks run down at the end of the finite horizon. Finally, it is very important to specify initial values from which the numerical solver can start a successful search for the optimum. Quite often the solver fails to find an optimal solution simply because of bad initial values. Furthermore, instability of the model may be a reason why the solver cannot find a solution. For example, Benhabib and Perli (1994) show

---

[52] We shall discuss this model in Chapter 4.

[53] Closely related to this point: the adaptation process must be completed approximately within the chosen time horizon. Obviously, the longer the observed period of time the more difficult it is for the solver to find a solution.

that the saddle-point stability of the Uzawa–Lucas model *with* human capital spillovers depends on parameter values. For the purpose of the numerical simulations we use the solver MINOS 5 of the software package GAMS (General Algebraic Modelling System), release 2.25, which is suitable for solving systems of nonlinear difference equations.[54] For the mathematical analysis we use continuous time models. This is certainly an idealized representation of reality as decisions mostly are made in discrete steps. For the numerical simulation we reformulate the continuous time models to corresponding discrete time models, which can be solved by GAMS.

---

[54] For a description of GAMS and for the used algorithms of MINOS 5, see Brooke et al. (1992).

Chapter 3

Environmental Policy in the Linear Growth Model

3.1 Introduction

In this chapter we analyse the consequences of fiscal policy on economic growth and other core variables in the simplest endogenous growth model. We thereby combine different approaches of the literature in a consistent analytical framework. The simplest endogenous growth model is called the *Rebelo* model or – according to its production function – the *AK* model. Since production is linear in the only input (capital), it is also known as the *linear* growth model. The models described in this chapter are closely related to the existing literature. We therefore depart from the usual procedure of the following chapters and skip the main results and the survey of the literature in the introduction, but we shall refer in every section to the relevant literature.

We start in Section 3.2 with the basic linear model which does not include an environmental dimension. The basic model is enriched by incorporating the natural environment and allowing for pollution in Section 3.3. In Section 3.4 we additionally allow for either private or public pollution abatement activities. In Section 3.5 we enlarge the closed economy setup and analyse the strategic interactions between two countries

41

in the presence of international environmental and knowledge spillovers. Finally, Section 3.6 summarizes the results and concludes this chapter.

3.2   The Basic Linear Model

We start with the simplest endogenous growth model, the linear one-sector growth model, and ignore the natural environment. The properties of the model are discussed by Jones and Manuelli (1990), King and Rebelo (1990) and Rebelo (1991). For simplicity we do not consider changes in the population size.[1] However, this simplification does not change the qualitative results but complicates the analysis.

3.2.1   The Analytical Framework

Technology

An obvious requirement for infinite growth is the avoidance of the decreasing marginal product of the accumulating input factors. In the Rebelo model the marginal product of the accumulating factor is constant as the production function is linear in the only input factor which is capital. Therefore, the production function exhibits both constant returns to scale and constant marginal product to capital:[2]

$$Y_t = AK_t, \quad \text{where } A, K, Y > 0 \tag{3.1}$$

Parameter A reflects the level of the technology, variables Y and K represent the final good and the stock of capital, respectively, and t is the time index. This simple production function violates the usual conditions for a neoclassical production function since the marginal product of capital is constant.[3] The specification of one single input factor and

---

[1] See Rebelo (1992) for the effects of exogenous population growth rates changes on growth in the linear growth model.

[2] Furthermore, the marginal product is identical to the average product of capital.

[3] The production function is called neoclassical if the following properties are satisfied. First, the production function must exhibit positive but diminishing marginal products with respect to each input factor:

$$\frac{\partial F}{\partial X} > 0, \quad \frac{\partial^2 F}{\partial X^2} < 0.$$

the absence of diminishing returns may seem to be unrealistic. It implies a world where computers produce computers (see Solow 1991). The assumption becomes plausible if we think of capital in a broader sense which includes human capital.[4] However, this implies that the ratio of physical to human capital is fixed and there are no substitution possibilities between human and physical capital. According to Aghion and Howitt (1998, Ch. 1.4.1) the Harrod–Domar model (see Harrod 1939 and Domar 1946) is an early variant of the linear model as it assumes that labor input grows automatically in proportion to capital.

The flow resource constraint of the closed economy is given by

$$Y_t = C_t + \dot{K}_t + \delta K_t. \tag{3.2}$$

Final output Y is a perfectly malleable good: it can be used without any frictions for consumption C and net investment in the capital stock $\dot{K}$. Parameter δ denotes the exogenous depreciation rate of the capital stock.

Firms

The economy consists of a large number of identical and competitive firms. Firms rent capital from the households at the interest rate r and use this input factor to produce a final good under the linear production technology described by equation (3.1). Firms' profit condition π in every period is given by

$$\pi_t = Y_t - r_t K_t.$$

The firms' zero profit condition reads

$$r_t = A. \tag{3.3}$$

Second, the production function must exhibit constant returns to scale. Third, the marginal product of the input factor approaches infinity as the input factor goes to zero and approaches zero as the input factor goes to infinity. These conditions are called Inada conditions, following Inada (1963). In the case of physical and human capital, the Inada conditions read

$$\lim_{K \to 0} \frac{\partial F}{\partial K} = \lim_{H \to 0} \frac{\partial F}{\partial H} = \infty \quad \text{and} \quad \lim_{K \to \infty} \frac{\partial F}{\partial K} = \lim_{H \to \infty} \frac{\partial F}{\partial H} = 0.$$

[4] According to Barro and Sala-i-Martin (1995, p. 39), Knight (1944) stressed the idea that diminishing returns might not apply to a broad concept of capital.

Equation (3.3) states that the gross return r must be equal to the marginal product of capital A. Condition (3.3) demonstrates a weakness of the linear one-sector growth model. In this model firms cannot adjust their marginal product of capital to a changing interest rate since it is constant and exogenously determined.

Households

The instantaneous utility of the identical, atomistic agents is assumed to be increasing in consumption at a decreasing rate

$$U\left(C_t\right) = \frac{C_t^{1-1/\varepsilon} - 1}{1 - 1/\varepsilon}, \quad \text{for} \quad \varepsilon > 0, \ \varepsilon \neq 1 \tag{3.4}$$

$$U\left(C_t\right) = \ln C_t, \quad \text{for} \quad \varepsilon = 1 \tag{3.5}$$

Parameter ε represents the elasticity of intertemporal substitution between current and future consumption. Such preferences imply that households expand their consumption at a constant rate whenever the real interest rate is constant.[5] Households maximize their lifetime utility, given by the integral of the discounted instantaneous utility function

$$U_0 = \int_{t=0}^{\infty} U\left(C_t\right) e^{-\rho t} dt, \tag{3.6}$$

subject to the households' flow budget constraint

$$\left(1 - \tau_K\right) r_t W_t + T_t = \left(1 + \tau_C\right) C_t + \dot{W}_t, \tag{3.7}$$

where parameter ρ denotes the exogenous rate of time preference and variable W indicates households' wealth. The symbols τ_C and τ_K denote the tax rates on consumption and capital income, respectively, and T indicates the lump-sum transfer of the government. Equation (3.7) shows that the sum of wealth income net-of-tax and the lump-sum transfers from the government (left-hand side) is used for gross consumption and wealth accumulation (right-hand side). Since we assume a closed economy, wealth is equal to holdings of business capital, thus households own

---

[5] The choice of preferences and production technologies consistent with a balanced growth path can be justified with the Kaldor (1961) stylized facts of economic growth. For a discussion of these facts, see Romer (1989).

the factor of production. Therefore we can rewrite equation (3.7) as

$$(1 - \tau_K) \, r_t K_t + T_t = (1 + \tau_C) \, C_t + \dot{K}_t + \delta K_t. \qquad (3.8)$$

Following the literature on fiscal policy and economic growth, depreciation of capital is assumed not to be tax deductible.[6] However, the tax deduction of capital depreciation would not change the qualitative results of this study as depreciation is exogenous and the tax rates are given for households.

Government

The government is introduced in a minimal fashion. To concentrate on the growth effects of taxes we abstain from public consumption or public production goods; instead, all revenue is redistributed to the household in a (non-distorting) lump-sum manner.[7] The government flow budget constraint is given by

$$T_t = \tau_C C_t + \tau_K r_t K_t. \qquad (3.9)$$

Public spending has to be financed solely by taxing consumption or capital income because the government does not issue bonds. Hence the government is forced to run a balanced budget in every period. However, ignoring public debt does not change the results in this framework.[8]

The Market Solution

The representative household chooses the path of consumption C which maximizes its lifetime utility (3.6) subject to its flow budget constraint (3.8) given the time paths of the interest rate r, the lump-sum transfer T, and the tax rates τ_C and τ_K. Formally the optimization problem is given by

---

[6] See, for example, Pecorino (1993), Corsetti and Roubini (1996) and Milesi-Ferretti and Roubini (1998a).

[7] See Turnovsky (1996) for a linear growth model with a public consumption good and, for example, Barro (1990) for a similar model with a public production factor.

[8] For the debt structure in a linear growth model, see, for example, Turnovsky (1996).

$$\max_{C_t} U_0 \;=\; \int_{t=0}^{\infty} U\left(C_t\right) e^{-\rho t} dt,$$

$$\text{s.t. } \dot{K} \;=\; \left(1 - \tau_K\right) r_t K_t + T_t - \left(1 + \tau_C\right) C_t - \delta K_t,$$

$$C_t, K_t \;\geqslant\; 0 \;\forall t, \; K_0 \text{ given.}$$

The corresponding current-value Hamiltonian for this optimization problem takes the form

$$\max_{C_t} \mathcal{H}_t = U\left(C_t\right) + \lambda_t \left[\left(1 - \tau_K\right) r_t K_t + T_t - \left(1 + \tau_C\right) C_t - \delta K_t\right].$$

The first-order conditions with respect to C, K and λ become

$$\frac{\partial \mathcal{H}_t}{\partial C_t} \;=\; C_t^{-\frac{1}{\varepsilon}} - \left(1 + \tau_C\right) \lambda_t \overset{!}{=} 0, \tag{3.10}$$

$$\frac{\partial \mathcal{H}_t}{\partial K_t} \;=\; \lambda_t \left[\left(1 - \tau_K\right) r_t - \delta\right] \overset{!}{=} \lambda_t \rho - \dot{\lambda}_t, \tag{3.11}$$

$$\frac{\partial \mathcal{H}_t}{\partial \lambda_t} \;=\; \left(1 - \tau_K\right) r_t K_t + T_t - \left(1 + \tau_C\right) C_t - \delta K_t \overset{!}{=} \dot{K}_t, \tag{3.12}$$

where λ denotes the shadow price of capital in terms of utility. Equation (3.10) implies that the marginal utility of consumption in every period should equal the after-tax shadow price of capital. The Euler equation (3.11) implies that the rate of change in the shadow price of capital should be equal to the interest rate net of tax minus the sum of the rate of capital depreciation and the rate of time preference.[9] Equation (3.12) represents the households' flow budget constraint. Taking logs of equation (3.10) and differentiating it with respect to time yields

$$\frac{1}{\varepsilon} \hat{C}_t = -\hat{\lambda}_t. \tag{3.13}$$

After eliminating the shadow price in the Euler equation (3.11) by using equation (3.13), we get the Keynes–Ramsey rule describing the optimal

---

[9] The Euler equation is also known as the equation of motion.

consumption over time for the given tax rates:[10]

$$\hat{C}_t = \varepsilon\left[(1 - \tau_K)r - \delta - \rho\right]. \tag{3.14}$$

According to equation (3.14) consumption grows, remains constant, or declines if the interest rate net of tax is larger than, equal to, or smaller than the sum of the rate of depreciation and the rate of time preference. Substituting for the lump-sum transfer T from the households' budget constraint (3.12) into the governments' budget constraint (3.9) yields again the flow resource constraint of the economy:

$$\hat{K}_t = A - \frac{C_t}{K_t} - \delta \quad \Leftrightarrow \quad \hat{K}_t + \delta = \left(1 - \frac{C_t}{Y_t}\right)\frac{Y_t}{K_t}. \tag{3.15}$$

Equation (3.15) corresponds to the Harrod–Domar condition, that is, the rate of growth plus capital depreciation equals the saving rate of the economy divided by the capital-output ratio.

A balanced growth path is characterized as a state where all variables grow at a constant, possibly zero rate. Therefore, derivatives of growth rates with respect to time are zero along a balanced growth path. By taking logs and derivatives with respect to time of equation (3.15), and the production function (3.1), and under consideration of equation (3.13) we see that consumption, output and the capital stock grow at the same constant rate g:

$$g \quad \equiv \quad \hat{C} = \hat{K} = \hat{Y} = -\varepsilon\hat{\lambda}. \tag{3.16}$$

Because of condition (3.16), the consumption-capital ratio C/K is constant along a balanced growth path. If one tax is greater than zero, the lump-sum transfer T grows with the rate g as well. In the following, time indices are skipped when no ambiguity arises.

Using equations (3.3), (3.14) and condition (3.16) we can derive the reduced form of the growth rate g:

$$g = \varepsilon\left[(1 - \tau_K)A - \delta - \rho\right] \quad \equiv \quad \varepsilon\left[R - \rho\right]. \tag{3.17}$$

---

[10] In the model under consideration the Keynes–Ramsey rule is a specific representation of the Euler equation. In more complex models the maximization problem may result in more than one Euler equation. However, the Keynes–Ramsey rule describes only the optimal consumption path.

For our further analysis it is useful to define $R = (1 - \tau_K)\,A$ as the real marginal product of capital net of tax. According to equation (3.17) the economic growth rate is increasing in the intertemporal elasticity of substitution ε and the level of the technology A, but decreasing in the capital income tax τ_K, the rate of the capital depreciation δ and the rate of time preference ρ. A higher capital income tax affects adversely the intertemporal incentive to invest in capital by reducing the net-of-tax interest rate which lowers growth.

We can derive the reduced form of the consumption-capital ratio by using equations (3.15) and (3.17), and condition (3.16):

$$\frac{C}{K} = A - \delta - \varepsilon \left[\left(1 - \tau^K\right) A - \delta - \rho \right]. \tag{3.18}$$

Before we derive the effects of tax and parameter changes on the consumption-capital ratio it is useful to disclose the restrictions on parameters to ensure the existence of a balanced growth path. For the existence of a balanced growth path we must rule out negative values of the growth rate and the consumption-capital ratio. Obviously a permanent negative growth rate cannot be consistent with the definition of a balanced growth path since the capital stock sooner or later becomes zero. From equations (3.17) and (3.18) we see that the nonnegativity requirements are fulfilled if

$$A \quad \geqslant \quad \frac{\delta + \rho}{(1 - \tau_K)}, \tag{3.19}$$

$$\varepsilon \quad < \quad \frac{A - \delta}{(1 - \tau_K)\,A - \delta - \rho}. \tag{3.20}$$

According to equation (3.18) the effects of A and δ on the consumption-capital ratio depend on whether ε is larger than, equal to, or smaller than unity. From equation (3.20) it is seen that the intertemporal elasticity of substitution can be both smaller or larger than unity. The latter is true at least for small capital income tax rates. Consequently, the consumption-capital ratio is increasing, unaffected, or decreasing in the rate of capital depreciation for ε smaller than, equal to, or larger than unity. The consumption-capital ratio is increasing, unaffected, or decreasing in the level of the technology for ε smaller than, equal to, or larger than $1/(1 - \tau_K)$. Furthermore, the consumption-capital ratio is increasing in the rate of time preference, the capital income tax rate, but decreasing in the intertemporal elasticity of substitution. Finally, the consumption tax does not influence the consumption-capital ratio. By assuming the special case of a logarithmic utility function (3.5) with an intertemporal elasticity of substitution equal to one, the consumption-capital ratio (3.18) simplifies and only depends positively on the rate of time preference. The effects of changes in the tax rates and the parameters on economic growth and the consumption-capital ratio are summarized in Table 3.1.

Table 3.1: Effects of tax and parameter changes on core variables

	τ_C	τ_K	A	δ	ε	ρ
$\frac{\partial g}{\partial x}$	0	$-$	$+$	$-$	$+$	$-$
$\frac{\partial (C/K)}{\partial x}$	0	$+$	$+$; 0 ; $-^\circ$	$-$; 0 ; $+^*$	$-$	$+$

$^\circ$ Signs are obtained for $\varepsilon <$; $=$; $> 1/(1 - \tau_K)$.

* Signs are obtained for $\varepsilon <$; $=$; > 1.

In the following it is explained how certain tax and parameter changes affect economic growth and the consumption-capital ratio:

- A consumption tax does not affect the intertemporal incentive to invest in capital since R is unaffected. Hence, it does not affect the consumption-capital ratio as long as the consumption tax revenues are redistributed as a lump sum to households. Consequently, the consumption tax is a lump-sum tax since it affects neither the intratemporal nor the intertemporal allocation.

- A capital income tax reduces the real marginal product of capital net of tax R and therefore the intertemporal incentive to invest in capital. Households are willing to consume rather than to invest if a capital income tax is introduced or increased. As a consequence, the consumption-capital ratio increases and the growth rate decreases.

- A higher level of technology A increases the real marginal product of capital net of tax R and therefore stimulates growth.

- A higher capital depreciation rate δ works in exactly the opposite direction as an increased level of the technology.

- A higher intertemporal elasticity of substitution ε polishes the curvature of the instantaneous utility function and therefore makes future consumption more valuable. Capital accumulation increases at the expense of today's consumption, therefore, the consumption-capital ratio decreases and growth rises.

- When the rate of time preference ρ increases, individuals value future utility less and consumption rises at the expense of capital accumulation. As a consequence, the consumption-capital ratio increases and the growth rate decreases.

The Central Planner Solution

We now derive the central planner solution as a first-best reference point. By comparing the first-order conditions of the market solution with the corresponding first-order conditions of the central planner solution we are able both to identify the distortionary effects of taxes and to determine the optimal tax rates. A benevolent central planner chooses consumption in order to maximize the discounted lifetime utility (3.6) of the representative household subject to the flow resource constraint of the economy (3.2). The current-value Hamiltonian for this optimization problem reads

$$\max_{C} \mathcal{H} = U(C) + \lambda (AK - C - \delta K).$$

The first-order conditions of the maximization problem with respect to C, K and λ are given by

$$\frac{\partial \mathcal{H}}{\partial C} = C^{-\frac{1}{\gamma}} - \lambda \stackrel{!}{=} 0, \tag{3.21}$$

$$\frac{\partial \mathcal{H}}{\partial K} = \lambda (A - \delta) \stackrel{!}{=} \lambda \rho - \dot{\lambda}, \tag{3.22}$$

$$\frac{\partial \mathcal{H}}{\partial \lambda} = AK - C - \delta K \stackrel{!}{=} \dot{K}. \tag{3.23}$$

After eliminating the shadow price of capital by using equations (3.21) and (3.22), the Keynes–Ramsey rule for the central planner solution can be derived:

$$\hat{C} = \varepsilon \left(A - \delta - \rho \right). \qquad (3.24)$$

Using condition (3.16) we see that the Keynes–Ramsey rule (3.24) corresponds to the reduced form of the growth rate. It implies that the growth rate is increasing in the intertemporal elasticity of substitution and the level of the technology, but decreasing in the rate of capital depreciation and the rate of time preference. The reduced form of the consumption-capital ratio can be derived by using equations (3.23), (3.24) and under consideration of condition (3.16):

$$\frac{C}{K} = A - \delta - \varepsilon \left(A - \delta - \rho \right). \qquad (3.25)$$

It is seen that the Keynes–Ramsey rule, the reduced form of the growth rate and the reduced form of the consumption-capital ratio are identical to the market solution for $\tau_K = 0$.[11] The effects of the technology level and capital depreciation on the consumption-capital ratio (3.25) depend on whether the intertemporal elasticity of substitution is smaller than, equal to or larger than unity. However, it can be seen that the consumption-capital ratio is increasing in the rate of time preference and decreasing in the intertemporal elasticity of substitution. The effects of parameter changes on the growth rate and the consumption-capital ratio in the social planner solution are identical to those of the market solution for $\tau_K = 0$ (see Table 3.1).

Optimal Tax Rates

Since the consumption tax τ_C is a lump-sum tax it does not distort the intratemporal or the intertemporal allocation of consumption and capital accumulation, irrespective of the tax rate. Thus, in the model without endogenous labor supply, an exogenous government budget requirement can be financed with the consumption tax in a lump-sum fashion. However, the lump-sum character vanishes as soon as the leisure-work

---

[11]Therefore, by using equations (3.24) and (3.25) we see that the parameter restrictions to ensure the existence of a balanced growth path are identical to that of the market solution for $\tau_K = 0$, see equations (3.19) and (3.20).

decision of the households is taken into account. In Section 2.3.1 we discussed three different types of leisure: raw time, quality time and home production. However, as capital in the linear growth model is assumed to be an agglomeration of different types of capital and as labor is not modeled explicitly, the only reasonable type of leisure is home production. Considering raw time and quality time is just possible if human capital (tight to labor) is modeled explicitly. Without changing the production function, raw time or quality time can be introduced only by assuming that capital is identical to human capital. If home production is incorporated into the framework, the lump-sum character of the consumption tax vanishes. It can be shown that the consumption tax affects leisure and the consumption-capital ratio, but it does not affect economic growth.[12]

As mentioned above, by setting the capital income tax equal to zero $\left(\tau_K^{opt} = 0\right)$, a market economy can reach a first-best solution.[13] Any positive tax rate on capital income reduces growth and decreases welfare.[14] Thus, it can be stated that the outcome of the unregulated market economy is Pareto optimal and welfare maximization is equivalent to growth maximization.

3.2.2   Conclusions

The linear model possesses no transitional dynamics. Changing behavior of economic agents due to exogenous shocks or to changes in the tax rates takes place immediately and creates no adaptation processes. Hence, the economy is always on a balanced growth path.[15] It is possible to introduce transitional dynamics and to retain the feature of constant return to capital in the long run. A production function which possesses these properties can be obtained by additively combining the linear production

---

[12]See Section A.1 (page 223) in the appendix for the linear model with home production.

[13]This becomes obvious by comparing the first-order conditions of the market solution (3.17) and (3.18) with the corresponding first-order conditions of the central planner solution (3.24) and (3.25).

[14]Furthermore, Rebelo (1991) shows that an investment tax reduces the real interest rate net of tax and hence the rate of growth, similar to a capital income tax.

[15]For a formal proof, see Barro and Sala-i-Martin (1995, Ch. 4.1.4).

function with the neoclassical production function:

$$Y = AK + BK^{\alpha}L^{1-\alpha}.$$

This specification has been proposed by Jones and Manuelli (1990). Sala-i-Martin (1990a, p. 17) calls this production process intuitively 'Sobelow' since it is a mixture of Solow's neoclassical and Rebelo's linear models.

The linear growth model requires no increasing returns to scale to give rise to durable economic growth; only constant returns to scale are required. Economic growth is determined by the intertemporal elasticity of substitution, the level of the technology which is identical to the marginal product of capital, the capital income tax, the rate of capital depreciation, and the rate of time preference.

This economy illustrates two features that are shared by all endogenous growth models: (i) in contrast to the neoclassical growth model the real rate of return does not decline towards zero as the capital stock increases without having to assume an exogenous labor-augmenting technical progress. (ii) there is a close relation between the real rate of return to investment and the rate of growth. If the real rate of return goes down, the rate of capital accumulation declines and so does the rate of growth.

3.3   The Linear Model with Pollution

The model described in Section 3.2 ignores the environment. It implicitly assumes that no pollution is produced by the economic process, or alternatively, that if any pollution is generated it can be disposed of at no cost to the community. In this section we enrich the basic linear growth model by incorporating the natural environment and allowing for pollution. The model in this section is based on Ligthart and van der Ploeg (1994). In contrast to Ligthart and van der Ploeg we use a more general utility function which allows additionally for an intertemporal elasticity of substitution unequal to unity. Furthermore, we analyse both the market solution and the central planner solution. Finally, we also allow for a nonlinear relation between the externality generating factor and pollution. We shall see that the effects of fiscal policy on core variables depend on the intertemporal elasticity of substitution and that the level of the elasticity of pollution with respect to capital is one of the parameters which determines the level of the optimal growth rate.

3.3.1   The Analytical Framework

Technology

The linear production function (3.1) and the flow resource constraint of the economy (3.2) are unchanged. We now additionally assume that the capital stock K used in production causes a negative environmental externality as a side product.[16] The flow externality is assumed to affect individuals' utility, but does not harm the production process, that is, there are no positive spillovers of a better environment to the production of goods. Aggregated pollution P is assumed to be a public 'bad'. The pollution function P possesses the functional form

$$P_t = K_t^\chi, \qquad (3.26)$$

where exponent $\chi > 0$ is the elasticity of pollution with respect to capital.

Firms

Firms rent capital from households at the interest rate r and use this input to produce a final good with the technology described by equation (3.1). In contrast to Section 3.2 firms must pay a pollution tax τ_P on capital. The firms' profit condition in every period is given by

$$\pi_t = Y_t - r_t K_t - \tau_P K_t.$$

The firms' zero profit condition reads

$$r = A - \tau_P. \qquad (3.27)$$

According to equation (3.27), the gross rate of the capital return must be equal to the private marginal product of capital minus the pollution tax rate.

---

[16] Alternatively, pollution could be generated by output. However, as output is linear to the capital stock it does not change the qualitative results.

Government

The government taxes consumption, capital income and pollution, but redistributes the revenue in a lump-sum manner to households. The government flow budget constraint reads

$$T_t = \tau_C C_t + \tau_K r_t K_t + \tau_P K_t. \tag{3.28}$$

Households

Unlike Section 3.2, the identical, atomistic agents' utility depends not only positively on consumption but also negatively on pollution:

$$U(C_t, P_t) \;=\; \frac{\left(C_t P_t^{-\eta_P}\right)^{1-1/\varepsilon} - 1}{1 - 1/\varepsilon} \quad \text{for} \quad \varepsilon > 0,\; \varepsilon \neq 1, \tag{3.29}$$

$$U(C_t, P_t) \;=\; \ln C_t - \eta_P \ln P_t, \quad \text{for} \quad \varepsilon = 1. \tag{3.30}$$

Utility is seen to be increasing in consumption at a decreasing rate, $U_C > 0, U_{CC} < 0$, while it is decreasing in aggregate pollution $U_P < 0$. Utility is decreasing in aggregate pollution at an increasing rate $U_{PP} > 0$, at a constant rate $U_{PP} = 0$, or at a decreasing rate $U_{PP} < 0$ for ε larger than, equal to, or smaller than $\eta_P/(1 + \eta_P)$. The positive parameter η_P represents the weight of pollution in utility. Economic agents' discounted lifetime utility is given by

$$U_0 = \int_{t=0}^{\infty} U(C_t, P_t) e^{-\rho t} dt. \tag{3.31}$$

The flow budget constraint of the households is unchanged and given by equation (3.8).

The Market Solution

The representative household maximizes lifetime utility (3.31) by choosing the path of consumption C subject to the flow household budget constraint (3.8), given the time paths of the interest rate r, the tax rates on consumption τ_C and capital income τ_K, and the lump-sum transfer T. As pollution is assumed to be a pure public 'bad', rationally acting households ignore it in their maximization problem. The current-value Hamiltonian for this optimization problem reads

$$\max_{C} \mathcal{H} = U(C, P) + \lambda \left[(1 - \tau_K) rK + T - (1 + \tau_C) C - \delta K \right].$$

The first-order conditions of the maximization problem with respect to C and K are given by

$$\frac{\partial \mathcal{H}}{\partial C} \overset{!}{=} 0 \quad : \quad -(1 + \tau_C) \lambda = C^{-1/\varepsilon} P^{-\eta_P (1 - 1/\varepsilon)}, \quad (3.32)$$

$$\frac{\partial \mathcal{H}}{\partial K} \overset{!}{=} \lambda \rho - \dot{\lambda} \quad : \quad -\hat{\lambda} = (1 - \tau_K) r - \delta - \rho, \quad (3.33)$$

respectively. After eliminating the shadow price of capital and replacing the interest rate r by equation (3.27), the first-order condition is given by

$$
\begin{aligned}
\hat{C} &= \varepsilon \left[(1 - \tau_K)(A - \tau_P) - \delta - \rho \right] + \eta_P (1 - \varepsilon) \hat{P} \quad (3.34) \\
&\equiv \varepsilon (R - \rho) + \eta_P (1 - \varepsilon) \hat{P}.
\end{aligned}
$$

Ignoring the last term, equation (3.34) can be recognized as the Keynes–Ramsey rule describing the optimal consumption over time in a decentralized economy. Equation (3.34) states that consumption growth depends not only on the parameters ε, A, δ, ρ, and the taxes on capital income and pollution, but also on the endogenously determined growth rate of pollution $\hat{P}$. Note that the growth rate of pollution can be replaced by $\chi \hat{K}$ (see equation (3.26), which in turn is a function of the mentioned parameters and tax rates). The last term of the Keynes–Ramsey rule vanishes as the level of pollution is constant over time (implying $\hat{P} = 0$) or for an intertemporal elasticity of substitution ε equal to unity. According to the first term of equation (3.34) consumption grows, remains constant, or declines if the return of capital net of tax is larger than, equal to, or smaller than the sum of the rate of capital depreciation and the rate of time preference. Considering the last term we see that for an intertemporal elasticity of substitution smaller than unity, consumption grows faster, *ceteris paribus*, the larger the growth rate of pollution. The opposite is true for an intertemporal elasticity larger than unity or for a declining pollution growth rate.

Along a balanced growth path it can be shown that consumption output, and the capital stock grow at the same constant rate g, whereas pollution grows at the rate g/χ. Taking logs and differentiating with respect to time, the production function (3.1), the flow resource constraint of the economy (3.2) and the pollution function (3.26), yields

$$g \equiv \hat{C} = \hat{K} = \hat{Y} = \hat{P}/\chi. \tag{3.35}$$

Condition (3.35) implies that the consumption-capital ratio C/K is constant along the balanced growth path. From condition (3.35) we see that pollution is rising over time. For an elasticity of pollution with respect to capital χ equal to one, pollution growth is equal to economic growth. If pollution is a strictly convex function of the capital stock $(\chi > 1)$, pollution growth is higher than economic growth. The opposite holds if pollution is a strictly concave function of the capital stock $(\chi < 1)$.

The reduced forms of the growth rate g and the consumption-capital ratio C/K for the market solution along a balanced growth path are given by

$$g = \frac{\varepsilon\left[(1-\tau_K)(A-\tau_P)-\delta-\rho\right]}{1+\eta_P\chi(\varepsilon-1)}, \tag{3.36}$$

$$\frac{C}{K} = A-\delta-\frac{\varepsilon\left[(1-\tau_K)(A-\tau_P)-\delta-\rho\right]}{1+\eta_P\chi(\varepsilon-1)}, \tag{3.37}$$

respectively, where the flow resource constraint (3.2), the Euler equation (3.34), and condition (3.35) have been used. Ignoring environmental pollution – setting η_P or χ and τ_P equal to zero – the reduced forms (3.36) and (3.37) are identical to those of the basic model without pollution (see equations (3.17) and (3.18)). According to equations (3.36) and (3.37) higher taxes on capital income and pollution reduce the real marginal product of capital net of tax and therefore the intertemporal incentive to invest in capital. Households are willing to consume rather than to invest. Therefore, the consumption-capital ratio increases and economic growth decreases. Again, the consumption tax is a lump-sum tax since it does not distort the consumption-capital ratio and the growth rate.[17]

---

[17] Along a balanced growth path the growth rate and the consumption-capital ratio

The Central Planner Solution

For determining the optimal tax system we now derive the central planner solution as a first-best reference point. A benevolent central planner chooses consumption C in order to maximize the lifetime utility of the representative household (3.31), subject to the flow resource constraint of the economy (3.2). In contrast to households, the benevolent planner takes into account the negative side-effects of production. The current-value Hamiltonian for this optimization problem takes the form

$$\max_{C} \mathcal{H} = U\left(C, P\right) + \lambda\left(AK - C - \delta K\right).$$

After eliminating the shadow price of the capital stock, the first-order condition is given by

$$\hat{C} = \varepsilon \left(A - \eta_P \chi \frac{C}{K} - \delta - \rho \right) + \eta_P \left(1 - \varepsilon\right) \hat{P}. \qquad (3.38)$$

The term $A - \eta_P \chi C / K$ in the Keynes–Ramsey rule (3.38) represents the social return to capital which consists of the private marginal product of capital A and the optimal marginal damage of pollution $\eta_P \chi C / K$, which is external to firms in the market economy. Ignoring the last term in equation (3.38) for a moment, this indicates that optimal consumption grows, remains constant, or declines if the social return to capital is larger than, equal to, or smaller than the sum of the rate of capital depreciation and the rate of time preference. Considering the last term we see that for an intertemporal elasticity of substitution ε smaller than unity, consumption grows faster, *ceteris paribus*, the larger the endogenously determined growth rate of pollution. The opposite is true for an intertemporal elasticity larger than unity.

We can derive the reduced forms of the growth rate and the consumption-capital ratio by using the flow resource constraint of the econ-

---

cannot be negative. From equations (3.36) and (3.37) we see that these requirements can only be fulfilled for

$$A \;\geqslant\; \frac{\delta + \rho + (1 - \tau_K)\tau_P}{(1 - \tau_K)}, \quad 1 > \eta_P \chi \quad \text{and}$$

$$\varepsilon \;<\; \frac{(A - \delta)(1 - \eta_P \chi)}{(1 - \tau_K - \eta_P \chi)A - (1 - \tau_K)\tau_P - (1 - \eta_P \chi)\delta - \rho}.$$

omy (3.2), condition (3.35), and the first-order condition (3.38):

$$g \;=\; \varepsilon\left(A - \frac{\eta_P \chi \rho}{1 - \eta_P \chi} - \delta - \rho\right), \tag{3.39}$$

$$\frac{C}{K} \;=\; A - \delta - \varepsilon\left(A - \frac{\eta_P \chi \rho}{1 - \eta_P \chi} - \delta - \rho\right). \tag{3.40}$$

Along a balanced growth path, the growth rate and the consumption-capital ratio cannot be negative. From equations (3.39) and (3.40) we see that these requirements can only be fulfilled by imposing the following parameter restrictions

$$A \;\geqslant\; \frac{\rho + (1 - \eta_P \chi)\,\delta}{1 - \eta_P \chi}, \tag{3.41}$$

$$\varepsilon \;<\; \frac{(A - \delta)\,(1 - \eta_P \chi)}{(A - \delta)\,(1 - \eta_P \chi) - \rho}, \tag{3.42}$$

$$1 \;>\; \eta_P \chi. \tag{3.43}$$

It is seen from equation (3.39) that optimal economic growth is increasing in the level of the technology A and the intertemporal elasticity of substitution ε, but decreasing in the capital depreciation rate δ, the rate of time preference ρ, the elasticity of pollution with respect to capital χ, and the weight factor of pollution in utility η_P. In the market solution we have seen that there is a trade-off between growth and pollution, the latter determined by the pollution tax. In analogy, in the central planner solution there is a trade-off between growth and the weight factor of pollution in utility: the more households value the environment, the lower is optimal economic growth. According to equation (3.40), the effects of the level of the technology and the capital depreciation rate on the consumption-capital ratio depend on whether the intertemporal elasticity of substitution is smaller than, equal to, or larger than unity. From equation (3.42) in connection with equation (3.43) it is seen that ε can be smaller and larger than unity. The consumption-capital ratio is unambiguously negatively affected by the intertemporal elasticity of substitution and positively by parameters η_P, ρ and χ. Finally we can state that the optimal response to greener preferences (higher η_P) is a decrease in economic growth, an increased consumption-capital ratio and a lower pollution growth rate. The effects of parameter changes on growth and the consumption-capital ratio are summarized in Table 3.2.

Table 3.2: Effects of parameter changes on core variables

	A	δ	ε	η_P	ρ	χ
$\frac{\partial g}{\partial x}$	$+$	$-$	$+$	$-$	$-$	$-$
$\frac{\partial (C/K)}{\partial x}$	$+\,;\,0\,;\,-^\diamond$	$-\,;\,0\,;\,+^\diamond$	$-$	$+$	$+$	$+$

$^\diamond$ Signs are obtained for $\varepsilon <\,;\,=\,;\,>. 1$.

Optimal Tax Rates

We now determine the optimal tax rates of the economy. In order to derive the first-best tax rates we compare the first-order condition of the market solution with the first-order condition of the social planner solution.[18] Comparison of equations (3.34) and (3.38) reveals the following condition for a first-best solution:

$$(1 - \tau_K)(A - \tau_P) \overset{!}{=} A - \eta_P \chi \left(\frac{C}{K}\right)^{cps}.$$

The superscript '*cps*' denotes the central planner solution. There are at least two possibilities to fulfill this condition and hence to achieve a first-best solution in a market economy (see Table 3.3).

Case 1: A first-best solution can be reached by setting the tax on capital income equal to zero and the tax on pollution equal to the optimal marginal damage of pollution. In this case the pollution tax corresponds to a Pigouvian tax. *Case 2:* Additionally, there is another way to reach

---

[18]This implicit solution is possible as long as we are interested in first-best tax rates. However, the determination of second-best tax rates (for example, in the case of a government revenue requirement which must be financed by means of distortionary taxes) works differently. The government could choose tax rates so as to maximize the household's indirect utility function, subject to the first-order condition of the household's maximization problem (see, for example, Chamley 1986). Note that the determination of second-best tax rates in the case of many taxes quite often constitutes an unsolvable theoretical problem.

Table 3.3: Optimal tax rates, when $P = f(K)$

	τ_K	τ_P
Case 1	0	$\eta_P \chi \left(\frac{C}{K}\right)^{cps}$
Case 2	$\frac{\eta_P \chi}{A} \left(\frac{C}{K}\right)^{cps}$	0

a first-best solution by setting the pollution tax equal to zero and the capital income tax equal to the optimal marginal damage of pollution, divided by the marginal product of capital. This is not surprising as capital is the dirty and the only input factor. The difference between the two approaches consists in the tax base. A tax on capital is levied on the capital income which consists of the marginal product of capital A times the capital stock K, whereas the tax on pollution is levied solely on the physical capital stock K. Therefore it is necessary to correct the tax-base differences of the two taxes when capital is used. The reduced forms of the optimal taxes on capital income and pollution can be obtained by replacing the optimal consumption-capital ratio in Table 3.3 by its reduced form (3.40). Finally, it can be stated that in an unregulated market economy (that is, all taxes are zero), growth of pollution and economic growth is too high from a welfare point of view.

3.3.2 Conclusions

In the above model a consumption tax is a lump-sum tax and a capital income tax reduces growth in the model without environment (see Section 3.2). Furthermore, a pollution tax reduces growth. Therefore, growth maximization is no longer equal to welfare maximization. There is a trade-off between economic growth which is maximal in an unregulated market and environmental protection. In an unregulated market economy, economic growth and pollution growth are too high from a welfare point of view. The government can reach a first-best solution either by imposing a pollution tax equal to the optimal marginal damage of pollution or by setting the capital income tax equal to the optimal marginal damage of pollution divided by the marginal product of capital. The latter is necessary to correct for the tax-base differences between a capital income tax and a pollution tax. We find that the optimal response to a shift towards greener preferences will imply a decrease in the economic growth rate and a lower rate of pollution growth.

The results of the presumed economy are pessimistic in the sense that economic growth is always accompanied by an increasing pollution level. If we think of a renewable natural resource with a certain absorption capacity due to natural regeneration it is obvious that a rising pollution level sooner or later exceeds the absorption capacity which leads to a collapse of the resource. Obviously this applies even more to an exhaustible resource. To guarantee sustainable development, following our definition as a path with a non-declining environmental quality (see page 12) this implies a stationary economy if the economy as a whole is assumed to be a renewable resource. The pessimistic result can be explained by recalling the central assumptions of the model: pollution is tied to the use of the only input factor of production, which is capital. Since factor substitution is not possible in the one-sector linear growth model and abatement activities are not taken into consideration, there must be a trade-off between pollution and production. The desire for less pollution is accompanied by lower production and hence reduced capital accumulation.

3.4 The Linear Model with Pollution and Abatement

In this section we shall show that durable economic growth may be compatible with a sustainable environment. As before, pollution is a by-product of economic activity but can be reduced by spending part of the aggregate output on abatement. The effects of environmental policy in a one-sector linear growth model with pollution and abatement activities are analysed by Gradus and Smulders (1993) for a centrally planned economy by varying the weight factor on pollution in the utility function, and by Ligthart and van der Ploeg (1994) for a decentralized economy by changing the pollution tax and the provision of the public abatement activities. Furthermore, there is a comprehensive analysis of environmental policy in the linear growth model by Smulders and Gradus (1996). In contrast to the above-mentioned literature, they investigate the following points. (i) They analyse the effects of environmental policy with a multiplicative separable utility function. (ii) They derive the results for a market solution and for a central planner solution. (iii) They model pollution not only as a flow but also as stock. (iv) They assume that the environment not only has an amenity value but also a productive value and furthermore acts as a life-support system.[19] (v) Abatement activities are assumed to be private in nature. In the following we ignore point (iii) as modeling pollution as a stock phenomenon does not change the qualitative results but complicates the analysis (see Section 2.1). Furthermore, we do not consider productive environmental externalities formally, since their influence on the results can be easily discussed. Finally, we analyse both private and public abatement activities.

This section is structured as follows: In Subsection 3.4.1 the general model is laid out and both the market solution with private abatement activities and the central planner solution are derived. Optimal tax rates of all taxes in a first-best setting and the reduced forms of all core variables are presented in Subsection 3.4.2. In Subsection 3.4.3 we additionally analyse the case of public abatement activities. Subsection 3.4.4 summarizes the results and concludes.

3.4.1 The Analytical Framework

Technology

The linear production function $Y_t = AK_t$ is unchanged. However, adding the possibility of abatement measures to reduce pollution, the flow resource constraint of the economy now reads

$$Y_t = C_t + \dot{K}_t + Z_t + \delta K_t. \qquad (3.44)$$

The perfect malleable good Y can be used without any frictions not only for consumption C and net investment in the capital stock $\dot{K}$, but additionally for abatement activities Z. We still assume that the capital stock K used in production causes a negative environmental externality as a side product. The externality is assumed to affect individuals' utility

---

[19] For a discussion of these concepts, see Section 2.1.

negatively, but does not harm the production process, that is, there are
no positive spillovers of a better environment to the production of goods.
Of course it is conceivable that pollution directly affects the productivity
of production. Although this aspect is not analysed formally, we discuss
it in Section 3.4.2. Aggregate pollution P is a public 'bad' which can
be reduced by means of private abatement activities Z which in turn
consume a part of output, in line with the flow resource constraint (3.44).
Both P and Z are modeled as flow quantities. The modeling of pollution
and/or abatement activities as stock values does not change the results
along a balanced growth path but complicates the analysis. We assume
that if Z increases, the capital stock pollutes less, no matter if old or
new. One can think of some end-of-pipe technology, for example filters,
being used up within one period. Hence, abatement activities have to
be renewed in each period. The pollution function P has the functional
form

$$P_t = \left(\frac{K_t}{Z_t}\right)^\chi, \tag{3.45}$$

where $\chi > 0$ is the exogenous elasticity of P with respect to the capital-
abatement ratio K/Z. According to equation (3.45), pollution is increasing in capital and decreasing in abatement activities, $P_K > 0$
and $P_Z < 0$. For further discussion about the chosen pollution specification and their impacts, see Section 2.1.

Firms

Firms rent capital from the households at the interest rate r and use
this input to produce a final good with the linear production technology
described by equation (3.1). In contrast to Section 3.2, firms additionally
must pay a pollution tax τ_P according to their pollution P and choose
the level of private abatement activities Z. The firms' profit condition
in every period is given by

$$\pi_t = Y_t - r_t K_t - Z_t - \tau_P P_t.$$

The level of pollution and hence the pollution tax liability depends on
the employed stock of capital K and the level of private abatement activities Z. Abatement is assumed to be a private good which enables

firms in principle to increase output without causing more pollution. Firms are assumed to maximize their profits by choosing K and Z. The first-order conditions of the firms' maximization problem are given by

$$r = A - \frac{Z}{K},\tag{3.46}$$

$$\frac{Z}{K} = \left(\chi\frac{\tau_P}{K}\right)^{1/(1+x)} \quad \Leftrightarrow \quad 1 = \tau_P\chi\frac{P}{Z}.\tag{3.47}$$

Firms rent capital up to the point where its marginal cost equals the private marginal product of capital minus the abatement-capital ratio Z/K, which is determined by the pollution tax in equation (3.47). Equation (3.47) shows that abatement measures are chosen such that their marginal costs correspond to the marginal liability of the pollution tax. Note that the former is unity since we assume a one-to-one technology which allows us to transform output into abatement activities without additional costs. Without a pollution tax ($\tau_P = 0$), firms would ignore the negative side-effect of capital in the production process and abatement activities would be zero.

Government

The government's task is solely to correct the market failure caused by the environmental externality. As the abatement activities are private in nature, we still assume that the revenue is redistributed in a lump-sum manner to households. The government levies a consumption tax, a capital income tax and a pollution tax. The government flow budget constraint reads

$$T_t = \tau_C C_t + \tau_K r_t K_t + \tau_P P_t.\tag{3.48}$$

The Market Solution

The maximization problem of the representative household is identical to that of Section 3.3. Households maximize lifetime utility (3.31) by choosing the path of consumption C subject to the flow household budget constraint (3.8), given the time paths of the interest rate r, the tax rates on consumption τ_C and capital income τ_K, and the lump-sum transfer T.

For convenience, the first-order conditions with respect to C and K are replicated:

$$(1 + \tau_C)\,\lambda = C^{-1/\varepsilon} P^{-\eta_P(1-1/\varepsilon)},$$

$$-\hat{\lambda} = (1 - \tau_K)\,r - \delta - \rho.$$

After eliminating the shadow price for capital and replacing the interest rate r by equation (3.46), the first-order conditions become

$$\hat{C} = \varepsilon \left[(1 - \tau_K) \left(A - \frac{Z}{K} \right) - \delta - \rho \right] + \eta_P (1 - \varepsilon)\,\hat{P}. \qquad (3.49)$$

Equation (3.49) is the Keynes–Ramsey rule for the market economy determining the optimal consumption over time for the given tax rates. Note that the abatement-capital ratio Z/K is determined by the pollution tax (see equation (3.47)), and the growth rate of pollution $\hat{P}$ can be rewritten as $\chi(\hat{K} - \hat{Z})$ (see equation (3.45)).

The Central Planner Solution

In order to get a first-best solution as a reference point for determining the optimal taxation rule, we derive in this section the centrally planned solution. In contrast to the representative household, a benevolent central planner takes the negative side-effects of production into account. Consumption C and abatement activities Z are chosen in order to maximize the lifetime utility of the representative household (3.31) subject to the flow resource constraint of the economy (3.44). The current-value Hamiltonian for this optimization problem takes the form

$$\max_{C,Z} \mathcal{H} = U\,(C, P) + \lambda\,(AK - C - Z - \delta K),$$

where utility and pollution are defined by equations (3.29) and (3.45), respectively. After eliminating the shadow price of the capital stock, the first-order conditions are given by

$$\frac{Z}{K} = \chi \eta_P \frac{C}{K}, \qquad (3.50)$$

$$\hat{C} = \varepsilon \left(A - \frac{Z}{K} - \delta - \rho \right) + \eta_P (1 - \varepsilon)\,\hat{P}. \qquad (3.51)$$

Equation (3.51) represents the Keynes–Ramsey rule for the central planner solution describing the optimal consumption over time. The last term vanishes if the level of pollution is constant over time (implying $\hat{P} = 0$), that is, the growth rate of capital is equal to the growth rate of abatement,[20] and as well for an intertemporal elasticity of substitution ε equal to unity. The term $A - Z/K$ represents the social return to capital which consists of the private marginal product of capital A and the optimal marginal damage of pollution Z/K, which is external to firms in the market economy. Given a constant level of pollution, consumption grows, remains constant, or declines if the social return to capital is larger than, equal to, or smaller than the sum of the rate of depreciation and the rate of time preference. In addition, for an intertemporal elasticity of substitution smaller than one, consumption grows faster, *ceteris paribus*, the larger the growth rate of pollution. The opposite is true for an intertemporal elasticity larger than unity or for a declining pollution growth rate. Ignoring the capital income tax, the Keynes–Ramsey rule of the market solution seems to be identical with that of the central planner solution. However, the term Z/K in both equations is determined differently. For the market solution it is determined by equation (3.47), whereas for the central planner solution it is determined by equation (3.50). Equation (3.50) shows that for a social optimum the marginal utility of consumption and abatement must be equalized.

3.4.2   Results Along a Balanced Growth Path

It is shown in the following that all variables grow at the same constant rate g along a balanced growth path. Taking logs and differentiating with respect to time, equation (3.50) and the linear production function (3.1) yields

$$\hat{C} = \hat{Z} \quad \text{and} \quad \hat{K} = \hat{Y}, \tag{3.52}$$

respectively. Substituting the ratio C/K from equation (3.50) into the flow resource constraint of the economy (3.44), taking logs and differen-

---

[20] From equation (3.45), it follows that $\hat{P} = \chi(\hat{K} - \hat{Z})$.

tiating with respect to time gives

$$\hat{K} = \hat{Z}. \tag{3.53}$$

Together, conditions (3.52) and (3.53) show that the following variables grow at the same rate g along a balanced growth path:

$$g \equiv \hat{C} = \hat{K} = \hat{Y} = \hat{Z}. \tag{3.54}$$

Condition (3.54) implies that the consumption-capital ratio C/K and the abatement-capital ratio Z/K are constant. Therefore, pollution P is constant along a balanced growth path as well. A constant level of pollution is in accordance with sustainable development if the ecosystem is assumed to be a renewable resource and the level of pollution does not exceed its absorption capacity. Thus, along a balanced growth path the term $\eta_P (1 - \varepsilon) \hat{P}$ becomes zero in the Keynes–Ramsey rules (3.49) and (3.51). Here it becomes obvious that modeling pollution as a flow is a useful simplification: it does not change the qualitative results of the analysis along a balanced growth path.[21] It is seen that a growing economy can in principle produce an increasing number of abatement activities to stabilize environmental pollution.

Optimal Tax Rates

In order to derive the first-best tax rates, we compare the first-order conditions of the market solution (3.47) and (3.49) with the corresponding first-order conditions of the central planner solution (3.50) and (3.51). By comparing equations (3.47) and (3.49) with (3.50) we can compute the optimal pollution tax rule if the capital income tax is equal to zero:

$$\tau_P^{opt} (t) = \chi^{-1} K_t \left[\left(\frac{Z}{K} \right)^{cps} \right]^{1+\chi}. \tag{3.55}$$

The optimal environmental tax $\tau_P^{opt} (t)$ must rise in accordance with the evolution of the physical capital stock. In equation (3.55) the optimal

---

[21] If the environment were modeled as a renewable environmental resource, pollution would have to be constant and should not exceed the natural regeneration capacity along a balanced growth path to guarantee sustainable growth according to our definition.

abatement-capital ratio, indicated with the superscript '*cps*', is constant along a balanced growth path and parameter χ is the constant pollution elasticity, but the physical capital stock K increases over time (see equation 3.54). For that reason the Pigouvian tax rate must increase over time with the growth rate of the economy. This result becomes intuitive by remembering that the optimal level of pollution is constant along a balanced growth path. To keep the level of P constant, the pollution tax must rise over time because the capital stock, which is responsible for pollution, accumulates over time. Firms only increase abatement activities over time if they have the incentive to do this via an increasing pollution tax. For further analysis it is useful to separate trend and level of the pollution tax. Therefore we normalize it by the capital stock and define

$$\bar{\tau}_P \equiv \frac{\tau_P}{K}, \tag{3.56}$$

which is constant along a balanced growth path. Thus we assume that the government can adjust the pollution tax in accordance with the evolution of the physical capital stock in order to contain a certain level of pollution in the presence of economic growth.[22]

Because pollution is the only distortion in the decentralized economy, a first-best solution is reached by setting the Pigouvian tax according to taxation rule (3.55). In contrast to Section 3.3, in this economy a capital income tax would fail to internalize the externality because it creates no incentive for firms to engage in abatement activities.

Reduced Forms of the Market Solution

The reduced forms of the growth rate for the market solution can be derived by using equations (3.47), (3.49), (3.54) and definition (3.56):

$$g = \varepsilon \left\{ (1 - \tau_K) \left[A - (\chi \bar{\tau}_P)^{1/(1+\chi)} \right] - \delta - \rho \right\}. \tag{3.57}$$

Additionally, using equations (3.44), (3.47), (3.54), (3.57) and definition (3.56) we can derive the reduced form of the consumption-capital

---

[22] In Nielsen et al. (1995) the rising pollution tax is normalized by aggregate production.

ratio:

$$\frac{C}{K} = [1 - \varepsilon (1 - \tau_K)] \left[A - (\chi \bar{\tau}_P)^{1/(1+x)} \right] - (1 - \varepsilon) \delta + \varepsilon \rho. \qquad (3.58)$$

For the existence of a balanced growth path we must restrict parameters to rule out a negative consumption-capital ratio and a negative growth rate. From equations (3.57) and (3.58) we see that these requirements are fulfilled for

$$A \;\geqslant\; \frac{\delta + \rho + (1 - \tau_K)\,(\chi \bar{\tau}_P)^{1/(1+x)}}{(1 - \tau_K)}, \qquad (3.59)$$

$$\varepsilon \;\leqslant\; \frac{A - (\chi \bar{\tau}_P)^{1/(1+x)} - \delta}{(1 - \tau_K) \left[A - (\chi \bar{\tau}_P)^{1/(1+x)} \right] - \delta - \rho}. \qquad (3.60)$$

The reduced form of the growth rate (3.57) shows that g is increasing in the level of the technology and the intertemporal elasticity of substitution, but decreasing in the capital income tax, the pollution tax, the depreciation rate of capital, and the rate of time preference. The higher the pollution tax, the lower is the real return to capital net of tax and thus economic growth. The reason is that abatement activities crowd out investment and consumption. From equation (3.58) it is seen that the consumption-capital ratio is increasing in the capital income tax and the rate of time preference. As is shown in equation (3.60), the intertemporal elasticity can be larger than unity, at least for a small capital income tax. Consequently the effects of the pollution tax, the capital depreciation rate and the level of the technology depend on the level of ε. Equation (3.47) shows that the abatement-capital ratio is increasing in the normalized pollution tax $\bar{\tau}_P$. The effects of changes in taxes and parameters on core variables are summarized in Table 3.4. In an unregulated market economy (that is, all taxes are zero) there is too much pollution, too little abatement and too much growth as there is a negative relationship between growth and environmental quality. An efficient solution requires a positive pollution tax (see tax rule (3.55)) which lowers growth and pollution. If one allows for abatement activities, however, growth is compatible with a renewable ecosystem as long as the level of pollution does not exceed the natural regeneration capacity.

Table 3.4: Effects of tax and parameter changes on core variables

	τ_C/η_P	τ_K/ρ	$\bar{\tau}_P/\chi$	A	δ	ε
$\frac{\partial g}{\partial x}$	0	−	−	+	−	+
$\frac{\partial(C/K)}{\partial x}$	0	+	$-\,;0\,;+^\circ$	$+\,;0\,;-^\circ$	$-\,;0\,;+^*$	−
$\frac{\partial(Z/K)}{\partial x}$	0	0	+	0	0	0

$^\circ$ Signs are obtained for: $\varepsilon <\,;=\,;>1/(1-\tau_K)$.

* Signs are obtained for: $\varepsilon <\,;=\,;>1$.

In the preceding analysis the possibility of productive environmental spillovers of a better environment has not been taken into account. However, an improvement in the environmental quality may increase the productivity of production (see Section 2.1). Formally, this case could have been analysed in the present setup by adding a multiplicative term $P^{-\epsilon}$ on the right-hand side of the production function (3.1). The positive parameter ϵ represents the strength of the negative impact of pollution on production. It is possible to discuss productive environmental spillovers also without a formal analysis: along a balanced growth path the productive effect of a better environmental quality is equivalent to a higher level of the technology A because the level of pollution is constant along a balanced growth path. From Table 3.4, an increase in the level of technology is seen to increase economic growth. Hence, environmental improvements stimulate economic growth, *ceteris paribus*. Whether this positive growth-rate effect dominates the above-mentioned negative growth-rate effect depends solely on parameter values and thus is an empirical question. Another possibility as to how environmental quality may affect economic growth is via the capital depreciation rate. If the depreciation rate is an increasing function of pollution, a better environmental quality is equivalent to a lower δ. Hence, a better environmental quality stimulates growth *ceteris paribus* (see Table 3.4). Again, whether this effect dominates the above-mentioned negative growth effect depends on the strength of this spillover.

The Reduced Forms of the Social Planner Solution

Using equations (3.44), (3.50), (3.51) and (3.54) we can derive the reduced forms of the growth rate, the consumption-capital ratio and the abatement-capital ratio of the central planner solution:

$$g = \frac{\varepsilon\left(A - \chi\eta_P\rho - \delta - \rho\right)}{1 + \chi\eta_P\left(1 - \varepsilon\right)}, \tag{3.61}$$

$$\frac{C}{K} = \frac{A - \delta - \varepsilon\left(A - \delta - \rho\right)}{1 + \chi\eta_P\left(1 - \varepsilon\right)}, \tag{3.62}$$

$$\frac{Z}{K} = \frac{\chi\eta_P\left[A - \delta - \varepsilon\left(A - \delta - \rho\right)\right]}{1 + \chi\eta_P\left(1 - \varepsilon\right)}. \tag{3.63}$$

According to equations (3.61)–(3.63), the optimal response to greener preferences – a higher η_P – is a decrease in economic growth, a reduction of the consumption-capital ratio, and an increase in the abatement-capital ratio. The latter implies a reduction in pollution.

Substituting the reduced form of the optimal abatement-capital ratio (3.63) in the optimal pollution tax rule (3.55) yields its reduced form

$$\bar{\tau}_P^{opt} = \left\{\chi^{\frac{x}{1+x}}\frac{\eta_P\left[A - \delta - \varepsilon\left(A - \delta - \rho\right)\right]}{1 + \chi\eta_P\left(1 - \varepsilon\right)}\right\}^{1+x}. \tag{3.64}$$

The optimal pollution tax (3.64) is an increasing function of η_P and ρ, whereas the effects of A and δ depend on whether ε is larger than, equal to, or smaller than unity.

3.4.3   Public Abatement Activities

So far, it has been assumed that abatement activities are a private good. In this section we model abatement as a public good, as in Ligthart and van der Ploeg (1994) and Nielsen et al. (1995). Public abatement can be interpreted as knowledge about clean production methods. The analysis of public abatement activities is based on Sections 3.4.1 and 3.4.2. Since the Technology section is identical to that of Section 3.4.1 we shall skip it here. Furthermore, the results for the central planner solution in Sections 3.4.1 and 3.4.2 can still be used as a first-best reference. To model public abatement activities, basically we have to modify only the firms' profit condition and the government flow budget constraint. Thus the sections on Firms, Government and the Market Solution have to be adapted to the case of public abatement measures.

Firms

In the case when abatement activities are public in nature, firms must pay a pollution tax τ_P levied on the pollution-generating factor. Hence firms cannot reduce pollution by means of abatement activities as assumed in Section 3.4.1, but only by reduction of production. The firms' profit condition π in every period is given by

$$\pi = Y - rK - \tau_P K.$$

The zero profit condition implies that

$$r = A - \tau_P. \tag{3.65}$$

The gross return of capital must be equal to the marginal product of capital minus the pollution tax rate. This result is identical to that of Section 3.3, where we did not allow for abatement activities.

Government

Since it is from an individual perspective irrational for single agents to purchase a non-rival good but to rely on free-riding, we now give up the assumption that tax revenues are redistributed in a lump-sum manner as only the government can provide the efficient level of abatement measures. The government flow budget constraint now reads

$$\tau_c C + \tau_k r K + \tau_P K = Z. \tag{3.66}$$

Note that the government's single task to internalize the negative environmental effect can be divided into two subproblems since it faces an externality and a collective good problem: the first is to impose an efficient pollution tax; the second is to provide an optimal level of public abatement measures.

The Market Solution

The maximization problem and the first-order conditions of the market solution are identical to Section 3.4.1. For convenience we replicate the first-order conditions with respect to C and K:

$$(1 + \tau_C)\lambda = C^{-1/\varepsilon}P^{-\eta_P(1-1/\varepsilon)},$$

$$-\hat{\lambda} = (1 - \tau_K)r - \delta - \rho.$$

After eliminating the shadow price for capital and replacing the interest rate r by equation (3.65), the first-order conditions reduce to

$$\hat{C} = \varepsilon\left[(1 - \tau_K)(A - \tau_P) - \delta - \rho\right] + \eta_P(1 - \varepsilon)\hat{P}. \qquad (3.67)$$

Equation (3.67) is the Keynes–Ramsey rule for the market solution. Using condition (3.54) we can rewrite equation (3.67) to the reduced form of the growth rate in the market economy:

$$g = \varepsilon\left[(1 - \tau_K)(A - \tau_P) - \delta - \rho\right]. \qquad (3.68)$$

By using the resource constraint of the economy (3.44), the government flow budget constraint (3.66), the first-order condition of the firms (3.65), and the reduced form of the growth rate (3.68) we can derive the reduced forms of the consumption-capital ratio and the abatement-capital ratio:

$$\frac{C}{K} = \frac{(1 - \varepsilon)(1 - \tau_K)(A - \tau_P) + (\varepsilon - 1)\delta + \varepsilon\rho}{1 + \tau_C}, \qquad (3.69)$$

$$\frac{Z}{K} = \frac{[\tau_C + \tau_K - \tau_C\varepsilon(1 - \tau_K)]A}{1 + \tau_C} \qquad (3.70)$$
$$+ \frac{(1 + \tau_C\varepsilon)(1 - \tau_K)\tau_P + \tau_C(\varepsilon - 1)\delta + \tau_C\varepsilon\rho}{1 + \tau_C}.$$

The effects of changes in tax rates and parameters on the growth rate, the consumption-capital ratio and the abatement-capital ratio are summarized in Table 3.5.[23] The effects of changes in tax rates and parameter values in case of public abatement activities are similar to the case of

---

[23] Parameters η_P and χ have no effect on the growth rate or on the consumption-capital or abatement-capital ratios, thus they are skipped in Table 3.5.

Table 3.5: Effects of tax and parameter changes on core variables

	τ_C	τ_K	τ_P	A	δ	ε	ρ
$\frac{\partial g}{\partial x}$	0	−	−	+	−	+	−
$\frac{\partial(C/K)}{\partial x}$	−	$-;0;+^\circ$	$-;0;^\circ+$	$+;0;-^\circ$	$-;0;+^\circ$	−	+
$\frac{\partial(Z/K)}{\partial x}$	+	+	+	$+;0;-^*$	$-;0;+^\circ$	−	+

$\diamond$ Signs are obatained for $\varepsilon < ; = ; > 1$.

$*$ Signs are obtained for $\varepsilon < ; = ; > \frac{\tau_C + \tau_K}{\tau_C(1-\tau_K)}$.

$\circ$ Signs are obtained for $\varepsilon < ; = ; > 1$.

private abatement activities (see Table 3.4). However, certain effects of parameter changes differ as neither Table 3.4 nor 3.5 show the optimal implications. The different pollution tax base in the case of private and public abatement activities is responsible for the differences. Apart from that there is another interesting difference. Although the consumption tax is a lump-sum tax it influences the consumption-capital ratio and the abatement-capital ratio and hence the level of pollution. To explain this we must distinguish between the government revenue and its expenditure as in the model under consideration both issues are associated. The *revenue* of a consumption tax does not distort the economy, hence it possesses the characteristics of a lump-sum tax. However, since the revenue is not *redistributed* as a lump sum but used for the provision of the public good, it affects the allocation of the economy. The provision of the public abatement activities crowds out consumption and reduces pollution.

Optimal Tax Rates

In this section we derive the optimal tax rates of the economy. In order to derive the first-best tax rates, we compare the first-order condition of the market solution with the first-order condition of the social planner solution. Comparison of equations (3.67) and (3.51) reveals the following condition

$$(1 - \tau_K)(A - \tau_P) \ \overset{!}{=} \ A - \left(\frac{Z}{K}\right)^{cps}. \tag{3.71}$$

Along a balanced growth path the optimal abatement-capital ratio is constant and determined by equation (3.63). Remember that the environmental externality is the only distortion in this economy. To correct this market failure the government has three tax instruments available. In principle there may be degrees of freedom in the choice of tax instruments. In the following we shall see that there are at least two possibilities to fulfill condition (3.71) and hence to achieve a first-best solution in a market economy (see Table 3.6).

Table 3.6: Optimal tax rates, when $P = f(K,Z)$

	τ_C	τ_K	τ_P
Case 1	0	0	$\left(\frac{Z}{K}\right)^{cps}$
Case 2	0	$\frac{1}{A}\left(\frac{Z}{K}\right)^{cps}$	0

Case 1: A first-best solution can be reached by setting the taxes on capital income and consumption equal to zero and the tax on pollution equal to the optimal marginal damage of pollution. In this case the pollution tax corresponds to a Pigouvian tax. *Case 2:* A first-best solution can also be reached by setting the taxes on pollution and consumption equal to zero and the capital income tax equal to the optimal marginal damage of pollution divided by the marginal product of capital. It can be seen that the effects of a capital income tax are similar to the effects of a tax on pollution. This is not surprising since physical capital is the dirty input factor; however the tax base is different. A tax on capital is levied on the capital income which consists of the marginal product of capital times the physical capital stock, whereas the tax on pollution is levied solely on the physical capital stock K. Therefore, it is necessary to correct the optimal marginal damage of pollution by A^{-1} in order to equate the tax-base differences of the two taxes, when a capital income tax is used.

Although a tax on consumption affects the abatement-capital ratio positively (see Table 3.5), it fails to internalize the externality. A consumption tax does not influence the marginal product net of tax and hence growth which is necessary for a first-best solution.

A first-best environmental policy requires that the marginal liability of the optimal tax equals the marginal costs of providing the public abatement measures. Since we assume a one-to-one technology by which the final good (tax revenue) can be transformed into the public good (see equation (3.44)), the first-best taxation instantaneously raises the public revenue necessary to provide the optimal level of abatement. Hence in our setting the optimal pollution tax (case 1) or the optimal capital tax (case 2) fulfill two tasks at the same time. They lower the inefficiently high growth rate and generate the exact amount of public revenues to provide the optimal level of abatement activities. This can be proved by inserting the optimal tax rates in the government's budget constraint (3.66).

3.4.4 Conclusions

In this section we have shown that a growing economy can in principle produce a growing number of abatement activities to stabilize environmental pollution. Hence, durable growth may be compatible with a sustainable natural environment. In the presumed economy a higher pollution tax lowers the real return of capital net of tax and thus economic growth if the environment has an amenity value only. The reason is that abatement crowds out investment and consumption. In an unregulated market economy there is too much pollution, too little abatement and too much growth. Welfare maximization is not equivalent to growth maximization. Growth is maximal in an unregulated market economy and welfare is maximal if the environmental externality is fully internalized. The optimal response to greener preferences is a decrease in economic growth. However, if environmental quality additionally affects either the productivity or the depreciation of capital, then a higher pollution tax stimulates economic growth, *ceteris paribus*. Whether this positive growth effect dominates the above-mentioned negative growth effect depends on parameter values. If the growth-stimulating effect dominates, growth would be too low in an unregulated market economy.

A capital income tax is growth reducing since it lowers the real marginal product of capital net of tax and therefore the intertemporal incentive to invest.

We analysed both private and public abatement activities. In the case of private abatement activities the pollution tax is levied on firms' pollution, and government revenues are redistributed in a lump-sum manner. In principle, every single firm is enabled to increase output without causing more pollution. With this specification we found that the optimal pollution tax is rising over time with the growth rate. Only a rising pollution tax creates the incentive to firms to increase their abatement activities. On the other hand, when abatement is public in nature the pollution tax is imposed on the pollution-generating factor, capital. Government revenues are here used to finance public abatement measures. At the firm level, pollution reduction is only possible through a reduction of output. However, on the economy level, increasing output is possible without causing more pollution. This requires an increase in abatement activities. With this specification there are at least two possibilities for achieving a first-best solution. An optimal solution in a decentralized economy can be reached either by setting a pollution tax equal to the optimal marginal damage of pollution or by setting the capital income tax equal to the optimal marginal damage of pollution divided by the marginal product of capital. Apart from the optimal tax structure, it is seen that the qualitative results do not depend on whether abatement activities possess the character of a private or public good. Therefore, in the following chapters we analyse alternately the former and the latter cases.

3.5   The Open Economy

So far, we have investigated the effects of environmental policy on growth and welfare in a closed economy. The fact that many environmental problems, as for example acidification or pollution of rivers and lakes, are international rather than national in nature implies that environmental externalities will not be fully internalized by means of national tax policies. Many of the most pressing environmental problems, such as the anthropogenic greenhouse effect or the destruction of the ozone layer, even possess a global character.[24] In the case of global externalities and given the existence of a supranational authority vested with the required competencies – for example, to introduce global environmental taxes – the model of a closed economy analysed in Section 3.4 could be used to analyse the effects of a global environmental policy on growth and welfare. Then the world economy could be interpreted as a closed economy. However, for the time being national governments are not willing to install supranational authorities vested with the required competencies to internalize global externalities.

In addition to international environmental spillovers there may exist other *non*-environmental transboundary externalities. In fact, empirical evidence suggests that foreign cumulative R&D is an important determinant of domestic productivity. For example, Coe and Helpman (1995) find by using pooled time-series/cross-section data of 21 OECD countries plus Israel during the period 1971-90 that foreign R&D capital stock has important effects on the total domestic factor productivity, and these are stronger the more open an economy is to foreign trade. Cumulative R&D expenditure is here used as a proxy for the stock of knowledge. The benefits from foreign R&D, for instance, consist of learning about new technologies and materials, production processes, or organizational methods. As R&D capital is a specific form of human capital associated with innovation, Engelbrecht (1997) additionally distinguishes between R&D and 'general' human capital, measured as average years of schooling of the labor force. His study supports the statistically significant results of Coe and Helpman and finds the same effects for general human capital.

The above observations lead us to study the strategic interactions between two countries within the framework of a differential game and to answer the question how pollution, economic growth and welfare are influenced by international policy coordination. We assume that every country is mutually affected by negative international environmental spillovers generated by the production process and by positive inter-

---

[24]For surveys on international environmental problems, see Måler (1990) or Sandler (1997).

national knowledge spillovers associated with capital accumulation. The welfare of the representative agent in every country is negatively affected by environmental pollution of the domestic and the foreign countries, whereas the production in every country is an increasing function of the domestic capital stock and foreign capital spillovers. Households invest in the stock of knowledge which has the character of an international public good in the absence of international patent markets. For simplicity, we assume two identical countries, implying that international trade and capital flows are absent. We derive both the noncooperative open-loop Cournot–Nash equilibrium where countries are assumed not to take into account the effects of their actions on the other country and the full cooperative outcome, corresponding to supranational planning. The open-loop Nash solution assumes that players have only initial state information and that the period of commitment is equal to the entire planning horizon. Every country is represented by a national benevolent central planner. Therefore, countries are treated as unit actors and the internal national decision-making process is ignored.

The underlying assumptions imply that important aspects of international environmental cooperations are ignored. Assuming that the period of commitment is equal to the entire planning horizon implies that stability problems are ruled out. Since we consider only two countries, cooperative equilibria with only a subgroup of countries participating are not possible either.[25] Finally, due to the assumption of identical countries all environmental agreements are cost efficient.[26] Nevertheless, we analyse not only the noncooperative and the full cooperative solutions, but also partial environmental or knowledge cooperations.

The analysis of this section is based on van der Ploeg and Ligthart (1994). They analyse the strategic interaction between two identical countries in an endogenous growth model where growth is driven by

---

[25] See, for example, Barrett (1994) for the issues of stability and coalition size of international environmental agreements in static and dynamic games of identical countries. For agreements of subcoalitions including side payments between identical countries, see Carraro and Siniscalco (1993), and between heterogeneous countries, see Petrakis and Xepapadeas (1996) and Schmidt (1997).

[26] For the problems of cost-effectiveness in international environmental agreements, see Hoel (1993) and Schmidt (2000) in static, and Kverndokk (1993) in dynamic frameworks.

infrastructure.[27] They take into account three international spillovers: knowledge spillovers, externalities resulting from government spending on a productive public good and environmental externalities. Furthermore, pollution is modeled as a stock variable. On the one hand we simplify this analysis by ignoring productive government spending and hence externalities associated with it and by modeling pollution as a flow. However, the former does not change the effects of the other spillovers and the latter does not change the qualitative results along a balanced growth path but simplifies the analysis. On the other hand, we generalize the analysis by assuming a multiplicatively separable and not an additively separable utility function. Furthermore, we evaluate the outcome of the partial cooperations from a welfare point of view.

In the following Section 3.5.1, we first describe the model setup for the open economy. In order to determine the cooperation effects, we derive in Section 3.5.2 the noncooperative open-loop Cournot–Nash equilibrium and in Section 3.5.3 the cooperative outcome which would result under supranational planning. By comparing the reduced forms of the noncooperative and the cooperative outcomes in Section 3.5.4 we estimate the effects of cooperation on growth, pollution and welfare.

3.5.1 The Analytical Framework

Technology

We consider a global economy consisting of two identical countries, the home country and the foreign country, the latter being indicated by an asterisk '*'. The home country produces one homogeneous good by using domestic capital K and foreign capital $\overset{*}{K}$. The latter is exogenously given for the home country and reflects the international knowledge spillover. The perfectly malleable output of the home country can be used without any frictions for consumption, for net investment in the capital stock, and for abatement activities. The production function and the resource constraint of the home country are given by, respectively,

$$ Y = AK^\alpha \overset{*}{K}^{1-\alpha}, \tag{3.72} $$

---

[27]It is a Barro type of model, that is, with a productive public good.

$$Y = C + Z + \dot{K} + \delta K, \qquad (3.73)$$

where $0 < \alpha \leqslant 1$. Parameter α denotes the exogenous share of domestic capital in production where A reflects the level of the technology.

As in Section 3.4, the capital stock used in production causes a negative environmental externality as a side product which can be reduced by abatement activities. However, we now distinguish between pollution generated in the home country p, pollution caused in the foreign country $\overset{*}{p}$ and total pollution P:

$$p = \left(\frac{K}{Z}\right)^{\chi}, \qquad (3.74)$$

$$P = p + (1 - \eta_F)\overset{*}{p}, \qquad (3.75)$$

where $0 \leqslant \eta_F \leqslant 1$. By means of parameter η_F we can distinguish different types of externalities. In the case of a global externality such as the anthropogenic greenhouse effect it does not matter where pollution is generated and total pollution is the sum of national and foreign pollutions $(P = p + \overset{*}{p})$, obtained by setting parameter $\eta_F = 0$. However, in the case of acid rain, transboundary pollution depends on the strength and direction of the wind. In the model this can be illustrated by setting η_F somewhere between zero and unity. Finally, setting $\eta_F = 1$ reflects the case of a pure national externality such as noise or smog.

Households

The instantaneous and the lifetime utilities of households are given as before:

$$U = \begin{array}{ll} \frac{\left(CP^{-\eta_P}\right)^{(1-1/\varepsilon)} - 1}{1 - 1/\varepsilon} & \text{for} \quad \varepsilon > 1 \\ \ln C - \eta_P \ln P & \text{for} \quad \varepsilon = 1 \end{array}, \qquad (3.76)$$

$$U_0 = \int_{t=0}^{\infty} U(C, P) e^{-\rho t} dt. \qquad (3.77)$$

Note that P now indicates total pollution, given by equation (3.75).

3.5.2 The Noncooperative Solution

The strategic interaction over time between the two countries can be modeled as a differential game. For the noncooperative solution the countries are assumed to behave in a Cournot–Nash manner. Given the selected plan of the foreign government, the benevolent planner of the home country maximizes lifetime utility by choosing the time paths of domestic consumption and abatement subject to the domestic resource constraint (3.73). The current-value Hamiltonian for the domestic country is given by

$$\max_{C,Z} \mathcal{H} = U\left[C, P\left(p, \overset{*}{p}\right)\right] + \lambda\left(AK^\alpha \overset{*}{K}^{1-\alpha} - C - Z - \delta K\right).$$

Note that variables $\overset{*}{K}$ and $\overset{*}{p}$ are exogenously given for the domestic country reflecting the international knowledge and pollution spillovers from the foreign country, respectively. Analogously the current-value Hamiltonian for the foreign country is given by

$$\max_{\overset{*}{C},\overset{*}{Z}} \overset{*}{\mathcal{H}} = \overset{*}{U}\left[\overset{*}{C}, \overset{*}{P}\left(\overset{*}{p}, p\right)\right] + \overset{*}{\lambda}\left(A\overset{*}{K}^\alpha K^{1-\alpha} - \overset{*}{C} - \overset{*}{Z} - \delta\overset{*}{K}\right).$$

Here variables K and p are exogenously given. Since the two countries are identical it is sufficient to derive the first-order conditions for one country. The first-order conditions of the home country with respect to consumption, abatement, capital and the shadow price of capital are given by

$$\lambda = C^{-1/\varepsilon} P^{-\eta_P(1-1/\varepsilon)}, \tag{3.78}$$

$$\lambda = \eta_P \chi C^{1-1/\varepsilon} P^{-\eta_P(1-1/\varepsilon)-1} p Z^{-1}, \tag{3.79}$$

$$-\hat{\lambda} = \alpha A \left(\frac{K}{\overset{*}{K}}\right)^{\alpha-1} \tag{3.80}$$
$$-\lambda^{-1}\eta_P \chi C^{1-1/\varepsilon} P^{-\eta_P(1-1/\varepsilon)-1} p K^{-1} - \delta - \rho,$$

$$\hat{K} = A - \frac{C}{K} - \frac{Z}{K} - \delta. \tag{3.81}$$

Equations (3.78) and (3.79) imply that the shadow price of capital should be equal to the marginal utility of consumption and abatement, respectively. Equation (3.80) is the Euler equation and equation (3.81) represents the flow resource constraint of the economy.

Because of the assumed symmetry, the optimal conditions of the domestic and the foreign countries are analogous, hence the levels of the domestic variables are identical to the levels of the corresponding foreign variables. The symmetry condition reads

$$C = \overset{*}{C}, \ K = \overset{*}{K}, \ P = \overset{*}{P}, \ p = \overset{*}{p}, \ Z = \overset{*}{Z}, \ \lambda = \overset{*}{\lambda}. \tag{3.82}$$

In addition, along a balanced growth path consumption, the capital stock, output and abatement activities grow at the same constant rate g:

$$g \ \equiv \ \hat{C} = \hat{K} = \hat{Y} = \hat{Z} = -\hat{\lambda}\varepsilon. \tag{3.83}$$

Because of condition (3.83), the consumption-capital ratio and the abatement-capital ratio are constant, and therefore, pollution P is constant along a balanced growth path as well. Applying conditions (3.82) and (3.83) and eliminating the shadow price of capital we can rewrite the first-order conditions (3.78)–(3.81) and get

$$\frac{Z}{K} \ = \ \frac{\eta_P \chi}{(2 - \eta_F)} \frac{C}{K}, \tag{3.84}$$

$$g \ = \ \varepsilon \left(\alpha A - \frac{\cdot Z}{K} - \delta - \rho \right), \tag{3.85}$$

$$g \ = \ A - \frac{C}{K} - \frac{Z}{K} - \delta. \tag{3.86}$$

Equation (3.84) shows that the marginal utility of consumption and abatement must be equalized. Equation (3.80) is the Euler equation describing the optimal accumulation of capital from a national point of view, and equation (3.86) corresponds to the Harrod–Domar condition. In the absence of an international environmental externality ($\eta_F = 1$), and in the absence of international knowledge spillovers ($\alpha = 1$), equations (3.84) and (3.85) are identical to the central planner solution of the closed economy in Section 3.4.2.

We can derive the noncooperative reduced forms of the growth rate, the consumption-capital ratio and the abatement-capital ratio by using the first-order conditions (3.84)–(3.86):

$$g = \frac{\varepsilon\left[(\eta_P\chi + 2 - \eta_F)(\alpha A - \delta - \rho) - \eta_P\chi(A - \delta)\right]}{2 - \eta_F + \eta_P\chi(1 - \varepsilon)}, \quad (3.87)$$

$$\frac{C}{K} = \frac{(2 - \eta_F)\left[A - \delta - \varepsilon(\alpha A - \delta - \rho)\right]}{2 - \eta_F + \eta_P\chi(1 - \varepsilon)}, \quad (3.88)$$

$$\frac{Z}{K} = \frac{\eta_P\chi\left[A - \delta - \varepsilon(\alpha A - \delta - \rho)\right]}{2 - \eta_F + \eta_P\chi(1 - \varepsilon)}. \quad (3.89)$$

To identify the effects of a noncooperative solution we compare the reduced forms of the noncooperative solution with the reduced forms of the cooperative solution which we shall derive in the following.

3.5.3   The Cooperative Solution

In the full cooperative solution each national social planner takes into account the effects of their decisions on the other country, hence all international spillovers are internalized. The easiest way to derive the global optimum is to assume a supranational social planner who chooses the paths of $C, Z, \overset{*}{C}, \overset{*}{Z}$ to maximize the sum of both lifetime utility functions subject to the national resource constraints. The current-value Hamiltonian of this maximization problem reads

$$\max_{C,Z,\overset{*}{C},\overset{*}{Z}} \mathcal{H} = U(C,P) + \overset{*}{U}\left(\overset{*}{C},\overset{*}{P}\right)$$

$$+ \lambda\left[AK^\alpha \overset{*}{K}^{1-\alpha} - C - Z - \delta K\right]$$

$$+ \overset{*}{\lambda}\left[A\overset{*}{K}^\alpha K^{1-\alpha} - \overset{*}{C} - \overset{*}{Z} - \delta\overset{*}{K}\right]$$

After eliminating the shadow prices of the domestic capital stock λ and foreign capital stock $\overset{*}{\lambda}$, and after imposing the symmetry conditions (3.82), the first-order conditions along a balanced growth path are given by

$$\frac{Z}{K} = \eta_P\chi\frac{C}{K}, \quad (3.90)$$

$$g = \varepsilon\left(A - \frac{Z}{K} - \delta - \rho\right), \quad (3.91)$$

$$g \;=\; A - \frac{C}{K} - \frac{Z}{K} - \delta. \tag{3.92}$$

Comparing equation (3.84) with (3.90) and (3.85) with (3.91), we see that the marginal utility of abatement and the marginal product of capital are increased in the cooperative solution, respectively – remember that $0 \leqslant \eta_F \leqslant 1$ and $0 < \alpha \leqslant 1$. This policy corresponds to a positive shock in consumers' preferences for environmental quality η_P and in the level A of the production technology. In the noncooperative solution the national central planner does not take into account the international environmental spillovers, that is, that domestic pollution creates a disutility in the foreign country as well. Therefore, the marginal utility of abatement is too low from a global welfare point of view. Furthermore, in the noncooperative solution the central planner does not take into account the beneficial effects of domestic capital accumulation for the foreign country. Hence, in the noncooperative solution the return to capital is too low from a global welfare point of view.

It is seen that the first-order conditions of the cooperative outcome are identical to the optimal first-order conditions of a closed economy in Section 3.4.2. In the full cooperative outcome all existing external effects are internalized. Hence, using equations (3.90)–(3.92) we get the same reduced forms of the growth rate, the consumption-capital ratio and the abatement-capital ratio as in the central planner solution of the closed economy:

$$g \;=\; \frac{\varepsilon\left(A - \chi\eta_P\rho - \delta - \rho\right)}{1 + \chi\eta_P\left(1 - \varepsilon\right)}, \tag{3.93}$$

$$\frac{C}{K} \;=\; \frac{A - \delta - \varepsilon\left(A - \delta - \rho\right)}{1 + \chi\eta_P\left(1 - \varepsilon\right)}, \tag{3.94}$$

$$\frac{Z}{K} \;=\; \frac{\chi\eta_P\left[A - \delta - \varepsilon\left(A - \delta - \rho\right)\right]}{1 + \chi\eta_P\left(1 - \varepsilon\right)}. \tag{3.95}$$

After having calculated the noncooperative and the cooperative outcomes we are able now to determine the cooperation effects on growth, pollution and welfare.

3.5.4 Cooperation Effects on Growth, Pollution and Welfare

We now can distinguish three different scenarios of cooperation: knowledge cooperation, environmental cooperation and full cooperation. The latter is the globally first-best solution described above. What are the reasons for analysing partial cooperations? First, it is likely that the negotiation costs differ between the two international spillovers. Second, the public is well informed about one spillover but not about the other because there is less uncertainty about it, or the consequences are more visible. In the extreme, the countries do not know about the second spillover.[28] Finally, partial cooperations are advantageous from a technical point of view since it is easier to show isolated cooperation effects of one spillover.

To assess the effects of the three different cooperative solutions on growth, pollution, the consumption-capital ratio and welfare we compare the reduced forms of the noncooperative solution (3.87)–(3.89) with the reduced forms of the cooperative solution (3.93)–(3.95). We see that the noncooperative solution is identical to the cooperative solution in the absence of international spillovers ($\alpha = 1$ and $\eta_F = 1$). There are two possibilities for computing the effects of the different cooperative outcomes. (i) The effects of knowledge cooperation on core variables are similar to the effects of a higher α in the reduced forms of the noncooperative outcome. The effects of environmental cooperation on core variables are similar to the effects of a higher η_F in the reduced forms of the noncooperative solution. Finally, the effects of full cooperation on core variables are similar to the effects of a simultaneous increase of α and η_F in the reduced forms of the noncooperative outcome. Unfortunately, the partial derivatives of the reduced forms with respect to a simultaneous increase of α and η_F are impossible to obtain. (ii) The other possibility to figure out the effects on core variables for a full cooperation is to compare the reduced forms of the noncooperative solution with the reduced forms of the cooperative solution. For the partial cooperations this is

---

[28] International spillovers could affect the countries asymmetrically, which complicates the negotiation and the success of a full cooperation. However, since we assume identical countries, this is not possible in our framework.

Economic Growth and Environmental Policy

done as follows. We can mimic the cooperative outcome for the separate knowledge and pollution agreements by setting $\alpha = 1$ and $\eta_F = 1$ in the reduced forms of the noncooperative solution, respectively. For example, to derive the effects of knowledge cooperation we compare every reduced form of the noncooperative solution for $0 < \alpha < 1$ with itself, but setting $\alpha = 1$. By doing so we obtain the effects of knowledge cooperation on pollution, growth and the consumption-capital ratio. Similarly this can be done for the environmental cooperation as well. The effects on growth, pollution and the consumption-capital ratio of knowledge, environmental and full cooperation are summarized in Table 3.7 in rows 2-4. The superscript 'nc' indicates the noncooperative solution whereas 'c' indicates the cooperative outcome. In order to analyse welfare changes

Table 3.7: Cooperation effects on core variables in the linear model

	knowledge coop.	environmental coop.	full coop.
growth	$g^{nc} < g^c$	$g^{nc} > g^c$	ambiguous
poll.	$P^{nc} < P^c$	$P^{nc} > P^c$	ambiguous
ratio	$\left(\frac{C}{K}\right)^{nc} > \left(\frac{C}{K}\right)^c$	$\left(\frac{C}{K}\right)^{nc} \gtreqless \left(\frac{C}{K}\right)^c$ for $\varepsilon \gtreqless 1$	ambiguous
welfare	ambiguous	ambiguous	$U^{nc} < U^c$

we integrate the discounted lifetime utility function (3.77) for $\varepsilon \neq 1$ and $\varepsilon = 1$, respectively:

$$U_0 = \frac{1}{1 - \frac{1}{\varepsilon}} \left\{ \frac{P^{-\eta_P \left(1 - \frac{1}{\varepsilon}\right)} \left(\frac{C}{K}\right)^{1-\frac{1}{\varepsilon}} K_0^{1-\frac{1}{\varepsilon}}}{[\rho - g\left(1 - 1/\varepsilon\right)]} - \rho \right\} \text{ for } \begin{matrix} \varepsilon > 0 \\ \varepsilon \neq 1 \end{matrix},$$

$$U_0 = \frac{1}{\rho} \ln \frac{C}{K} + \frac{1}{\rho} K_0 - \frac{1}{\rho} \eta_P \ln P + \frac{1}{\rho^2} g \text{ for } \varepsilon = 1, \quad (3.96)$$

where the term $[\rho - g\left(1 - 1/\varepsilon\right)]$ must be positive to rule out explosive consumption paths.[29] From the present-value utility function (3.96) we see that the discounted lifetime utility is a rising function of the

---

[29] This is shown, for example, by Barro and Sala-i-Martin (1995, p. 156). The requirement corresponds to the bounded utility condition and rules out explosive consumption paths.

consumption-capital ratio and the rate of growth but a decreasing function of pollution. K_0 represents the exogenous initial capital stock at period 0. Inserting the results of Table 3.7 (rows 2–4) in function (3.96) we are now able to analyse the different agreements from a welfare point of view. Unfortunately, we see that the effects on welfare in most cases are ambiguous. Before we derive the cooperation effects, recall that in the noncooperative solution all existing *national* externalities are internalized as we have assumed a national benevolent planner.

Knowledge cooperation: National governments internalize the external international effect of capital accumulation on the other country. The marginal product of capital increases which stimulates growth in the cooperative solution. Due to higher economic growth, the level of pollution rises and the consumption-capital ratio decreases. The effect on welfare is ambiguous since higher pollution and a decreased consumption-capital ratio decrease welfare but a higher growth rate increase welfare, *ceteris paribus* (see equation (3.96)).

Environmental cooperation: The governments internalize the negative international external effect of pollution, which increases the marginal utility of abatement and lowers the social marginal product of capital $(\alpha A - Z/K)$. A lower social marginal product reduces growth (see equation (3.85)). The consumption-capital ratio decreases, remains constant or increases depending on whether we assume the intertemporal elasticity of substitution to be larger than, equal to, or smaller than unity. Again the effects on welfare depend on the parameter values, not only because of the ambiguous effect on the consumption-capital ratio. *Ceteris paribus*, higher pollution increases welfare whereas lower growth decreases welfare (see equation (3.96)).

Full cooperation: Since countries are identical and a full cooperation is equivalent to a global first-best solution we know that welfare is maximized in the cooperative outcome. However, the effects on economic growth and pollution of full cooperation depend on the parameter values. Hence, optimal pollution may even rise in the cooperative outcome. If there exists just one international spillover, every partial cooperation would be identical to a full cooperation and hence corresponds to a first-best solution. In such cases the welfare effect would be unambiguously positive.

Spillovers exist because of missing markets. Knowledge spillovers, for instance in the form of new inventions, can be internalized by the creation of patent markets. Obviously international knowledge spillovers require a supranational patent authority vested with the required competencies to guard and to enforce international patent treaties. To a large extent such organizations exist. For instance the 'European Patent Office' (EPO), established in 1977, protects patents within 18 European countries. Furthermore, European patents are also granted on the basis of international applications filed under the 'Patent Cooperation Treaty'. The Patent Cooperation Treaty is one of the various multilateral treaties dealing with the legal and administrative aspects of intellectual property rights which are administrated by the intergovernmental 'World Intellectual Property Organization' (WIPO). State membership of WIPO was more than 170 in August 1998.[30] In addition, the EPO possesses a trilateral cooperation with the 'Japanese Patent Office' and the 'United States Patent and Trademark Office' which cover 80 per cent of the world patents.[31] Given these facts it seems plausible to state that many international knowledge spillovers are already internalized. However, apart from the Montreal Protocol on the protection of the ozone layer (1986) no substantial international environmental cooperation has been implemented so far. Thus one can argue that knowledge cooperation best describes the real world in our model. From our analysis it is seen that knowledge cooperation unambiguously boosts growth but causes deterioration in the environmental quality. Thus our model suggests that among other things the creation of international patent markets is responsible for environmental degradation. Furthermore, the effects on welfare of knowledge cooperation are ambiguous and depend on parameter values. This is a typical second-best result: the correction of one distortion in the presence of other distortions does not necessarily improve welfare (see Lipsey and Lancaster 1956). Hence the internalization of the knowledge spillover by means of an international patent market

---

[30] Data is taken from the official web site of the World Intellectual Property Organization (http://www.wipo.org/eng/main.htm).

[31] Data and information is taken from the official web site of the European Patent Office (http://www.european-patent-office.org).

may decrease welfare. Finally we can state that the presence of international patent markets may even increase the need for environmental cooperation which would then unambiguously increase welfare.

3.6 Summary of the Results

In this chapter we discussed different versions of the linear growth model. Table 3.8 summarizes the results concerning the growth effects of taxes, the required optimal tax instruments to support a first-best solution, and whether pollution is rising or not. Columns 2 and 3 represent the results of the basic linear model and the model with leisure where we abstained from environmental issues. The model enriched by the natural environment is represented in columns 4–6. It was shown that a tax on consumption does not affect growth; furthermore it possesses the characteristics of a lump-sum tax (denoted by 'ls') as long as leisure is not endogenously determined (row 2). If leisure is incorporated, the lump-sum character of the consumption tax vanishes (column 3). Independent of the assumed linear model, a tax on capital reduces the return to investment and hence economic growth (row 3). We found that without

Table 3.8: Results of the linear growth model

	basic	with l	with P	with P / Z^{priv}	with P / Z^{pub}
$\frac{\partial g}{\partial \tau_C}$	0; ls	0	0; ls	0; ls	0; ls
$\frac{\partial g}{\partial \tau_K}$	−	−	−	−	−
$\frac{\partial g}{\partial \tau_P}$			−	−	−
τ^{opt}	none	none	τ_K, τ_P	$\bar{\tau}_P$	τ_K, τ_P
$\hat{P}$	no	no	+	0	0

government intervention pollution is too high in a closed market economy. This is true because pollution is a public bad and hence ignored in the individual maximization problem. A tighter environmental policy is always accompanied by a decrease in economic growth as long as the environment acts solely as an amenity good and does not directly affect the production process (row 4). Similar to a tax on capital income, the pollution tax reduces the return to investment and growth. It is seen that a tighter environmental policy increases welfare in spite of the negative growth effect as long as the pollution tax is below the Pigouvian level. Hence optimal growth is lower than maximal growth. Due to the linear production function, the qualitative results do not depend on whether pollution is generated by the use of capital or by production. Optimal pollution rises over time if abatement activities are not available and if the environment is not modeled as a life-support system (column 4). Obviously this contradicts a sustainable development. If the environment is modeled as a life-support system, optimal pollution may not rise over time as life is not possible above a critical pollution level (see Smulders and Gradus 1996). In a world without abatement activities this would imply a stationary economy. However, allowing for abatement activities in a growing economy can in principle produce a growing number of abatement activities to stabilize environmental pollution (columns 5 and 6). If abatement activities are private in nature (Z^{priv}) only a rising pollution tax can serve as a first-best instrument (column 5). However, if abatement is public (Z^{pub}) there are in principle two possibilities for achieving an optimal solution. An efficient outcome can be reached either by setting the pollution tax equal to the optimal marginal damage of pollution or by setting the capital income tax equal to the optimal marginal damage of pollution divided by the marginal product of capital (column 6).

In the last part of this chapter we studied the strategic interactions between two identical countries within a framework of a differential game. By doing so we have taken into account the fact that many of the most pressing environmental externalities are international rather than national in nature and no supranational authority exists vested with the required competencies to internalize these externalities. Furthermore, we have taken into consideration the effects of international knowledge spillovers on total factor productivity, as empirical evidence suggests. Every country was mutually affected from positive international knowledge spillovers and negative international environmental externalities. It was argued that the creation of an international patent market aiming for internalization of international knowledge spillovers could be responsible among other things for environmental degradation and may even lower welfare in the worst case. Furthermore, it was shown that due to knowledge spillovers the environmental quality could deteriorate in the case of a full cooperation compared to the noncooperative outcome, although welfare increases.

From the analysis in this chapter it is obvious that growth in GDP is an unsatisfactory welfare indicator. It is not able to reflect welfare properly nor is it a good approximation. Although consumption growth does not reflect welfare properly either, it is still closer to the welfare criteria. Following the results of this chapter, governments should not strive for maximizing economic growth or consumption if they are interested in welfare maximization. Feasible growth is determined solely by technology, however optimal growth is determined additionally by preferences. In all analysed models with environment, optimal growth was lower than maximal growth.

Finally it can be stated that the one-sector linear growth model predicts neither absolute nor conditional convergence. The former takes place when poorer countries grow faster than richer ones – without conditioning on any other characteristics of the economy – whereas there is conditional convergence when a country grows faster the farther it is below its own steady state. Suppose that two countries possess the same parameter values $(A, \delta, \varepsilon, \eta_P, \rho, \chi)$ but differ in their initial capital stock K_0. Since both countries grow always at the same constant rate g, the poor country will always be poorer at each level and never catch up. Furthermore, a different technology level implies that a low-growth country remains a low-growth country.[32] These results are in contrast to the neoclassical growth model where poorer countries tend to grow faster outside the balanced growth path. For a comparison between the neoclassical growth model and the linear growth model concerning the empirical evidence, see Aghion and Howitt (1998, Ch. 1.5).

Concerning the growth effects of taxes, we mentioned in Section 2.3.2 that it is important to distinguish between the direct and indirect tax

---

[32] Other convergence mechanisms are possible by modifying the model setup. For example, a linear growth model with an endogenously determined time preference possesses transitional dynamics and can explain growth convergence, as shown by Zee (1997).

effects. In the models under consideration the former is usually negative while the latter usually softens the direct tax effect through factor substitution. However, in the one-sector linear growth model there is only one explicit input. Hence, factor substitution is absent as the ratio of physical to human capital is fixed implicitly. Therefore, the linear model tends to overdraw the tax effect on growth. We shall see in the next chapters that this is true for the taxes on capital income and pollution. Furthermore, in the next chapters we remove another unrealistic shortcoming of the linear growth model, namely the absence of transitional dynamics.

Chapter 4

Environmental Policy in the Uzawa–Lucas Model

4.1 Introduction

In Chapter 3 we justified the simple linear production function by the assumption that capital in a wide sense includes physical and human capital components. In this chapter we now work out a two-sector model in which the accumulation of physical capital is separated from the accumulation of human capital. We shall see that allowing for substitution between physical and human capital in the production process changes the effects of fiscal policy substantially as indirect tax effects are then possible. The model used in this chapter is based on Gradus and Smulders (1993). Actually it is a Uzawa–Lucas model, formulated by Uzawa (1965) and Lucas (1988), extended by a technological environmental externality. By using this model we remove another unrealistic shortcoming of the linear growth model, namely the absence of transitional dynamics. Economic agents do not respond to exogenous shocks or changes in tax rates immediately but trigger adaptation processes. This chapter consists of three different parts which complement each other mutually: the analysis of the closed economy along a balanced growth path; the numerical simulation of its transitional dynamics; and finally the analysis of the open economy. In the following we review the relevant literature and outline our main results.

Gradus and Smulders (1993) show for a centrally planned closed economy by varying the weight factor of pollution in the utility function, that environmental care does not influence optimal growth. We show in this chapter that the non-interference of economic growth due to a change in environmental policy is also true for a decentralized economy by explicitly modeling households' and firms' decisions and additionally assuming a more general utility function.[1] Furthermore, we show that this non-interference is not special to a pollution tax but also valid for taxes on consumption, labor income and capital income. The independency of non-environmental taxes on growth has already been shown by Lessat (1994, Ch. III.3) and Milesi-Ferretti and Roubini (1994) in similar models but without environment. Finally, we compare the market-driven path with the optimal path in order to determine a tax system that is suitable for internalizing the environmental externality.

Whereas most of the literature on environmental policy and growth examines the long-run effects, little has been done so far to analyse the short- and medium-term effects. Neglecting the transitional dynamics can be problematic and may lead to wrong policy recommendations (see Section 2.4). However, there are a few exceptions in the literature. Van der Ploeg and Ligthart (1994) derive the transitional dynamics of a linear growth model extended by a renewable environmental resource. They find that the fall in the short-run growth rate of the economy is bigger than in the long-run growth rate. Note that the introduction of an environmental stock into the framework of the linear model is responsible for this result and alone determines the transitional dynamics of the economy. Perroni (1995) gets a similar result in a two-sector growth model where the composite of two final goods can be used for consumption and investment in both physical and human capital. In such a model an environmental tax is growth reducing in the long run. By means of a numerical simulation, Perroni finds that short-run growth losses are even bigger. Bovenberg and Smulders (1996) compute analytically the

---

[1]Unlike Gradus and Smulders (1993) we assume a multiplicative instead of an additive separable utility function.

transitional dynamics of a two-sector model consisting of a consumption good and an R&D sector which generates knowledge about pollution-augmenting techniques. The renewable environmental resource acts both as an amenity good and as a public input into production – the latter is identical to a productive spillover of a better environment (see Section 2.1). They find that if the environment acts mainly as an amenity good, a tighter environmental policy reduces growth in both the long run and the short run. But if a better environmental quality solely increases the productivity of the production process, long-run growth rises but short-run growth is reduced. The latter applies as households anticipate the long-run productivity gains and raise short-run consumption at the expense of saving. Reduced saving harms the accumulation of humanmade capital and hence hurts income growth. In this chapter we simulate numerically the transitional dynamics of the above mentioned Uzawa–Lucas model with environment. Thus we complete the long-term analysis of the first part of the chapter by simulating the short- and medium-term effects. Since at least the quantitative results of the numerical simulation depend on the choice of the parameter values, we calibrate the model so as to capture empirical stylized facts of industrialized countries. We simulate both the optimal adaptation paths caused by increased preferences for a clean environment and the transitional dynamics of a decentralized economy after a change in the pollution tax rate. Furthermore we compare the effects of unexpected and announced policy measures. We find that the adaptation of the growth rates to the new balanced growth path are non-monotonous: except for a sharp decline in the period when the policy action takes place, growth rates of the national product are above their equilibrium value during the whole adaptation process. For environmental policy being suboptimal in the initial equilibrium, welfare in every period is higher compared to the 'business-as-usual' scenario, which means there are no intergenerational problems. Hence, from a welfare point of view, not only in the long run but also in the short run there is no reason to refrain from a tighter environmental policy. The announcement of the policy measure produces growth effects already in the year of announcement. After the announcement period we observe a path similar to that in the scenario without announcement. However, the negative deflections from the balanced growth rate are smaller, which could be interesting from a political economy point of view.

In the third section of this chapter we open up the economy and develop a new model by considering international knowledge and international environmental spillovers in a framework with Uzawa–Lucas production processes. By doing so we continue the analysis of Section 3.5. Again we analyse the strategic interactions between two countries within the framework of a differential game and in a two-country world and examine the effects of different kinds of cooperations. As the Uzawa–Lucas model possesses a separate education sector it allows now for a proper modeling of the knowledge spillover. We shall see that the results of cooperation in a Uzawa–Lucas economy differ from the results of Section 3.5.4 and depend on whether physical capital or final good production is responsible for pollution. In the Rebelo model this distinction does not matter since there is a linear relation between the capital stock and production. In the open economy model with a linear production function, welfare effects of partial cooperations are ambiguous because of the model's inherent trade-off between growth and pollution (see Section 3.5.4). If output is responsible for pollution we confirm the results of the linear model to a large extent. However, environmental cooperation no longer hampers growth, and increases welfare unambiguously. Concerning environmental degradation the results become more optimistic if pollution is generated by physical capital. Environmental cooperation does not affect growth but reduces pollution and increases welfare. Both knowledge cooperation and full cooperation reduce pollution and increase growth and welfare unambiguously.

The chapter is structured as follows. In Section 4.2 we describe the model and analyse the effects of environmental policy in a closed Uzawa–Lucas economy along a balanced growth path. Section 4.3 is devoted to the transitional dynamics of an environmental policy measure. After the calibration of the model we simulate numerically the adaptation process both for the central planner and the market economy. Additionally we compare unexpected and announced policy measures and finally perform a sensitivity analysis. In Section 4.4 we open up the economy by allowing international spillovers but again restrict the analysis to the balanced growth path. As the cooperation results depend on the pollution specification we analyse both plausible cases. Section 4.5 summarizes the results and concludes this chapter.

4.2 The Closed Economy

4.2.1 The Analytical Framework

We assume a two-sector endogenous growth model of a closed economy. The first sector produces a perfectly malleable good, which can be used for consumption, abatement activities and investment in the physical capital stock. The second sector is the education sector where human capital is accumulated. Human capital is embodied in people and assumed to be a private good, which is both rival and excludable (see Section 2.3.2). Apart from the production technologies, the present model is identical to that of Section 3.4. The new or different equations are explained in detail; similar or identical equations are replicated for convenience but not explained again.

Technology

In the first sector, the final good Y is produced with a Cobb–Douglas technology that possesses constant returns to scale with respect to physical capital K and effective labor (uH) but diminishing returns to both factors separately:

$$Y_t = AK_t^\alpha \left(u_t H_t\right)^{1-\alpha}, \tag{4.1}$$

where $A, H, K, Y > 0, 0 < \alpha < 1$, and $0 \leqslant u \leqslant 1$. Effective labor is defined as the product of u – the fraction of the unit time budget that is devoted to production of the final good – and human capital H. Parameter α denotes the exogenous share of physical capital and parameter A reflects the exogenously given level of the technology. Unlike Lucas (1988), we ignore the possibility of a spillover from the average stock of human capital to final good production.[2] The flow resource

---

[2]Unlike the original Lucas model, there is no externality in human capital to reflect the assumption that people are more productive when they are around clever people.

constraint of the economy is given by

$$Y_t = C_t + \dot{K}_t + Z_t + \delta_K K_t, \tag{4.2}$$

where $C, \dot{K}, Z, \delta_K \geqslant 0$. Final output Y can be used for consumption C, for net investment in the physical capital stock $\dot{K}$, for public abatement activities Z, or to prevent current physical capital stock from depreciation $\delta_K K$.

In the education sector, human capital is produced with a constant returns to scale technology which utilizes human capital whereas physical capital is negligible:

$$\dot{H}_t = [B(1 - u_t) - \delta_H] H_t, \tag{4.3}$$

where $B, H, \delta_H \geqslant 0$. Parameter B is the studying productivity, $(1 - u)$ is the fraction of the unit time budget devoted to education $(0 \leqslant u \leqslant 1)$, and parameter δ_H is the depreciation rate of human capital. The maximum growth rate of human capital is given by $B - \delta_H$, for $u = 0$ where the whole unit time budget is devoted to studying. According to equation (4.3) new human capital is accumulated by using time and old human capital. As the production is assumed to be constant returns to scale, new human capital is a linear function of old human capital as long as studying time is constant. Thus we assume that future generations take advantage of the growing human capital stock, because it improves the quality of education. This coincides with the idea that children gain from the human capital stock of their parents. Note, however, that future generations may replace old by new human capital since it depreciates over time. Hence future generations have not only a higher but also a different stock of human capital. It is important for the economic interpretation of equation (4.3) that it implicitly models an intergenerational spillover of human capital.

The specifications of the final good production function (4.1) and the human capital accumulation function (4.3) ensure that diminishing returns do not arise when physical capital K and human capital H grow at

---

Formally this can be modeled by the following production function

$$Y = AK^\alpha (uH)^{1-\alpha} \bar{H}^\varsigma,$$

where $\bar{H}^\varsigma$ represents the externality from average human capital.

the same rate. Therefore, falling marginal products to one factor can be avoided. Furthermore, since both inputs H and K can be accumulated infinitely, unlimited growth is in principle possible.[3] Note that human capital accumulation is assumed to be a non-market sector and is thus not subject to factor income taxation (see Section 2.3.2).

The capital stock K used in production causes a negative environmental externality as a side product which can be reduced by means of public abatement activities which in turn absorb a part of output, in line with the flow resource constraint (4.2). Unlike Chapter 3.4 where we analysed both private and public abatement measures, we analyse only the latter in this chapter. However, the results concerning growth and welfare would not change at all if abatement is assumed to be a private good. The pollution function P is identical to that of Section 3.4 and possesses the functional form

$$P_t = \left(\frac{K_t}{Z_t}\right)^{\chi}. \tag{4.4}$$

Pollution is increasing in physical capital but decreasing in abatement activities, $P_K > 0$ and $P_Z < 0$. Parameter $\chi > 0$ is the exogenous elasticity of P with respect to ratio K/Z.[4]

Firms

The economy consists of a large number of identical and competitive firms. These rent physical capital from households at the interest rate r and hire human capital at the wage rate w. Firms use these input factors to produce final goods with the technology described by equation (4.1). They must pay a pollution tax τ_P according to their pollution-generating input factor, physical capital. Firms are assumed to maximize their profits in every period by choosing effective labor uH and the physical capital stock K, given the pollution tax τ_P levied on the physical capital

---

[3] Caballé and Santos (1993) illustrate that the standard neoclassical model is a special case of the Uzawa–Lucas framework. This can be seen by fixing the fraction of time devoted to production u. The second sector then corresponds to the exogenous labor-augmenting technical progress.

[4] For a further explanation of the pollution function, see Section 2.1.

stock K. The representative firms' profit condition is given by

$$\pi_t = Y_t - w_t \left(u_t H_t \right) - r_t K_t - \tau_P K_t. \tag{4.5}$$

The profit is maximized when the marginal cost of each factor equals its after-tax marginal product:

$$r_t \;=\; \alpha \frac{Y_t}{K_t} - \tau_P \;=\; \alpha A \left(\frac{K_t}{u_t H_t} \right)^{\alpha-1} - \tau_P, \tag{4.6}$$

$$w_t \;=\; (1-\alpha) \frac{Y_t}{u_t H_t} \;=\; (1-\alpha) A \left(\frac{K_t}{u_t H_t} \right)^{\alpha}. \tag{4.7}$$

Households

The utility function of the identical, atomistic agents with perfect foresight over an infinite time horizon is given by[5]

$$U \left(C_t, P_t \right) \;=\; \frac{\left(C_t P_t^{-\eta_P} \right)^{1-1/\varepsilon} - 1}{1 - 1/\varepsilon} \quad \text{for} \quad \varepsilon > 0,\; \varepsilon \neq 1, \tag{4.8}$$

$$U \left(C_t, P_t \right) \;=\; \ln C_t - \eta_P \ln P_t, \quad \text{for} \quad \varepsilon = 1. \tag{4.9}$$

Economic agents allocate their unit time budget in every period between production time u and studying time $(1-u)$. They rent human and physical capital to firms. Consumption and the allocation of time are chosen in order to maximize the lifetime utility, given by the integral of the discounted instantaneous utility

$$U_0 = \int_{t=0}^{\infty} U \left(C_t, P_t \right) e^{-\rho t} dt, \tag{4.10}$$

subject to the human capital accumulation constraint (4.3) and the flow budget constraint

$$(1 - \tau_K) \, r_t K_t + (1 - \tau_H) \, w_t \left(u_t H_t \right) = (1 + \tau_C) \, C_t + \dot{K}_t + \delta_K K_t, \tag{4.11}$$

where τ_C, τ_H and τ_K are the tax rates on consumption, labor income and capital income, respectively. The left-hand side of equation (4.11) represents the different sources of income, the right-hand side the uses of income.

---

[5] For an explanation of such a utility function, see page 26.

Government

The government's task in this economy is to correct the market failure caused by the environmental externality. It does so by taxing consumption, physical capital income, labor income and pollution and by providing non-rival abatement activities. The government flow budget constraint reads as

$$\tau_C C_t + \tau_H w_t \left(u_t H_t \right) + \tau_K r_t K_t + \tau_P K_t = Z_t. \tag{4.12}$$

In the following, time indices of variables are ignored where unnecessary.

The Market Solution

The representative household chooses consumption C and the allocation of human capital u in order to maximize lifetime utility (4.10) subject to the human capital accumulation function (4.3) and the flow budget constraint (4.11), taking the time paths of r, w and the tax rates τ_C, τ_H, τ_K and τ_P as given. Since pollution is assumed to be a public 'bad', rationally acting economic agents ignore it in their individual maximization problem. The current-value Hamiltonian for this optimization problem takes the form

$$
\begin{aligned}
\max_{C,u} \mathcal{H} \;=\;& U\left(C, P \right) \\
&+\; \lambda \left[\left(1 - \tau_K \right) rK + \left(1 - \tau_H \right) w\left(uH \right) - \left(1 + \tau_C \right) C - \delta_K K \right] \\
&+\; \mu \left[B\left(1 - u \right) H - \delta_H H \right].
\end{aligned}
$$

The first-order conditions are given by

$$\frac{\partial \mathcal{H}}{\partial C} \overset{!}{=} 0 \;:\; \left(1 + \tau_C \right) \lambda = C^{-1/\varepsilon} P^{-\eta_P (1 - 1/\varepsilon)}, \tag{4.13}$$

$$\frac{\partial \mathcal{H}}{\partial u} \overset{!}{=} 0 \;:\; \mu B = \left(1 - \tau_H \right) w\lambda, \tag{4.14}$$

$$\frac{\partial \mathcal{H}}{\partial K} \overset{!}{=} \lambda \rho - \dot{\lambda} \;:\; -\hat{\lambda} = \left(1 - \tau_K \right) r - \delta_K - \rho \equiv R - \rho, \tag{4.15}$$

$$\frac{\partial \mathcal{H}}{\partial H} \overset{!}{=} \mu \rho - \dot{\mu} \;:\; -\hat{\mu} = B - \delta_H - \rho, \tag{4.16}$$

where λ and μ are the shadow prices of physical capital and human capital, respectively. For further analysis it is useful to define R as the real return to capital net of tax. Equation (4.13) implies that the marginal utility of consumption in every period should equal the after-tax shadow price of physical capital. Equation (4.14) shows that the marginal product of human capital in the education sector times the shadow price of human capital must be equal to its marginal product in the final good production net of tax times the shadow price of physical capital. The first Euler condition (4.15) implies that the rate of change in the shadow price of physical capital should equal the real interest rate of capital net of tax R minus the rate of time preference. The second Euler condition (4.16) says that the rate of change in the shadow price of human capital should equal the marginal product of human capital in the education sector minus the human capital depreciation rate and the rate of time preference. The Keynes–Ramsey rule describing the optimal consumption path for given tax rates is derived by using equations (4.13) and (4.15), where r is replaced by equation (4.6):

$$\hat{C} = \varepsilon \left[(1 - \tau_K) \left(\alpha \frac{Y}{K} - \tau_P \right) - \delta_K - \rho \right] + \eta_P (1 - \varepsilon) \hat{P} \quad (4.17)$$
$$\equiv \varepsilon (R - \rho) + \eta_P (1 - \varepsilon) \hat{P}.$$

The Central Planner Solution

In contrast to the market solution, a central planner maximizes the utility of the representative economic agent and takes into account the negative side-effects of physical capital (pollution) on utility. The central planner maximizes lifetime utility by choosing consumption C, abatement measures Z, and the allocation of human capital u subject to the flow resource constraint of the economy (4.2) and the human capital accumulation constraint (4.3). The current-value Hamiltonian for this optimization problem takes the form

$$\max_{C,Z,u} \mathcal{H} = U(C, P)$$
$$+ \lambda \left[AK^\alpha (uH)^{1-\alpha} - C - Z - \delta_K K \right]$$
$$+ \mu \left[B(1 - u)H - \delta_H H \right].$$

The first-order conditions are given by

$$\frac{\partial \mathcal{H}}{\partial C} \stackrel{!}{=} 0 \quad : \quad \lambda = C^{-1/\varepsilon} P^{-\eta_P(1-1/\varepsilon)}, \tag{4.18}$$

$$\frac{\partial \mathcal{H}}{\partial Z} \stackrel{!}{=} 0 \quad : \quad \lambda = \eta_P \chi C^{1-1/\varepsilon} P^{-\eta_P(1-1/\varepsilon)} Z^{-1}, \tag{4.19}$$

$$\frac{\partial \mathcal{H}}{\partial u} \stackrel{!}{=} 0 \quad : \quad \mu B u H = \lambda (1-\alpha) Y, \tag{4.20}$$

$$\frac{\partial \mathcal{H}}{\partial K} \stackrel{!}{=} \lambda \rho - \dot{\lambda} \quad : \quad -\hat{\lambda} = \alpha \frac{Y}{K} - \frac{Z}{K} - \delta_K - \rho, \tag{4.21}$$

$$\frac{\partial \mathcal{H}}{\partial H} \stackrel{!}{=} \mu \rho - \dot{\mu} \quad : \quad -\hat{\mu} = B - \delta_H - \rho. \tag{4.22}$$

Elimination of λ from equations (4.18) and (4.19) yields

$$\frac{Z}{K} = \eta_P \chi \frac{C}{K}. \tag{4.23}$$

It requires that for an optimal solution the marginal utility of consumption and abatement must be equalized. This result is already known from Section 3.4.1. We shall see that this optimality condition is independent of the assumed production technologies and whether physical capital or final output is responsible for pollution. From (4.20) it is seen that the marginal product of human capital in the education sectors times the shadow price of human capital must be equal to its marginal product in the final good production times the shadow price of physical capital. The first Euler equation (4.21) implies that the rate of change of the shadow price of physical capital should be equal to the social marginal product of capital in the final good sector minus the rate of capital depreciation and the rate of time preference. The second Euler condition (4.22) is identical to that of the market solution.

By using equations (4.18) and (4.21) we can derive the Keynes–Ramsey rule:

$$\begin{aligned}
\hat{C} &= \varepsilon \left(\alpha \frac{Y}{K} - \frac{Z}{K} - \delta_K - \rho \right) + \eta_P (1-\varepsilon) \hat{P} \tag{4.24} \\
&\equiv \varepsilon (R_S - \rho) + \eta_P (1-\varepsilon) \hat{P},
\end{aligned}$$

The real social return to capital investment, denoted by R_S, equals the private return to capital $\alpha Y/K$ corrected by the optimal marginal damage of pollution Z/K which is external to firms in the market economy. The last term of equation (4.24) vanishes if the level of pollution is constant over time, that is, the growth rate of capital is equal to the growth rate of abatement,[6] or if the intertemporal elasticity of substitution ε equals unity. According to the first part of equation (4.24) consumption grows, remains constant, or declines if the real social return to capital is larger than, equal to, or smaller than the rate of time preference. Considering the last term of equation (4.24) we see that for an intertemporal elasticity of substitution smaller than one, the growth rate of consumption increases with the growth rate of pollution. The opposite holds for an intertemporal elasticity of substitution larger than one or for a negative pollution growth rate.

4.2.2   Results Along a Balanced Growth Path

Along a balanced growth path, consumption, abatement activities, output, the human capital stock and the physical capital stock grow at the same constant rate g, whereas the fraction of time devoted to production is constant over time.[7]

$$g \equiv \hat{C} = \hat{H} = \hat{K} = \hat{Y} = \hat{Z} = -\hat{\lambda}\varepsilon = -\hat{\mu}\varepsilon, \quad 0 = \dot{u}. \qquad (4.25)$$

Because of condition (4.25) the consumption-capital ratio C/K, the consumption-output ratio C/Y, the capital-labor ratio K/H, the output-capital ratio Y/K and the abatement-capital ratio Z/K are constant, and therefore, pollution P is also constant along a balanced growth path.

Optimal Tax Rates

In order to derive the optimal tax rates, the first-order conditions of the market solution are compared with the corresponding first-order conditions of the central planner solution. Comparison of equations (4.13) and (4.14) with (4.18) and (4.20) by using equation (4.7) show that a

---

[6] From equation (4.4) it follows that $\hat{P} = \chi(\hat{K} - \hat{Z})$.

[7] In the literature the formal proof is quite often ignored. For the interested reader we show the formal proof in Section A.2.1 (page 224) in the appendix.

first-best solution requires that the taxes on consumption and labor income are zero, $\tau_C = \tau_H = 0$. Furthermore, comparison of equation (4.15) with (4.21) using equation (4.6) reveals the following condition for a first-best solution

$$(1 - \tau_K)\left(\alpha\frac{Y}{K} - \tau_P\right) \;\overset{!}{=}\; \alpha\left(\frac{Y}{K}\right)^{cps} - \left(\frac{Z}{K}\right)^{cps}, \qquad (4.26)$$

where the superscript 'cps' denotes the central planner solution. As in the linear model with public abatement activities there are several possibilities for achieving a first-best solution in a market economy since condition (4.26) can be fulfilled in at least two ways (see Table 4.1).

Table 4.1: Optimal tax rates

	τ_C	τ_H	τ_K	τ_P
Case 1	0	0	0	$\left(\frac{Z}{K}\right)^{cps}$
Case 2	0	0	$\left(\frac{Z}{K}\right)^{cps}\left[\alpha\left(\frac{Y}{K}\right)^{cps}\right]^{-1}$	0

Case 1: A first-best solution can be reached by setting all non-environmental taxes equal to zero and the pollution tax equal to the optimal marginal damage of pollution. Such a pollution tax corresponds to a Pigouvian tax. Obviously a first-best environmental policy requires that the marginal liability of the pollution tax equals the marginal costs of providing the public abatement measures. Remember that we assume a one-to-one technology by which the final good (tax revenue) can be transformed into the public abatement activities. Thus the first-best taxation instantaneously raises the public revenue necessary to provide the optimal level of abatement. Thus the first-best solution can be reached in both cases without the use of a lump-sum instrument. This can be proved by inserting the optimal tax rates in the government's flow budget constraint (4.12). Hence, in case 1, for instance, the pollution tax fulfills two tasks at the same time: it corrects the inefficient physical capital-intensive final good production and generates the exact amount of public revenue to provide the optimal level of abatement.

Case 2: Another way to achieve a first-best solution is to set the taxes on consumption, labor income and pollution equal to zero and the capital income tax equal to the optimal marginal damage of pollution divided by the optimal marginal product of capital. As in the linear model it can be seen that the effects of a capital income tax are similar to the effects of a tax on pollution. However, the tax base is different: a tax on capital is levied on the capital income which consists of the marginal product of capital times the physical capital stock $(\alpha Y/K)\,K$, whereas the tax on pollution is levied solely on the physical capital stock K. Therefore, it is necessary to correct the optimal marginal damage of pollution by $(\alpha Y/K)^{-1}$ in order to equate the tax-base differences of the two taxes when a capital income tax is used for internalization.

In both cases, the optimal tax structure holds along and outside the balanced growth path. Outside the balanced growth path the optimal tax rates can change over time since the optimal ratios on abatement-capital and output-capital may vary over time. However, along a balanced growth path the tax rates are constant, since the ratios are constant (see condition (4.25) and its implications). Finally, it can be stated that there is a rationale for capital income taxation when capital is the dirty input factor and a pollution tax instrument is not available. However, the informational requirements for the pollution tax versus capital income tax may be asymmetric in practice. Suppose that marginal pollution damages are constant (as seems plausible for SO_2). To induce the optimal reduction in pollution under the pollution tax the government needs to have only an estimate of marginal environmental damages. In contrast, for the capital income tax solution the government would also need to know the elasticity of factor inputs with respect to price, and the elasticity of final output with respect to factor input quantities.

Reduced Forms of the Market Solution

In this section we analyse the long-term consequences of isolated tax and parameter changes for economic growth and other core variables. In doing so, we derive the reduced forms of all core variables along a balanced growth path. Along a balanced growth path, the differential equations of the market solution (4.15) and (4.16) can be rewritten by condition (4.25) and equation (4.6), as

$$g = \varepsilon \left[(1 - \tau_K) \left(\alpha \frac{Y}{K} - \tau_P \right) - \delta_K - \rho \right] \equiv R - \rho, \quad (4.27)$$

$$g = \varepsilon (B - \delta_H - \rho). \quad (4.28)$$

It is seen that equation (4.28) is already the reduced form of the growth rate. Using condition (4.25) we can rewrite the flow resource constraint of the economy (4.2) and the human capital accumulation constraint (4.3), respectively

$$g = \frac{Y}{K} - \frac{C}{K} - \frac{Z}{K} - \delta_K, \quad (4.29)$$

$$g = B(1 - u) - \delta_H. \quad (4.30)$$

Using equations (4.28) and (4.30) we can derive the reduced form of the fraction of time devoted to production

$$u = \frac{(1 - \varepsilon)(B - \delta_H) + \varepsilon \rho}{B}. \quad (4.31)$$

Substituting the growth rate in equation (4.27) by (4.28) we obtain the reduced form of the output-capital ratio

$$\frac{Y}{K} = \frac{B - \delta_H + \delta_K + (1 - \tau_K)\tau_P}{\alpha(1 - \tau_K)}. \quad (4.32)$$

Finally, for deriving the reduced forms of the consumption-capital ratio and the abatement-capital ratio we rewrite the flow budget constraint of the government (4.12) by using equations (4.6) and (4.7):

$$\tau_C \frac{C}{K} + [\alpha \tau_K + (1 - \alpha) \tau_H] \frac{Y}{K} + (1 - \tau_K)\tau_P = \frac{Z}{K}. \quad (4.33)$$

Insertion of the rewritten flow budget constraint of the government (4.33) into the flow resource constraint of the economy (4.2) yields either

$$\frac{C}{K} = \frac{[1 - \tau_K \alpha - (1 - \alpha)\tau_H]}{(1 + \tau_C)} \frac{Y}{K} - \frac{\delta_K + (1 - \tau_K)\tau_P + \varepsilon(B - \delta_H - \rho)}{(1 + \tau_C)},$$

$$(4.34)$$

or

$$\frac{Z}{K} = \frac{[\tau_C + \alpha \tau_K + (1 - \alpha)\tau_H]}{(1 + \tau_C)} \frac{Y}{K} \quad (4.35)$$

$$+\frac{(1-\tau_K)\tau_P - \tau_C\delta_K - \tau_C\varepsilon(B-\delta_H-\rho)}{(1+\tau_C)}.$$

By replacing the output-capital ratio in equations (4.34) and (4.35) by equation (4.32) we obtain the reduced forms of the consumption-capital ratio and the abatement-capital ratio, respectively. By means of equation (4.27) and the reduced forms (4.28) and (4.32), it is now explained through which channels taxes affect long-term growth.

- It is seen in equation (4.27) that the capital income tax and the pollution tax affect directly the incentive to invest in physical capital. For a given output-capital ratio this direct tax effect lowers the real return to capital net of tax R and hence growth. However, due to higher taxes on capital income and pollution, final good production becomes more human capital intensive. Analytically this corresponds to a higher output-capital ratio Y/K (see equation (4.32)). Thus, *ceteris paribus* the *gross* real interest rate and hence growth increases due to the indirect tax effect. To assess whether the direct or indirect effects dominate, we take a look at equation (4.28). From equation (4.28) we see that the long-term growth rate is not affected by any tax-rate changes. Therefore, the direct tax effect of increased taxes on capital income or pollution is exactly offset by its indirect tax effect. Hence, the real return to capital net of tax is totally independent of both tax rates. The explanation for this result is as follows. According to the constant returns to scale in the final good sector (4.1), both capital stocks have to grow with the same rate along a balanced growth path. However, the growth rate of human capital stock is determined solely in the education sector (4.3). Therefore, human capital is the engine of growth in the Uzawa–Lucas model. Recall that education is assumed to be a non-market sector, therefore it is not directly taxed by the capital income tax, or by the labor income tax, or by the consumption tax. In addition, since the pollution tax is levied on the dirty input physical capital which is not used in the education sector the marginal return of human capital in the education sector is not affected by any tax-rate changes. This implies that none of the analysed taxes affects economic growth.

- The taxes on consumption and labor are lump-sum taxes since they are absent in the first-order conditions (4.27) and (4.28) and hence do not distort the economy.

Even though the taxes on consumption and labor income are lump-sum taxes, they have a negative effect on the consumption-capital ratio and a positive effect on the abatement-capital ratio (see equations (4.34) and (4.35)). The reason is that although the imposition of both taxes is non-distorting, their revenues are used to provide public abatement activities which change the allocation of the economy. Although both taxes reduce pollution, they cannot yield a first-best solution since they do not correct the inefficient physical capital-intensive final good production (see equation (4.32)). From equation (4.35) it is seen that the taxes on capital income and pollution increase the abatement-capital ratio whereas their effects on the consumption-capital ratio cannot be signed unambiguously.

Milesi-Ferretti and Roubini (1994) analyse the growth effect of taxes on labor income and capital income in a Uzawa–Lucas model without environment. They show that the growth rate is independent of the tax rates on capital and labor income regardless of whether leisure is modeled as quality time or home production or in the absence of leisure as in our case. It is easy to show that the introduction of quality time or home production in our model does not change the non-interference of economic growth due to changes in fiscal policy. However, we shall see in Chapter 5 that leisure modeled as raw time will change these results significantly. In the following it is explained how certain parameter changes affect economic growth.

- A change in the level of the technology A does not affect long-term growth because it does not change permanently the productivity of the final good sector.
- A higher studying efficiency parameter B increases the productivity of the education sector. Increased human capital accumulation leads to a higher growth rate.
- A change of both η_P and χ does not affect long-term growth. Furthermore, these parameters are absent in the reduced forms of the market economy. The reason is that the public 'bad' pollution is

Economic Growth and Environmental Policy

ignored in the individual maximization problem. However, an optimal pollution tax is a positive function of η_P and χ. Hence, the qualitative effects of changes in η_P and χ are identical to changes in the pollution tax.

- When ρ increases, individuals value future utility less and consumption rises at the expense of capital accumulation. As a consequence, time devoted to production is increased at the expense of studying time – see equation (4.31) – which lowers growth.
- A higher depreciation rate of the human capital stock δ_H works exactly in the opposite direction to B. It reduces the productivity of human capital accumulation and lowers growth.
- A change in the physical capital stock δ_K does not affect growth because it does not change permanently the productivity of the final good sector.
- Since a higher intertemporal elasticity of substitution ε polishes the curvature of the utility function and therefore makes future consumption more valuable it works in the opposite direction to a higher ρ. Hence, time devoted to production decreases and growth increases.

The effects of changes in tax rates and parameters on core variables are summarized in Table 4.2.

Table 4.2: The effects of tax and parameter changes on core variables

	τ_C/τ_H	τ_K/δ_K	τ_P	$A/\eta_P/\chi$	B	α	δ_H	ε	ρ
$\frac{\partial g}{\partial x}$	0	0	0	0	+	0	−	+	−
$\frac{\partial u}{\partial x}$	0	0	0	0	−*	0	0*	−	+
$\frac{\partial(Y/K)}{\partial x}$	0	+	+	0	+	−	−	0	0
$\frac{\partial(Z/K)}{\partial x}$	+	+°	+	0	+°	0°	−°	−	0

° Signs are obtained by setting the lump-sum taxes equal to zero, $\tau_C = \tau_H = 0$.
* Signs are obtained for $\varepsilon = 1$.

In the formal analysis, the possibility of productive spillovers from a better environment has not been taken into account. As shown in

Section 3.4.2, it is possible to discuss these spillovers along a balanced growth path without a formal analysis since pollution is constant over time. Therefore, productive spillovers from a better environment to the final good sector or the education sector are formally equivalent to higher levels of A or B, respectively.[8] From Table 4.2 it is seen that the level of technology A does not influence long-term economic growth. Hence, productive spillovers to final good production triggered by a better environment are growth neutral. However, if pollution affects human capital accumulation negatively then environmental improvements stimulate growth. Another possibility as to how the environment may affect economic growth is via the depreciation rate of the human capital stock δ_H. If, for example, a lower level of pollution causes human capital to depreciate at a lower rate, then a better environmental quality increases the returns of the education sector and hence stimulates economic growth. This is shown analytically by Gradus and Smulders (1993) in a similar model for a centrally planned economy by varying the weight factor of pollution in the utility function.

Reduced Forms of the Central Planner Solution

Similar to the market solution we can derive the reduced forms of the central planner solution. Using the flow resource constraint of the economy (4.2), the human capital accumulation constraint (4.3), equations (4.22), (4.23) and (4.24), and the balanced growth path condition (4.25) we get the reduced forms

$$\frac{C}{K} = \frac{(1 - \alpha\varepsilon)(B - \delta_H - \rho) + (1 - \alpha)\delta_K + \rho}{\alpha + (\alpha - 1)\eta_P\chi}, \qquad (4.36)$$

$$\frac{Y}{K} = \frac{(1 - \varepsilon)(B - \delta_H - \rho) + \frac{1}{\chi\eta_P}(B - \delta_H + \delta_K) + \rho}{\alpha - 1 + \frac{\alpha}{\eta_P\chi}}, \qquad (4.37)$$

$$\frac{Z}{K} = \frac{(1 - \alpha\varepsilon)(B - \delta_H - \rho) + (1 - \alpha)\delta_K + \rho}{\alpha - 1 + \frac{\alpha}{\eta_P\chi}}, \qquad (4.38)$$

---

[8] Formally these cases could have been analysed in the present setup by adding a multiplicative term $P^{-\epsilon}$ in the production function of either the final good or the education sector.

where the reduced forms of the growth rate and the fraction of time devoted to production are identical to the market solution (see equations (4.28)) and (4.31). Thus, the second and third rows of Table 4.2 are also valid for the central planner solution. Since the Pigouvian tax must be equal to the optimal marginal damage of pollution Z/K (see Table 4.1), we can use equation (4.38) to derive the effects of parameter changes on the optimal pollution tax. The optimal pollution tax is an increasing function of η_P, ρ and χ but a decreasing function of α. The effects of B and δ_H depend on the level of ε, but they are positive for $\varepsilon = 1$. Finally, we show the optimal response to a positive shock to η_P. From equations (4.28) and (4.31) we see that a shock towards greener preferences does not influence growth and time devoted to production. But the optimal response to a higher η_P is a more labor-intensive final good production (equivalent to a higher Y/K ratio), less pollution (equivalent to a higher Z/K ratio) and a higher consumption-capital ratio C/K (see equations (4.36)–(4.38)). Hence, the qualitative effects of a higher η_P correspond to those of a higher τ_P in the market solution.

In this section, according to equation (4.4) pollution was assumed to be a function of the physical capital stock and abatement activities. We mentioned in Section 2.1 another pollution specification: pollution could be a function of total output and abatement activities. It is easy to show that this pollution specification would not change the results with regard to the closed economy's long-term growth rate as the reduced form of the growth rate is identical to equation (4.28). We skip the formal proof here as this pollution specification is analysed later in Section 4.4 on the Open Economy. However, we shall see in Chapters 5 and 6 that this distinction may change the results in more complex models.

4.3   The Simulation of the Transition Path

In Section 4.2 we investigated the effects of environmental policy on growth and core variables along a balanced growth path. Hence, we restricted our analysis to the long-term effects and ignored the transitional dynamics. We found that neither the pollution tax nor an optimal policy response due to a change in the weight of pollution in utility affect long-term economic growth. However, we shall see that growth rates are affected by environmental policy in the short and medium term. Because of an environmental policy measure, the initial ratio of both capital stocks is no longer optimal. This imbalance induces an adaptation process whereby the new optimal ratio is reached only gradually by investments which increase the relatively scarce capital stock. This section is based on Hettich (1995) and simulates numerically the transitional dynamics of the economy. The transitional dynamics describe the adaptation of an economy after an exogenous shock to its new balanced growth path. We investigate two kinds of shocks. For the centrally planned economy we simulate the optimal policy response due to a change in the weight of pollution in utility. A shock towards greener preferences can occur due to new scientific information about the impact of pollution on environmental quality. For the decentralized economy we analogously describe the adaptation process after a change in the pollution tax rate. In addition we compare unanticipated and announced policy scenarios for a decentralized economy.

As the numerical solver can solve only discrete time models we reformulate the model analysed in Section 4.2 as a discrete version.[9] According to Blanchard and Fischer (1989, p. 44), the empirical estimations of the intertemporal elasticity of substitution vary substantially, but usually lie around or below unity. For simplicity, we therefore assume for the simulation a logarithmic utility function and set $\varepsilon = 1$. The discrete maximization problem of the market solution and the system of difference equations both for the market and central planner solutions are represented in Section A.2.2 (page 225) in the appendix.[10]

The discrete reduced form of the growth rate along a balanced growth path both for the central planner solution and the market solution reads

$$g = \frac{B - \delta_H - \rho}{1 + \rho}. \tag{4.39}$$

---

[9] For the numerical simulations we use the solver MINOS 5 of the software package GAMS (General Algebraic Modelling System), release 2.25, which is suitable for solving nonlinear difference equations, as mentioned in Section 2.4.

[10] For an introduction to discrete dynamical systems and applications of discrete dynamic optimization problems, see, for example, Feichtinger and Hartl (1986, Ch. A.2), Stokey and Lucas (1993, part II) and Azariadis (1995).

Equation (4.39) is the discrete version of equation (4.28) for $\varepsilon = 1$.[11]

4.3.1   Calibration of Parameters

The quantitative results of numerical simulations depend on the particular choice of parameter values of the specified functional forms. Therefore, we select the parameters and calibrate the model so as to capture stylized empirical facts of industrialized countries. Additionally, for economically crucial benchmark parameters we use econometric estimates suggested in the literature.

We set the long-term economic growth rate equal to 2 per cent ($g = 0.02$), which corresponds to the average per capita growth rate of the real domestic product of Western Germany between 1971 and 1991.[12] Following Barro and Sala-i-Martin (1995, pp. 37 and 191) we set the rates of capital depreciation equal to 5 per cent ($\delta_x = 0.05$) and the rate of time preference equal to 2 per cent ($\rho = 0.02$). Using equation (4.39), calibration of the model implies a studying productivity parameter $B = 0.0904$. Following Lucas (1988, p. 26) we fix the share of physical capital in final good production at $\alpha = 0.25$. Since the level of the technology has no impact on the growth rate and other core variables along a balanced growth path (see Table 4.2), we set it equal to unity ($A = 1$). In Western Germany, pollution abatement and control expenditure in the private and public sector as a percentage of GDP were 1.6 per cent ($Z/Y = 0.016$) in the years 1987–90 (see OECD 1993, Table 14.2A, p. 294)). Therefore we calibrate the pollution elasticity χ and the weight of pollution in utility η_P such that abatement expenditures in our model reproduce this share with respect to GDP. This is fulfilled for $\chi = 0.8$ and $\eta_P = 0.0249$. Note that such a calibration assumes the

---

[11] Rearranging and taking logs of equation (4.39) yields $\ln(1 + g) = \ln(1 + B - \delta_H) - \ln(1 + \rho)$. Applying the approximation $x \approx \ln(1 + x)$ for small x ($x \ll 1$), we get $g \approx B - \delta_H - \rho$, which is identical to the reduced form (4.28) of the continuous time model for $\varepsilon = 1$.

[12] Actually the computed value is 1.969 per cent. For the computation we use the annual statistics of the OECD main indicators 13100310 (GDP, current prices, million DM, Western Germany), 13102512 (GDP implicit price level, I/90, Western Germany), and EUROSTAT 123000000 (total working population/male and female, Western Germany, 1000 Source). Also King and Rebelo (1990) and Devereux and Love (1994) calibrate their models in order to achieve a growth rate of 2 per cent.

real world to be on a balanced growth path, at least on average. Since the determination of the parameter values is somehow arbitrary we vary the share of physical capital in final good production α, the rate of time preference ρ and the pollution elasticity χ to test the robustness of the results in a sensitivity analysis. However, in all scenarios, parameter values are chosen such that the long-term growth rate remains at 2 per cent and pollution abatement is 1.6 per cent of output along the initial balanced growth path.

In the following we start with a simulation of the transitional dynamics caused by a shock towards greener preferences – a higher η_P – in the centrally planned economy. This scenario is called 'increased environmental care' scenario (IEC). The IEC scenario describes the optimal adaptation path to an unexpected change of η_P and is thus a first-best solution. To make the different simulations comparable we assume that the abatement-output share doubles from 0.016 to 0.032 along the new balanced growth path (from $\eta_P = 0.025$ to $\eta_P = 0.05$). Note that this implies a pollution reduction of 46 per cent. The scenario where no shocks take place at all is called the 'business-as-usual' scenario (BAU). The BAU path serves as a reference system for the IEC scenario. The chosen parameter values are summarized in Table 4.3. All our simula-

Table 4.3: Parameter levels for the BAU and the IEC scenarios

	A	B	α	δ_H	δ_K	ε	η_P	ρ	χ
BAU	1	0.0904	0.25	0.05	0.05	1	0.0249	0.02	0.8
IEC	1	0.0904	0.25	0.05	0.05	1	0.0500	0.02	0.8

tions cover 150 periods. Within this period of time all simulations have already reached the new balanced growth path.[13]

4.3.2 The Increased Environmental Care Scenario

In this section we simulate numerically the transitional dynamics for a centrally planned economy after a sudden unexpected shock of the pol-

---

[13]To be mathematically precise: the economy never actually reaches the new balanced growth path, but rather approaches it asymptotically.

lution disutility parameter η_P. A shock towards greener preferences can occur due to new scientific information about the impact of pollution on the environmental quality. The simulation starts with period one, when the central planner faces the new (higher) value of η_P. The stocks of human and physical capital are fixed in period one and correspond to the optimal initial BAU values of η_P. The central planner allocates the shares of human capital to the final good sector and to the education sector, chooses quantities of abatement measures, consumption and investment in physical capital so as to achieve the welfare-optimal transition path. Since the model is saddle-point stable, the economy asymptotically reaches the new balanced growth path.

Note that we do not take into account costs of installing investment goods. Thus an increase in the capital stock does not require additional costs per unit of investment which are used up in transforming goods into capital.[14] Furthermore, the allocation between time for studying and production can be altered without any friction. In reality this is certainly not the case. Imagine, for instance, a tax reform which alters the optimal ratio of both capital stocks. As we do not consider frictions, households in our model can reduce production time instantaneously to increase studying time or vice versa. Thus our simulation results tend to underestimate adjustment costs and adjustment time since we ignore both issues.

Figure 4.1 traces the growth of output, represented by the solid line, and growth of consumption, represented by the dashed line, during the transition after an increase in environmental care. The horizontal axis is the time axis, measured in years; the vertical axis represents the growth rates of output and consumption. Growth rates of output and consumption possess equilibrium values of 2 per cent along the initial balanced growth path in years –2 to 0 before the shock. In year 1, when the preferences become greener, output growth declines to a negative value of –0.75 per cent. But already from year 2 onwards it is positive again and even remains above its balanced growth path rate of 2 per cent until convergence. However, this turns out to be a pure baseline effect

---

[14] A standard specification is that investment is subject to convex installation costs which are a function of a firm's relative investment; see, for example, Blanchard and Fischer (1989, Ch. 2.4).

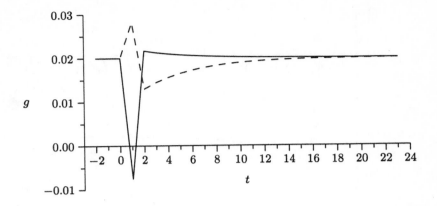

Figure 4.1: Growth rates of output (solid) and consumption (dashed)

as described in the following. Figure 4.2 shows the percentage deviation of the levels of output (solid), consumption (dashed) and fraction of time devoted to production (dotted), compared to the business-as-usual scenario. The level of output is below the BAU levels in all years (see Figure 4.2). Therefore growth rates above 2 per cent are due to the negative growth rate in year 1.

Growth of consumption is almost mirror inverted at the 2 per cent axis to the growth of output. In year 1, consumption growth increases above its long-term growth rate to 2.81 per cent. Although abatement activities are increased, it is optimal to enlarge consumption in period 1. Remember that the flow resource constraint must be fulfilled in every period, thus output minus abatement and net investment is equal to consumption. We know from the balanced growth path analysis (see Section 4.2.2) that in the long run final good production becomes more human capital intensive due to an increase in η_P (see page 114). To achieve the new capital-labor ratio in the final good sector, the central planner increases education time by decreasing production time (see Figure 4.2), which lowers output. Additionally, abatement activities are increased. Both effects lead *ceteris paribus* to a lower consumption. However, to achieve the new capital-labor ratio the central planner reduces physical investment almost to zero. In period 1, increased abatement

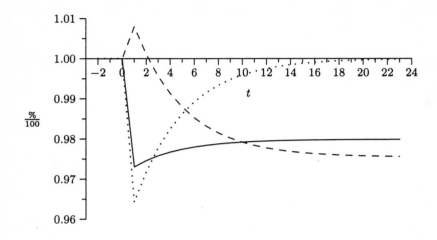

Figure 4.2: Levels of Y (solid), C (dashed) and u (dotted) as a percentage of BAU

activities and the decline of output do not offset reduced investments, hence consumption level and consumption growth are both above their BAU values. But already in year 2 the growth rate of consumption has declined to 1.3 per cent. From Figure 4.2 it is seen that apart from period 1 the level of consumption is below its BAU level.

The path of abatement growth is similar to the path of consumption growth, although its peaks are more extreme. In year 1 the growth rate of abatement increases up to 106.56 per cent, in year 2 it declines to 1.3 per cent, and then converges towards its steady-state growth rate. The intuition behind the similarity between consumption and abatement growth paths is that the marginal utility of consumption must be equal to the marginal utility of abatement (see equation (A.21) in the appendix, page 226).

As mentioned above, the share of physical to human capital in final good production must decrease in the long run because physical capital is the dirty factor. Investment in physical capital declines in year 1 and the fraction of time devoted to education $(1 - u)$ increases temporarily since u declines (see Figure 4.2). The former effect decreases physical capital accumulation, whereas the latter increases human capital accumulation. After year 1, the growth rates of human and physical capital and the fraction of time devoted to production converge back to their steady-state values. For the time path of the fraction of time devoted to production, see the dotted line in Figure 4.2; for the growth rates of physical and human capital, see Figure 4.3.

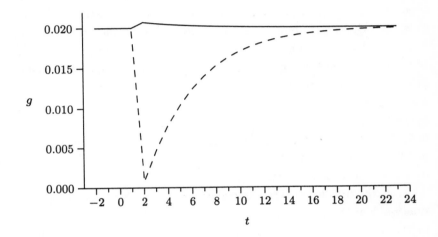

Figure 4.3: Growth rates of human (solid) and physical (dashed) capital

4.3.3   Different Environmental Policy Scenarios

In this section we analyse the transition paths of a decentralized economy in the case of unexpected and anticipated increases of the pollution tax. Although there is a symmetry between the central planner solution and the market solution it does not make sense to model announcement effects for a centrally planned economy.

Before we simulate announcement effects, we describe the 'environmental policy' scenario (EP). The EP scenario represents the transitional dynamics of the *market solution* caused by a sudden unexpected increase of the pollution tax. For simplicity and for a better comparability between the central planner and the market solution, we abstain from non-environmental taxes. Thus, the environmental externality is the only distortion in the market economy. Hence, for optimal values of the pollution tax the EP scenario is identical to the first-best IEC scenario and again the BAU path serves as a reference system for the EP scenario. For all simulations we assume that the pollution tax is below its optimal level on the initial balanced growth path. This reflects the widely shared belief that environmental externalities are currently not fully internalized. Moreover, it provides a rationale for the recently observed tightening of environmental policy in many industrialized countries. As mentioned above, optimal environmental policy requires that the share of abatement activities doubles from 1.6 per cent to 3.2 per cent of GDP. This implies a pollution reduction of 46 per cent. The higher abatement-output value of 3.2 per cent is chosen arbitrarily, but it is needed to make the different scenarios comparable and just concerns the normative part of the analysis. In the EP scenario, pollution tax rates of 0.62 per cent and 1.33 per cent guarantee an abatement-output share of 1.6 per cent and 3.2 per cent, and thus correspond to values of η_P of 0.0249 and 0.0500, respectively.

From the simulation of the central planner solution we get the optimal time path of the pollution tax rate. The pollution tax must be equal to the optimal abatement-capital ratio (see Table 4.1). The optimal

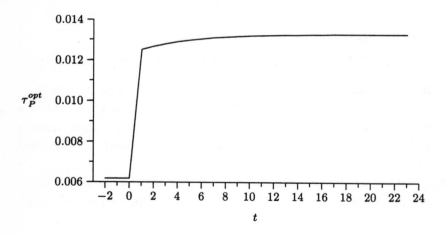

Figure 4.4: The optimal time path of the pollution tax

pollution tax suddenly increases from its BAU value of 0.62 per cent to

1.25 per cent at first in period one (see Figure 4.4). Then it converges slowly to its optimal long-term value of 1.33 per cent. In contrast to this optimal environmental policy we assume for the decentralized economy in the EP scenario that the government in period 1 increases the pollution tax from its previous level of 0.62 per cent directly to its long-term optimal value of 1.33 per cent. Thus, the time path of the pollution tax is simplified as a once-and-for-all jump. This procedure simplifies the programming for the simulation as the pollution tax takes only two instead of 150 values, while it does not change the qualitative results and hardly changes quantitative results.

We now assume that the economic agents know in period one that the policy will change a couple of years ahead. We neglect the issue of time inconsistency raised by Kydland and Prescott (1977) and assume that the individuals trust in the policy action.[15] In the following we compare two different announced environmental policy scenarios, EP_5 and EP_10, which describe announcement effects of 5 and 10 years, respectively, with the unanticipated environmental policy scenario EP. Furthermore, we describe the EP_grad scenario, where the government gradually increases the pollution tax. In the EP scenario the policy action takes place in period 1, whereas in the announced environmental policy scenarios the increase of the pollution tax is known from period 1.

In the following figures we compare the unanticipated EP scenario with the announced EP_5 and EP_10 scenarios. For better comparability we plot the time paths of key variables of the three scenarios in separate figures. In Figures 4.5 and 4.6, growth rates and levels of output are depicted as a percentage of BAU. In Figures 4.7 and 4.8, consumption and abatement levels are traced as a percentage of their corresponding BAU levels. In all four figures the unexpected environmental policy scenario EP is represented by solid lines, whereas the announced policy scenarios EP_5 and EP_10 are depicted by dashed and dotted lines, respectively. As seen in Figure 4.5, the announcement of the policy measure produces an additional effect already in the year of announcement. After the year when the policy action takes place (years 6 and 11, respectively) we observe similar adjustment patterns as in the EP sce-

---

[15] See Stokey (1991) for a discussion about time consistency.

nario without announcement. However, the strength of the deflections are different. For example, in Figure 4.5 we see that the negative deflections from the balanced growth rate become smaller the longer the period of announcement. In contrast to the unanticipated environmental policy with announcement there is no negative economic growth rate at any point of time. However, the positive deflections are larger in the announced scenarios. As can be seen in Figure 4.6 the levels of output

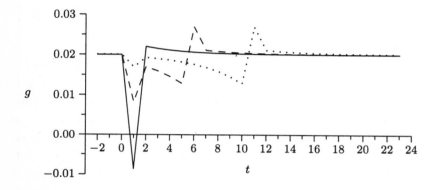

Figure 4.5: Growth of output in the EP scenarios

as a percentage of BAU are always below BAU. Furthermore, this figure indicates that the overall output losses due to the policy measure become smaller the longer the announcement period. In Figure 4.7 we see that the consumption levels are above their BAU levels during the period of announcement. However, they decline below the BAU level as soon as the policy action takes place. Figure 4.8 traces the levels of abatement as a percentage of BAU in the three EP scenarios. It is seen that the level of the abatement measures increases to over 200 per cent of the BAU level in the year when the policy action takes place.

In a further scenario, called the EP_grad scenario, the government gradually increases the pollution tax rate linearly within annual steps over 10 years. The time path of the policy action is known by the individuals in year 1 when the pollution tax is increased for the first time. Figure 4.9 describes the growth rates of output (solid), consumption (dashed) and abatement activities (dotted). The paths of the growth

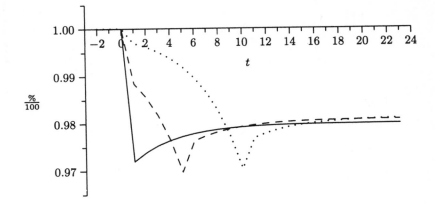

Figure 4.6: Levels of output as a percentage of BAU in the EP scenarios

rates are quite similar to those of the EP scenario. However, the deflections from the steady-state growth rates are smaller but stretched over 10 years, reflecting the gradual increase of the environmental costs between years 1 and 11. In the gradual tax reform scenario, output growth rates are below their equilibrium values not only in the first period (as in the EP scenario), but also within the first 10 years when the policy measures take place, however, without being negative. The growth rate of abatement declines from 13.70 per cent in year 1 slowly to 7.11 per cent in year 10, then it falls sharply to 1.49 per cent in year 11, and finally converges to its long-term rate of 2 per cent.

In Table 4.4 we compare the main results of the different EP scenarios. The table is structured as follows: transitional implications are split into effects on levels and welfare, and into political indicators. The BAU scenario serves as the benchmark case for all the different EP scenarios. Remember that the BAU scenario is calibrated such that the share of abatement to output is 1.6 per cent whereas the share of abatement to output in the different EP scenarios is 3.2 per cent in the long run. The scenarios differ only in the level of the pollution tax τ_P and the announcement period. All chosen parameters are represented in Table 4.3. *Column 2* represents the BAU scenario where no policy change takes

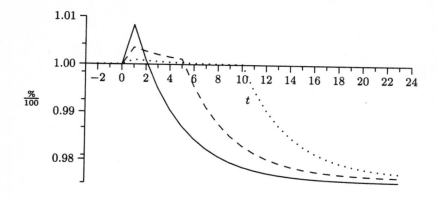

Figure 4.7: Levels of consumption as a percentage of BAU in the EP scenarios

place. The BAU scenario is always on a balanced growth path. The level of output, consumption, abatement and so on is normalized to 100 per cent and highest and lowest growth rates correspond to the balanced growth rate of 2 per cent. *Column 3,* representing the EP scenario, shows the results of an unanticipated increase of the pollution tax. Pollution abatement as a percentage of domestic product increases from 1.6 per cent (BAU scenario) to 3.2 per cent in the long run. Since the period of announcement is identical to the shock period there are no differences in its values. In year 1 when the policy measures take place, the level of output is 2.8 per cent below the BAU level. The levels of consumption C and abatement Z are 0.83 per cent and 114 per cent over their respective BAU levels. *Columns 4* and *5* represent the scenarios where the policy measure is announced 5 and 10 years in advance. Finally, *column 6* represents the scenario where the pollution tax is increased gradually over 10 years. All scenarios have some common characteristics: (i) In all EP scenarios welfare is above its BAU level. There are no hard times for economic agents from a welfare point of view. In all periods and scenarios the level of welfare is above its BAU level. Hence, during the transition process individuals do not suffer from the structural change because the material utility losses arising from the decline in consumption and output are more than offset by the immaterial util-

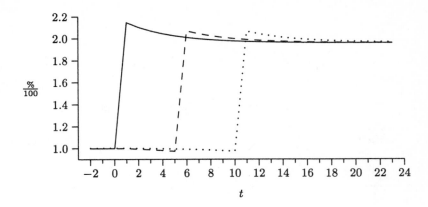

Figure 4.8: Levels of abatement as a percentage of BAU in the EP scenarios

ity gains from decreased pollution. The present-value of utility in all EP scenarios is above the BAU level. Hence, from a welfare point of view, not only in the long run but also in the short run there is no reason to refrain from environmental policy. (ii) In all EP scenarios, the highest output growth rate and the lowest consumption growth rate are in the year of shock, whereas the highest consumption growth rate is in the year of announcement.

Comparing the EP scenario with scenarios EP_5 and EP_10 where the policy action is announced 5 and 10 years in advance, we observe that the negative deflections of output and consumption growth rates become smaller the longer the announcement period. However, the present value of welfare decreases with the period of announcement. This is due to the fact that after the announcement the pollution tax rate remains unchanged at the initial level and abatement measures cannot increase compared with the BAU scenario, whereas in the EP scenario during this period the abatement measures have already been increased. Hence the welfare losses are not due to announcement but due to the lag of environmental policy. Thus from a welfare point of view the announcement period is a waste of time. In years 2 to 5 of the EP_5 scenario and in years 2 to 10 of the EP_10 scenario the abatement levels are even

Table 4.4: Results of the different EP scenarios

Scenario	BAU	EP	EP_5	EP_10	EP_grad
announcement (t)	–	0	5	10	0
Level effects as a percentage of BAU					
Y in t of announ.	100	97.2	98.85	99.7	98.41
Y in t of shock	100	97.2	97.63	97.68	98.41
C in t of announ.	100	100.83	100.35	100.09	100.48
C in t of shock	100	100.83	99.55	99.47	100.48
Z in t of announ.	100	214.68	100	100	111.47
Z in t of shock	100	214.68	206.97	206.42	111.47
$\sum_{t=1}^{T} \frac{Y_t}{(1+\rho)^t}$	100	97.96	98.06	98.13	98.05
$\sum_{t=1}^{T} \frac{C_t}{(1+\rho)^t}$	100	97.64	97.78	97.87	97.76
$\sum_{t=1}^{T} \frac{Z_t}{(1+\rho)^t}$	100	196.52	193.22	190.01	193.59
Welfare effects as a percentage of BAU					
year of announ.	100	101.53	100.14	100.04	100,36
year after announ.	100	101.23	100.11	100.03	100.42
year of shock	100	101.53	100.99	100.92	100,36
year after shock	100	101.23	100.82	100.77	100.42
$\sum_{t=1}^{T} \frac{Y_t}{(1+\rho)^t}$	100	100.25	100.23	100.21	100.240
Political indicators (growth rates in % (year of appearence))					
max. Y growth	2.00	2.20(2)	2.69(6)	2.68(11)	2.11(10)
max. C growth	2.00	2.84(1)	2.36(1)	2.1(1)	2.49(1)
min. Y growth	2.00	−0.86(1)	0.83(1)	1.28(10)	0.38(1)
min. C growth	2.00	1.25(2)	1.43(6)	1.46(11)	1.76(9)

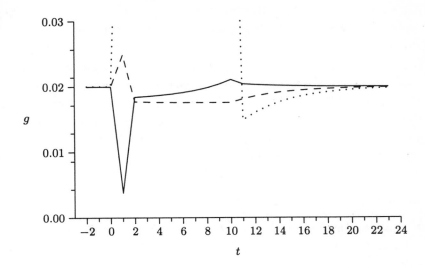

Figure 4.9: Growth of Y (solid), C (dashed) and Z (dotted) in the EP_grad scenario

below their BAU levels. This is the case since the tax base of pollution – physical capital – grows at a rate below the BAU rate. Nevertheless, there are overall welfare gains. In the EP_grad scenario the pollution tax increases gradually over ten years. Compared with the EP_5 and EP_10 scenarios, the EP_grad scenario yields a higher overall welfare gain, and the growth-rate deflections are smaller than in the EP scenario. From a pure welfare point of view there is no reason to announce the policy measure or to increase the pollution tax gradually. However, from a political economy point of view it may be interesting to know how growth rates of the national product behave after tightening environmental policy. According to a public opinion survey with 14 800 interviews, 69 per cent of the European Community's population believe that economic development must be ensured and the environment be protected at the same time (see OECD 1993, Table 14.1A). A government mainly striving for re-election and not maximizing economic agents' welfare thus will be very reluctant to tighten environmental policy if this is accompanied with substantial growth losses, since the re-election probabilities

depend on the economic performance of the economy. In order to keep
negative growth-rate deflections small, the government would prefer an
announced or a gradual tax reform. Following this train of thought it
would be rational for the government to arrange the announced policy
measure in such a way that it takes place one year before the election.
Economic growth would then be maximal in the year of election (see
Table 4.4). Assuming a purely rational government solely striving for
re-election may seem extreme, however such considerations are important for a government in power.

4.3.4   Sensitivity Analysis

A sensitivity analysis enables us to test how far the results in Sections
4.3.2 and 4.3.3 depend on the chosen parameter values. For the sensitivity analysis we vary the share of physical capital in production α,
the rate of time preference ρ and the capital depreciation rate δ. Table 4.5 shows the results of the sensitivity analysis, where first parameter
values, second ratios of variables along the new balanced growth path
and finally transitional implications are listed. The six sensitivity scenarios cannot be compared with the previous BAU scenario: different
parameter sets determine different BAU scenarios which are not listed.
Percentage deviations of key variables and welfare therefore relate to
their corresponding BAU scenarios. In the following we compare the
sensitivity scenarios with the EP scenario. All sensitivity scenarios are
calibrated such that the long-term growth rate is 2 per cent and abatement measures as a percentage of domestic product are initially 1.6 per
cent and 3.2 per cent along the new balanced growth path.

In the sensitivity scenarios $S\_\alpha1$ and $S\_\alpha2$, the share of physical
capital in final good production is varied. With $\alpha = 0.2$ the economy
is less, and with $\alpha = 0.4$ it is more, physical capital intensive. Given a
growth rate equal to 2 per cent and an abatement-output ratio equal to
1.6 per cent we must calibrate new values of the pollution tax rate τ_P. If
the economy is less physical capital intensive ($S\_\alpha1$) the consumption-
output ratio is higher, whereas the investment-output ratio and the
capital-labor ratio are lower than in the EP scenario, and vice versa
for a more physical capital-intensive economy $S\_\alpha2$. In the less physi-

Table 4.5: Results of the sensitivity scenarios

	EP	$S\_\alpha 1$	$S\_\alpha 2$	$S\_\rho 1$	$S\_\rho 2$	$S\_\delta 1$	$S\_\delta 2$
				Scenario			
Parameters							
τ_P (%)	1.33	4.25	0.79	1.18	1.48	1.18	1.47
B	0.090	0.090	0.090	0.080	0.101	0.080	0.100
α	0.25	0.1	0.4	0.25	0.25	0.25	0.25
ρ	0.02	0.02	0.02	0.01	0.03	0.02	0.02
δ	0.5	0.5	0.5	0.5	0.5	0.04	0.06
Ratios of variables along the new balanced growth path							
C/Y	0.80	0.92	0.68	0.77	0.82	0.81	0.79
I/Y	0.05	0.02	0.08	0.05	0.04	0.05	0.04
K/Y	2.41	0.75	4.07	2.71	2.17	2.71	2.17
K/H	0.72	0.16	2.34	0.48	0.85	0.96	0.57
Levels effects as a percentage of BAU							
Y_1	97.2	92.50	98.69	97.01	97.35	97.11	97.28
C_1	100.8	100.8	100.7	100.9	100.7	100.9	100.8
Z_1	214.9	247.1	208.7	214.7	214.7	214.7	214.7
$\sum \frac{Y_t}{(1+\rho)^t}$	97.96	97.92	97.61	97.81	98.05	98.00	97.94
$\sum \frac{C_t}{(1+\rho)^t}$	97.64	97.64	97.23	97.65	97.67	97.64	97.64
$\sum \frac{Z_t}{(1+\rho)^t}$	196.5	196.6	195.8	195.9	197.1	196.7	196.4
Welfare effects as a percentage of BAU							
U_1	101.5	101.1	102.3	101.7	101.4	101.6	101.5
U_2	101.2	100.6	102.0	101.4	101.1	101.3	101.2
$\sum \frac{U_t}{(1+\rho)^t}$	100.3	100.2	100.4	100.3	100.3	100.3	100.3
Political indicators (growth rates in % (year of appearance))							
max. Y	2.2(2)	5.3(2)	2.0(∞)	2.2(2)	2.2(2)	2.2(2)	2.2(2)
max. C	2.8(1)	2.8(1)	2.7(1)	2.9(1)	2.7(1)	2.9(1)	2.8(1)
min. Y	-0.9(1)	-5.7(1)	0.7(1)	-1.1(1)	-0.1(1)	-0.9(1)	-0.8(1)
min. C	1.5(2)	0.3(2)	1.5(2)	1.3(2)	1.2(2)	1.3(2)	1.2(2)

cal capital-intensive economy, a tighter environmental policy induces a smaller overall welfare increase and the deflections of the growth rates are larger than in the IEC scenario. For example, the growth rate of output falls to minus 5.65 per cent in period 1 but it jumps to 5.33 per cent in period 2. The opposite applies to the less physical capital-intensive economy. The sensitivity scenario $S\_\alpha 2$ has one special feature. During the transition we do not observe output growth rates above the equilibrium rate, as is the case for all other scenarios. Moreover, the output growth rates during the whole adaptation process are below the equilibrium value.

In the sensitivity scenarios $S\_\rho 1$ and $S\_\rho 2$, the rate of time preference is varied. Individuals value the future higher in the sensitivity scenario $S\_\rho 1$ and lower in $S\_\rho 2$. Given a growth rate equal to 2 per cent and an abatement-output ratio equal to 1.6 per cent we must calibrate the studying productivity parameter B and the pollution tax rate τ_P in those scenarios again. In the $S\_\rho 1$ scenario, the consumption-output ratio is lower and the investment-output ratio is higher compared with the EP scenario.[16] This is true since future consumption is valued higher the lower the rate of time preference. The opposite is true for the sensitivity scenario $S\_\rho 2$.

In the sensitivity scenarios $S\_\delta 1$ and $S\_\delta 2$ we vary the rate of depreciation. As in the S_ρ scenarios we must calibrate new values for the pollution tax τ_P and the studying efficiency parameter B. Finally, varying the elasticity χ only changes the pollution disutility parameters η_P, but does not change ratios, levels or political indicators. The sensitivity scenarios S_χ are therefore not included in Table 4.5.

Summarizing the results of the sensitivity analysis and given the fact that the model is always calibrated so as to yield an initial economic growth rate of 2 per cent and an abatement-output ratio of 1.6 per cent we see that the qualitative properties are unchanged and the quantitative results do not change substantially by varying the rate of time preference ρ, the rate of depreciation δ and the pollution elasticity χ. However, the results, especially those concerning the highest and lowest growth rates, seem to react sensitively to changes in the intensity of

---

[16]This cannot be seen in Table 4.5 because of rounding errors.

physical capital α.

4.4   The Open Economy

Empirical evidence suggests that foreign human capital is an important determinant of domestic factor productivity (see Section 3.5, page 79). Furthermore, environmental problems like global warming make clear the international dimension of certain environmental externalities. These observations motivated us in Section 3.5 to analyse the strategic interactions between two countries for the linear model. Analogously, in this section we study a differential game between two countries for the Uzawa–Lucas production processes.[17] Since the formal analysis is similar to Section 3.5, we shall keep it as short as possible. As in Section 3.5, every country is mutually affected by positive international knowledge spillovers associated with human capital accumulation, and negative international environmental spillovers generated by the production process. However, the Uzawa–Lucas model allows us to distinguish between human capital and physical capital and thus provides a better possibility for modeling knowledge spillovers. In Section 3.5 we assumed that the employment of foreign capital in foreign production increases the productivity of domestic production. In this section we assume that foreign human capital investment in the foreign education sector increases the productivity in the domestic education sector. We shall see that the distinction between physical capital and human capital in this two-sector model changes the results of cooperation. Furthermore, the cooperation effects depend on whether physical capital or final good production is responsible for pollution. In the Rebelo model this distinction does not matter since there is a linear relation between the capital stock and production.

In the following, we first describe in Section 4.4.1 the setup for the open economy. As in this model the effects of cooperation depend on the pollution specification, in Section 4.4.2 we choose physical capital as the polluting factor and in Section 4.4.3 final output as the polluting factor. In order to determine the cooperation effects, we derive in both sections

---

[17] For a discussion about the underlying assumptions, see Section 3.5.

the noncooperative open-loop Cournot–Nash equilibrium and the cooperative outcome which would result under supranational planning. By comparing the reduced forms we can assess the effects of cooperation on growth, pollution and welfare. Since the procedure is similar to Section 3.5, we shall concentrate mainly on the analytical differences and results.

4.4.1   The Analytical Framework

The production function and the flow resource constraint of the economy are identical to the previously analysed case of a closed economy (see Section 4.2.1). Each country produces one final good using physical capital and effective labor. The perfectly malleable output can be used without any friction for consumption, for net investment in the capital stock, and for abatement activities. Since countries are assumed to be identical, no trade will occur in equilibrium and international flows of commodities or capital can be ignored. For convenience we replicate the production function for the domestic country:

$$Y_t = A K_t^{\alpha} (u_t H_t)^{1-\alpha}, \tag{4.40}$$

$$Y_t = C_t + \dot{K}_t + Z_t + \delta_K K_t. \tag{4.41}$$

However, the human capital accumulation constraint is different. We still assume a constant return to scale technology, for example in the domestic country,

$$\dot{H}_t = B \left[(1 - u_t) H_t \right]^{\beta} \left[\left(1 - \overset{*}{u}_t \right) \overset{*}{H}_t \right]^{(1-\beta)} - \delta_H H_t, \tag{4.42}$$

where B reflects the exogenous level of the technology and $0 < \beta < 1$ is the exogenous domestic human capital share in education. However, due to our assumptions new human capital is produced not only by using domestic human capital but also by using foreign human capital, which is indicated by an asterisk '*'. The latter is exogenous for the home country and reflects the international human capital spillover.

As before, the utility function depends on the trade-off between consumption and pollution. For convenience we replicate the corresponding lifetime utility, which is given by

$$U_0 = \int_{t=0}^{\infty} \frac{\left(C_t P_t^{-\eta_P}\right)^{(1-1/\varepsilon)} - 1}{1 - 1/\varepsilon} e^{-\rho t} dt. \qquad (4.43)$$

Pollution generated by the home country p, and pollution caused by the foreign country $\overset{*}{p}$, contribute to total pollution P. Total pollution is given by

$$P_t = p_t + (1 - \eta_F) \overset{*}{p}_t, \qquad (4.44)$$

where $0 \leq \eta_F \leq 1$. By means of parameter η_F we can distinguish different kinds of externalities. See Section 3.5 (page 82) for a description and examples.

4.4.2 Physical Capital as the Polluting Factor

As before we assume that pollution is caused by using physical capital in production and can be reduced by abatement activities. Pollution generated by the domestic country is given by the pollution function

$$p = \left(\frac{K}{Z}\right)^{\chi}. \qquad (4.45)$$

For this pollution specification we derive in the following the noncooperative solution, the cooperative solution and finally the cooperation effects on core variables.

The Noncooperative Solution

The strategic interactions over time between the two countries are modeled as a differential game. For the noncooperative solution the symmetrical countries are assumed to behave in a Cournot–Nash manner: given the selected plan of the foreign government the benevolent planner of the home country maximizes lifetime utility (4.43) of the representative citizen by choosing the time paths of domestic consumption, abatement activities, physical and human capital accumulation, and the fraction of time devoted to production subject to the domestic resource constraint (4.41) and the human capital accumulation constraint (4.42).

The current-value Hamiltonian for the domestic optimization problem is given by

$$\max_{C,Z,u} \mathcal{H} = U\left[C, P\left(p, \overset{*}{p}\right)\right] \tag{4.46}$$

$$+ \lambda\left[AK^{\alpha}(uH)^{1-\alpha} - C - Z - \delta_K K\right]$$

$$+ \mu\left\{B\left[(1-u)H\right]^{\beta}\left[\left(1-\overset{*}{u}\right)\overset{*}{H}\right]^{(1-\beta)} - \delta_H H\right\}.$$

Analogously, the current-value Hamiltonian for the foreign central planner reads

$$\max_{\overset{*}{C},\overset{*}{Z},\overset{*}{u}} \overset{*}{\mathcal{H}} = \overset{*}{U}\left[\overset{*}{C}, \overset{*}{P}\left(\overset{*}{p}, p\right)\right]$$

$$+ \overset{*}{\lambda}\left[A\overset{*}{K}^{\alpha}\left(\overset{*}{u}\overset{*}{H}\right)^{1-\alpha} - \overset{*}{C} - \overset{*}{Z} - \delta_K \overset{*}{K}\right]$$

$$+ \overset{*}{\mu}\left\{B\left[\left(1-\overset{*}{u}\right)\overset{*}{H}\right]^{\beta}\left[(1-u)H\right]^{(1-\beta)} - \delta_H \overset{*}{H}\right\}.$$

Due to the assumed symmetry of the countries, the first-order conditions of the home and the foreign countries are equivalent. Furthermore, the domestic variables solving the domestic planning problem are identical to the corresponding foreign variables, hence

$$C = \overset{*}{C}, \ H = \overset{*}{H}, \ K = \overset{*}{K}, \ P = \overset{*}{P}, \ p = \overset{*}{p}, \ u = \overset{*}{u}, \ \mu = \overset{*}{\mu}, \ \lambda = \overset{*}{\lambda}. \tag{4.47}$$

In addition, along a balanced growth path the variables C, H, K, Y Z grow at the same constant rate g, whereas u is constant over time:

$$g \equiv \hat{C} = \hat{H} = \hat{K} = \hat{Y} = \hat{Z}, \quad 0 = \hat{u}. \tag{4.48}$$

Because of condition (4.48), the ratios C/K, Z/K, K/H, Y/K and Y/Z are constant, and therefore pollution P is constant along a balanced growth path as well. Using conditions (4.47) and (4.48), the first-order conditions along a balanced growth path determine the following system of equations:

$$\frac{Z}{K} = \frac{\chi\eta_P}{2-\eta_F}\frac{C}{K}, \tag{4.49}$$

$$g = \varepsilon\left(\alpha\frac{Y}{K} - \frac{Z}{K} - \delta_K - \rho\right), \tag{4.50}$$

$$g = \varepsilon\left(\beta B - \delta_H - \rho\right), \tag{4.51}$$

$$g = \frac{Y}{K} - \frac{C}{K} - \frac{Z}{K} - \delta_K, \tag{4.52}$$

$$g = B\left(1 - u\right) - \delta_H. \tag{4.53}$$

Equation (4.49) requires that the marginal utility of consumption and abatement must be equalized. Equations (4.50) and (4.51) represent the Keynes–Ramsey rule and the second Euler condition, respectively. Equation (4.52) is the flow resource constraint of the economy and equation (4.53) is the human capital accumulation constraint. Equation (4.51) is already the reduced form of g. The other reduced forms of the time devoted to production, the consumption-capital ratio, the output-capital ratio and the abatement-capital ratio can be derived immediately by using the first-order conditions (4.49)–(4.53):

$$u = \frac{B - \varepsilon\left(\beta B - \delta_H - \rho\right) - \delta_H}{B}, \tag{4.54}$$

$$\frac{C}{K} = \frac{(1 - \alpha\varepsilon)\left(\beta B - \delta_H - \rho\right) + (1 - \alpha)\delta_K + \rho}{\alpha + (\alpha - 1)\frac{\eta_P \chi}{2 - \eta_F}}, \tag{4.55}$$

$$\frac{Y}{K} = \frac{(1 - \varepsilon)\left(\beta B - \delta_H - \rho\right) + \frac{2 - \eta_F}{\chi \eta_P}\left(\beta B - \delta_H + \delta_K\right) + \rho}{\alpha - 1 + \frac{\alpha(2 - \eta_F)}{\eta_P \chi}}, \tag{4.56}$$

$$\frac{Z}{K} = \frac{(1 - \alpha\varepsilon)\left(\beta B - \delta_H - \rho\right) + (1 - \alpha)\delta_K + \rho}{\alpha - 1 + \frac{\alpha(2 - \eta_F)}{\eta_P \chi}}. \tag{4.57}$$

To compare the reduced forms of the noncooperative solution with the reduced forms of the cooperative solution we derive the latter in the following.

The Cooperative Solution

In the cooperative solution each national social planner takes into account the effects of his/her decision on the other country. The easiest way to derive the global optimum is to assume a supranational social planner. A supranational planner chooses $C, Z, u, \overset{*}{C}, \overset{*}{Z}, \overset{*}{u}$ in order to maximize the sum of lifetime welfare in both countries subject to the national resource and human capital accumulation constraints. The current-value Hamiltonian for this optimization problem is given by

$$
\max_{C,Z,u,\overset{*}{C},\overset{*}{Z},\overset{*}{u}} \mathcal{H} = U\left[C, P\left(p,\overset{*}{p}\right)\right] + \overset{*}{U}\left[\overset{*}{C}, \overset{*}{P}\left(\overset{*}{p},p\right)\right] \tag{4.58}
$$

$$
+ \ \lambda\left[AK^\alpha\left(uH\right)^{1-\alpha} - C - Z - \delta_K K\right]
$$

$$
+ \ \overset{*}{\lambda}\left[A\overset{*}{K}{}^\alpha\left(\overset{*}{u}\overset{*}{H}\right)^{1-\alpha} - \overset{*}{C} - \overset{*}{Z} - \delta_K \overset{*}{K}\right]
$$

$$
+ \ \mu\left\{B\left[(1-u)H\right]^\beta\left[\left(1-\overset{*}{u}\right)\overset{*}{H}\right]^{(1-\beta)} - \delta_H H\right\}
$$

$$
+ \ \overset{*}{\mu}\left\{B\left[\left(1-\overset{*}{u}\right)\overset{*}{H}\right]^\beta\left[(1-u)H\right]^{(1-\beta)} - \delta_H H\right\}.
$$

After eliminating the shadow prices and imposing the symmetry condition (4.47) the first-order conditions along a balanced growth path are given by

$$
\frac{Z}{K} = \chi\eta_P\frac{C}{K}, \tag{4.59}
$$

$$
g = \varepsilon\left(\alpha\frac{Y}{K} - \frac{Z}{K} - \delta_K - \rho\right), \tag{4.60}
$$

$$
g = \varepsilon\left(B - \delta_H - \rho\right), \tag{4.61}
$$

$$
g = \frac{Y}{K} - \frac{C}{K} - \frac{Z}{K} - \delta_K, \tag{4.62}
$$

$$
g = B\left(1-u\right) - \delta_H. \tag{4.63}
$$

Equation (4.61) is already the reduced form of the growth rate. By using equations (4.59)–(4.63) we can derive the reduced forms of u, C/K, Y/K K/Z:

$$
u = \frac{B - \varepsilon\left(B - \delta_H - \rho\right) - \delta_H}{B}, \tag{4.64}
$$

$$
\frac{C}{K} = \frac{(1-\alpha\varepsilon)\left(B - \delta_H - \rho\right) + (1-\alpha)\delta_K + \rho}{\alpha + (\alpha - 1)\eta_P\chi}, \tag{4.65}
$$

$$\frac{Y}{K} = \frac{(1-\varepsilon)(B-\delta_H-\rho) + \frac{1}{\chi\eta_P}(B-\delta_H+\delta_K) + \rho}{\alpha - 1 + \frac{\alpha}{\eta_P\chi}}, \quad (4.66)$$

$$\frac{K}{Z} = \frac{\alpha - 1 + \frac{\alpha}{\eta_P\chi}}{(1-\alpha\varepsilon)(B-\delta_H-\rho) + (1-\alpha)\delta_K + \rho}. \quad (4.67)$$

After having calculated the noncooperative and the cooperative outcomes we are able now to determine the cooperation effects on growth, pollution and welfare.

Cooperation Effects on Growth, Pollution and Welfare

In the following we distinguish between the effects of knowledge cooperation, environmental cooperation and full cooperation on growth, pollution and welfare. To analyse the effects of cooperation on core variables we compare the reduced forms of the noncooperative solution (4.51) and (4.54)–(4.57) with the corresponding reduced forms of the cooperative solution (4.61) and (4.64)–(4.67). We see that the noncooperative solution is identical to the full cooperative solution if international spillovers are absent ($\beta = 1$ and $\eta_F = 1$). The outcome for the knowledge cooperation and environmental cooperation can be mimicked by setting $\beta = 1$ and $\eta_F = 1$ in the reduced forms of the noncooperative solution, respectively. We now derive effects of the cooperations on growth, pollution and the consumption-capital ratio as described in Section 3.5.4. These effects are summarized in rows 2–4 of Table 4.6. The utility function applied in this model is identical to the one of Section 3.5 and we can replicate the integrated present-value utility function (3.96):

$$U_0 = \frac{1}{1-\frac{1}{\varepsilon}}\left[\frac{P^{-\eta_P\left(1-\frac{1}{\varepsilon}\right)}\left(\frac{C}{K}\right)^{1-\frac{1}{\varepsilon}}K_0^{1-\frac{1}{\varepsilon}}}{\rho - g(1-1/\varepsilon)} - \rho\right] \quad \text{for } \begin{array}{c} \varepsilon > 0 \\ \varepsilon \neq 1 \end{array},$$

$$U_0 = \frac{1}{\rho}\ln\frac{C}{K} + \frac{1}{\rho}K_0 - \frac{1}{\rho}\eta_P\ln P + \frac{1}{\rho^2}g \quad \text{for } \varepsilon = 1, \quad (4.68)$$

where $\rho - g(1-1/\varepsilon) > 0$. According to equation (4.68) the present-value of welfare is a positive function of economic growth and of the consumption-capital ratio but a negative function of pollution. Inserting the results of rows 2–4 of Table 4.6 into equation (4.68) we can moreover determine the cooperation effects from a welfare point of view. The effects on welfare are summarized in row 5 of Table 4.6.

Table 4.6: Cooperation effects on core variables, when $P = f(K,Z)$

	knowledge coop.	pollution coop.	full coop.
growth	$g^{nc} < g^c$	$g^{nc} = g^c$	$g^{nc} < g^c$
pollution	$P^{nc} > P^c$	$P^{nc} > P^c$	$P^{nc} > P^c$
ratio C/K	$\left(\frac{C}{K}\right)^{nc} < \left(\frac{C}{K}\right)^c$	$\left(\frac{C}{K}\right)^{nc} < \left(\frac{C}{K}\right)^c$	$\left(\frac{C}{K}\right)^{nc} < \left(\frac{C}{K}\right)^c$
welfare	$U_0^{nc} < U_0^c$	$U_0^{nc} < U_0^c$	$U_0^{nc} < U_0^c$

Knowledge cooperation: The national governments internalize only the external international effect of human capital accumulation to the other country. Therefore, the marginal product of studying increases, this boosts growth in the cooperative solution since the education sector is the engine of growth (see Section 4.2.2). Due to the fact that the marginal productivity of human capital increases, final good production becomes more human capital intensive. This leads to a reduced pollution and an increased consumption-capital ratio. Higher growth, a better environmental quality and an increased consumption-capital share increase unambiguously welfare in the knowledge cooperation (see equation (4.68)).

Environmental Cooperation: The governments internalize only the negative international external effect of pollution. The effects are equivalent to a higher pollution tax in the closed economy(see Section 4.2.2). The long-term growth rate is unchanged, pollution decreases, and the consumption-capital ratio increases. The effects on welfare in the case of environmental cooperation are unambiguously positive.

Full cooperation: Since the effects of the partial cooperations on core variables are the same, it is not surprising that the full cooperation (which is a combination of the partial cooperations) has the same effects. Growth rises, environmental quality increases and the consumption-capital ratio increases, which leads to a higher welfare.

4.4.3   Final Output as the Polluting Factor

In this section, pollution is assumed to be a function of total output Y and abatement activities Z. So instead of assuming physical capital to be the dirty factor responsible for generating a negative environmental externality, we now assume output to be responsible for pollution:

$$p = \left(\frac{Y}{Z}\right)^{\chi}. \tag{4.69}$$

The Noncooperative Solution

We will skip the maximization problem and the derivation of the first-order conditions since it is analogous to that of Section 4.4.2. Along a balanced growth path, the Keynes–Ramsey rule with this pollution specification is given by

$$g = \varepsilon \left[\alpha\left(\frac{Y}{K} - \frac{Z}{K}\right) - \delta_K - \rho\right], \tag{4.70}$$

where all other first-order conditions along a balanced growth path are identical to (4.49) and (4.51)–(4.53). The same applies for the reduced forms of the growth rate and the fraction of time devoted to production. They are identical to equations (4.51) and (4.54). However, the reduced forms of the consumption-capital ratio, of the output-capital ratio and of the output-abatement ratio are now given by

$$\frac{C}{K} = \frac{(1 - \alpha\varepsilon)(\beta B - \delta_H - \rho) + (1 - \alpha)\delta_K + \rho}{\alpha}, \tag{4.71}$$

$$\frac{Y}{K} = \frac{\Psi_3(\beta B - \delta_H + \delta_K) + \chi\eta_P\alpha[(\varepsilon - 1)\delta_K + \varepsilon\rho]}{\alpha(2 - \eta_F)}, \tag{4.72}$$

$$\Psi_3 \equiv [(2 - \eta_F) + \chi\eta_P(1 - \alpha\varepsilon)]$$

$$\frac{Y}{Z} = 1 + \frac{(2 - \eta_F)(\beta B - \delta_H + \delta_K)}{\chi\eta_P[(1 - \alpha\varepsilon)(\beta B - \delta_H - \rho) + (1 - \alpha)\delta_K + \rho]}. \tag{4.73}$$

The Cooperative Solution

The Keynes–Ramsey rule of the cooperative solution along a balanced growth path is identical to the one of the noncooperative solution (4.70);

note, however, that the output-capital ratio and the abatement-capital ratio are determined differently as we shall see in the following. The other first-order conditions are identical to equations (4.59) and (4.61)–(4.63). The reduced forms of the growth rate and of the fraction of time devoted to production are identical to (4.61) and (4.64), respectively. The remaining reduced forms of C/K, Y/K and Y/Z are given by

$$\frac{C}{K} = \frac{(1 - \alpha\varepsilon)(B - \delta_H - \rho) + (1 - \alpha)\delta_K + \rho}{\alpha}, \tag{4.74}$$

$$\frac{Y}{K} = \frac{\Psi_4(B - \delta_H + \delta_K) + \chi\eta_P\alpha[\varepsilon\rho + (\varepsilon - 1)\delta_K]}{\alpha}, \tag{4.75}$$

$$\Psi_4 \equiv [1 + \chi\eta_P(1 - \alpha\varepsilon)]$$

$$\frac{Y}{Z} = 1 + \frac{B - \delta_H + \delta_K}{\eta_P\chi[(1 - \alpha\varepsilon)(B - \delta_H - \rho) + (1 - \alpha)\delta_K + \rho]}. \tag{4.76}$$

Cooperation Effects on Growth, Pollution and Welfare

In the following we distinguish between the effects of knowledge cooperation, environmental cooperation and full cooperation. Comparing the reduced forms again we see that the noncooperative solution is identical to the full cooperative solution for $\beta = 1$ and $\eta_F = 1$. The cooperative outcome for the knowledge and environmental cooperations can be mimicked by setting $\beta = 1$ and $\eta_F = 1$ in the reduced forms of the noncooperative solution, respectively. The discounted present value of utility is identical to equation (4.68). The effects on growth, pollution, the consumption-capital ratio and welfare are summarized in Table 4.7.

Table 4.7: Cooperation effects on core variables, when $P = f(Y,Z)$

	knowledge coop.	environmental coop.	full coop.
growth	$g^{nc} < g^c$	$g^{nc} = g^c$	$g^{nc} < g^c$
pollution	$P^{nc} < P^c$	$P^{nc} > P^c$	ambiguous
ratio	$\left(\frac{C}{K}\right)^{nc} < \left(\frac{C}{K}\right)^c$	$\left(\frac{C}{K}\right)^{nc} = \left(\frac{C}{K}\right)^c$	$\left(\frac{C}{K}\right)^{nc} < \left(\frac{C}{K}\right)^c$
welfare	ambiguous	$U^{nc} < U^c$	$U^{nc} < U^c$

Due to *knowledge cooperation* the marginal product of studying increases which boosts growth in the cooperative solution since the education sector is the engine of growth. The increased marginal productivity of human capital in the education sector leads to a more human capital-intensive final good production and to an increased consumption-capital ratio. Since final good production increases – responsible for the environmental externality – pollution rises. The welfare effects are ambiguous due to the trade-off between growth and pollution. Higher growth and an increased consumption-capital ratio increase welfare, whereas higher pollution decreases welfare *ceteris paribus* (see equation (4.68)).

An *environmental cooperation* does not affect the engine of growth. Therefore, the long-term growth rate is unchanged. Pollution decreases but the consumption-capital ratio is unchanged. The effects on welfare in the case of environmental cooperation are unambiguously positive.

Under *full cooperation*, growth rises and the capital-consumption ratio increases; however, the effect on pollution is ambiguous. Depending on the relative strength of the two international spillovers, pollution may rise in the case of full cooperation. Nevertheless, welfare increases since full cooperation is equivalent to a first-best solution.

In the open economy model with a linear production function, the welfare effects of partial cooperations are ambiguous due to the model's inherent trade-off between pollution and growth (see Section 3.5.4). The models used in this section allow a more positive appraisal concerning welfare effects of partial cooperations and environmental protection. This is due to the more precisely specified final good production where physical and human capital are used in a substitutive relation. We showed that *environmental cooperation* improves welfare unambiguously since pollution reduction is possible without harming growth. However, the effects of *knowledge cooperation* depend on the chosen pollution function, that is, whether pollution is a side product of physical capital or of final good production. If output is responsible for pollution we confirm the results of the linear model: knowledge cooperation increases growth at the expense of environmental quality; hence the effects on welfare are ambiguous. Thus our model suggests that among other things the existence of international patent markets is partly responsible for the environmental degradation nowadays.[18] Therefore it is uncertain whether the creation of a patent market in the past increased welfare. However, if pollution is assumed to be a function of physical capital, the pessimistic result changes to a positive one. By assuming this pollution specification, knowledge cooperation boosts not only growth but also reduces pollution and increases welfare. If this pollution specification describes best the real world in our model, the creation of a patent market increased growth and at the same time increased environmental quality. Obviously, both effects raise welfare. Hence, whether the creation of international patent markets tends to improve or tends to reduce environmental quality depends on the pollution specification. Why are the results concerning the environment less optimistic in the case where pollution is a function of output? Given a certain level of output and abatement, with this specification there is no possibility of reducing pollution by choosing a different input ratio in final good production – similar to the Rebelo model. On the other hand if pollution is generated by physical capital, pollution can be reduced by a more labor-intensive production without lowering output or increasing abatement activities. This missing substitution possibility in the former is responsible for the different effects of cooperation on the environmental quality. Finally we compare the effects of full cooperation for both pollution specifications. Unlike the linear growth model, the model in this section suggests that full cooperation increases growth unambiguously independent of the pollution specification. However, whereas environmental quality increases if pollution is generated by physical capital, the effect becomes ambiguous and depends on the relative strength of both spillovers if pollution is generated by output.

4.5   Summary of the Results

This chapter consisted of three mutually complementing parts. We first focused on the effects of environmental policy of a closed economy along a balanced growth path. We then simulated numerically the corresponding

---

[18] For a discussion about the effects of the creation of international patent markets on growth, pollution and welfare, see also Section 3.5.4.

transitional dynamics. Finally, we analysed the strategic interactions between two countries in the presence of international spillovers but again restricted the analysis to the balanced growth path.

By varying the weight factor of pollution in the utility function, Gradus and Smulders (1993) show that environmental care does not influence optimal growth in a closed Uzawa–Lucas economy. We have shown in this chapter that the non-interference of economic growth due to a change in environmental policy is also true for a decentralized economy with non-rival abatement activities by explicitly modeling households' and firms' decisions and additionally assuming a more general utility function. Furthermore, we have shown that this non-interference is not special to a pollution tax but also valid for non-environmental taxes. Thus in contrast to the linear model long-term economic growth is not affected by a consumption tax, a labor income tax, a capital income tax, or a pollution tax. Furthermore, taxes on consumption and labor income possess the characteristics of a lump-sum tax. Concerning the growth-rate effects of taxes on capital income and pollution, there are two effects at work: both taxes reduce the growth rate directly through a drop in the net tax interest rate. However, the direct adverse tax effect is exactly offset by the positive indirect tax effect due to a more human capital intensive final good production. Hence the growth rate is unchanged. If, additionally, productive spillovers from a better environment to the education sector are taken into consideration there might be a stimulating growth effect of a tighter environmental policy. Recall that in the Rebelo model just one explicit input factor is used. Hence factor substitution and thus the indirect tax effect are absent as the ratio of physical to human capital is fixed implicitly. Therefore, the Rebelo model can explain only direct tax effects. However, the Uzawa–Lucas model allows for input substitution and can explain both the direct and indirect tax effects. We found, not surprisingly, that the decentralized outcome is inefficient without government intervention. There is too much pollution and the final good production is too physical capital-intensive since economic agents do not take into account the environmental externality. In principle, the government can reach a first-best solution by setting the pollution tax equal to the optimal marginal damage of pollution.

However, the environmental externality can also be internalized by setting the capital income tax equal to the optimal marginal damage of pollution divided by the optimal marginal product of capital. The latter correction is necessary to equate the tax-base differences between the capital income tax and the pollution tax. Since we assume a one-to-one technology which transforms the tax revenues into abatement the first-best solution can be achieved without the use of an additional lump-sum instrument since both taxes in principle fulfill two tasks at the same time. They correct the inefficient physical capital-intensive final good production and generate exactly the amount of public revenues needed for providing the optimal level of abatement. Finally it should be noted that the informational requirements for the government in the case of a capital income tax solution may be much higher in practice: To induce the optimal reduction in pollution under the pollution tax, the government needs to have only an estimate of marginal environmental damages. In contrast, for the capital income tax solution the government also needs to know the price elasticity of factor inputs and the elasticity of final output with respect to factor input quantities.

In the second part of this chapter we focused on the transitional dynamics of a change in environmental policy in the closed Uzawa–Lucas economy. For that purpose we simulated numerically the adaptation process of the calibrated model. We thus complemented the analytical long-term effects of environmental policy by their short- and medium-term effects. Since the quantitative results depend on the chosen parameter values, we calibrated the model and selected the parameters in order to capture stylized empirical facts of industrialized countries. We simulated the transitional dynamics for a centrally planned economy after a sudden unexpected shock of the pollution disutility parameter and the corresponding transitional dynamics of a market economy caused by a sudden unexpected increase of the pollution tax. Furthermore we compared the market-driven unexpected scenario with announced and gradual tax reforms. For all simulations we assumed that the share of abatement activities must double in the long term from 1.6 per cent to 3.2 per cent of GDP which implies that pollution is reduced by 46 per cent. In the market economy this target can be reached by increas-

ing the pollution tax from 0.62 per cent to 1.33 per cent. We showed
that the Uzawa–Lucas model extended by environmental pollution is
stable and converges to its balanced growth path, at least for consistent
and realistic parameter values. Caballé and Santos (1993) have already
proved the global convergence of every off-balance path. However, this
was done for the Uzawa–Lucas model without environment. The results
of the simulation are interesting from either a welfare or a political point
of view. Concerning welfare we have mentioned in Section 2.4 (page 36)
that although a policy measure could nevertheless be beneficial in the
long run it could be harmful in the short and medium term, so that
overall discounted welfare is negative compared to the business-as-usual
scenario. We have seen that this is not the case for our scenarios. Compared to the business-as-usual scenario, welfare is higher in *every* period
and is thus Pareto dominant. Hence, from a welfare point of view, not
only in the long run but also in the short run there is no reason to refrain
from environmental policy making. Furthermore from a welfare point of
view it is optimal to increase the pollution tax unexpectedly. However,
it must be noted that we did not take into account the costs of installing
investment goods. Furthermore, we assumed that the allocation between
time for studying and production could be altered without any frictions.
In reality this is certainly not the case as households cannot alter instantaneously their time allocation between studying and working because of
a policy measure. Since we expect investment costs and other frictions
to prevail in practice, from our point of view, the best policy recommendation is a gradual environmental policy scheme. First, the adjustment
processes are not as unsteady as under the three other environmental
policy schemes, because a gradual increase in the pollution tax extends
the adjustment processes over several years. Second, consumers' welfare is higher under the gradual environmental policy scheme than under the announced policy schemes, because there is no time lag before
environmental policy is implemented. Even though the simulations in
this chapter do not take adjustment costs of capital accumulation and
cost of frictions into account, we expect that these costs do not have
to be very high before it pays in terms of welfare to implement the
policy change gradually. Concerning the political relevance we should

consider that welfare is not directly measurable and therefore GDP is used quite often as a welfare indicator in public discussion. Whereas the long-term growth rate is not affected by a tighter environmental policy, there are non-monotonic movements of growth rates during the adaptation processes leading to the new balanced growth path. Apart from a sharp decline in the period when the policy is implemented, growth-rates of the national product are above their equilibrium value during the whole adaptation process. It is seen that a longer time span between announcement and implementation causes smaller negative growth rate deflections. If the government's re-election chances depend on economic performance it would be rational to keep the negative growth deflections small. Again, the gradual tax reform can be recommended from this point of view as well. Finally, the sensitivity analyses reveal that the share of physical capital in the final good sector is the key parameter to the understanding of the transitional dynamics in our two-sector growth model. The lower the share of capital in production, the more severe are the adjustment processes. Similar to Section 4.3, Svane and Hettich (1998) investigate the transitional dynamics of the *generalized* Uzawa–Lucas model caused by environmental policy, and confirm the above-mentioned qualitative results.[19]

In the third part of this chapter we opened up the economy and developed a new model by considering international knowledge and international environmental spillovers in a framework using Uzawa–Lucas production processes. Hence we extended the open economy analysis of Section 3.5 and took into account the presence of international spillovers which are justified by empirical evidence. Again we analysed the strategic interactions between two countries and considered a global economy consisting of two identical countries. Whereas the results for the closed economy do not depend on the pollution specifications, we established that the effects of different kinds of cooperation depend on it. In the Rebelo model the results do not depend on the pollution specification since there is a linear relation between the capital stock and production. Furthermore, in the Rebelo model, welfare effects of partial coopera-

---

[19]The generalized Uzawa–Lucas model is investigated in Chapter 6. However, the analysis is restricted to the balanced growth path.

tions are ambiguous because of the model's inherent trade-off between growth and pollution (see Section 3.5.4). In this section we found that the mentioned results of the linear model can be confirmed to a large extent in the Uzawa–Lucas model with the output-induced pollution specification. But, in contrast, an environmental cooperation does not hamper growth and increase welfare unambiguously. If, on the other hand, pollution is generated by physical capital, the results concerning environmental degradation become more optimistic: the pollution cooperation does not affect growth but lowers pollution and increases welfare. Both a knowledge cooperation and a full cooperation lower pollution and increase growth and welfare unambiguously.

In contrast to the standard neoclassical model, in the Uzawa–Lucas model there may exist different economies that grow at the same constant rate although their long-run levels of physical and human capital never converge. Moreover, the rate of growth is determined by the productivity of the human capital technology and consumers' preferences, and it remains invariant to the technology for final good production. Hence this model is not only suitable for explaining the empirical observed growth-rate diversity, as does the Rebelo model, but additionally explains conditional convergence.

By summarizing the results of the different parts of this chapter we can state that there is a need for further empirical investigation. Whereas the pollution specification does not alter the effects of fiscal policy in the closed economy, this is the case for an open economy. The growth effects of environmental policy in the open economy depend on whether pollution is generated by physical capital or output. This is also true for more complex closed Uzawa–Lucas economies analysed in the next chapters. Thus for policy recommendations we should know which pollution specification gives a better description of the real world. Furthermore, the size of adjustment costs, frictions concerning the allocation of time between production and studying, and the share of physical capital in final good production should be known in order to guarantee realistic simulations of the adaptation processes.

Chapter 5

Environmental Policy in the Uzawa–Lucas Model with Leisure

5.1 Introduction

In the present chapter we generalize the closed economy model in Section 4.2 by allowing for elastic labor supply. Thus, households not only decide how much time to devote to working and studying but also decide on the number of hours spent on leisure. We will see that this extension changes the results of Section 4.2 substantially. We restrict the analysis to the long-run effects along a balanced growth path and to a closed economy. We analyse the consequences of isolated tax changes and additionally of a revenue-neutral environmental tax reform. We will see again that the results differ for pollution due to capital utilization and pollution caused by output production. Although environmental quality does not affect production processes directly, it can be shown that a higher pollution tax boosts economic growth, whereas non-environmental taxes reduce long-term economic growth. Furthermore, it is shown that there might exist a *double growth dividend* to be reaped by an environmental

151

tax reform.[1]

In the literature on endogenous growth with human capital it is shown that a tighter environmental policy might have a stimulating growth effect. In Gradus and Smulders (1993), positive growth effects occur in a Uzawa–Lucas model where pollution reduces human capital depreciation.[2] Bovenberg and Smulders (1995) model a two-sector economy consisting of a consumption good and an R&D sector which generates knowledge about pollution-augmenting techniques. As better environmental quality improves factor productivity in the consumption good sector, positive growth effects of a tighter environmental policy are possible. In a pure human capital variant of the two-sector Lucas model, van Ewijk and van Wijnbergen (1995) find positive growth effects of a tighter environmental policy also by assuming that pollution affects the production process negatively. Hence, the existing literature has been able to explain only positive growth effects of a tighter environmental policy by assuming direct negative productivity effects of pollution either in the education or in the consumption good sector.

In contrast to the existing literature, it is shown in this chapter that in a Uzawa–Lucas model with leisure a higher pollution tax might boost long-term economic growth without assuming direct positive productivity effects of a cleaner environment. Pollution is modeled as an inevitable side product of the physical capital stock used in the final good production and it is assumed that it affects individuals' utility negatively. By means of costly private abatement activities, pollution can be reduced without lowering production. The pollution tax reduces leisure, increases studying time and hence boosts growth. The reason is that due to the increased pollution tax, firms increase their abatement activities, which reduces final output net of abatement at the expense of households' consumption. Households increase their marginal utility of leisure by substituting leisure through studying time to counteract reduced consumption which finally boosts growth. Hence, an improvement in the environment by means of a pollution tax leads to a positive growth effect. This is the *first* growth dividend. However, in a model variant where pollution is

---

[1] The formal analysis of this chapter is based on Hettich (1998).
[2] We have discussed this case in Section 4.2 (page 112).

a function of output – in contrast to physical capital – and abatement activities it is shown that a pollution tax does not affect growth. Hence with this alternative pollution specification there exists no first growth dividend.

Irrespective of the pollution specification, a tax on consumption, on capital income, or on labor income increases the demand for leisure at the expense of studying time and therefore reduces growth. These results have already been shown by Lucas (1990) in a model similar to that in this chapter, but without environment. Devereux and Love (1994) and Milesi-Ferretti and Roubini (1998b) confirm Lucas's results in more general models, but also without environment.[3]

The growth effects of an environmental tax reform where green taxes partly replace other taxes have been analysed by Bovenberg and de Mooij (1997) within a modified Barro model. They find that a tighter environmental policy may enhance growth if there exists a negative productivity effect of pollution or if the substitution elasticity between pollution and other input factors is rather low. Again the former effect is caused by a positive productivity effect of a better environment. In the latter case, an environmental tax is almost a lump-sum tax because its tax base is rather inelastic. A revenue-neutral environmental tax reform would shift the tax burden away from the net return on investment towards profits and hence stimulate growth.[4]

Even without the assumption of an inelastic substitution elasticity between pollution and other input factors, it is shown in this chapter for both pollution specifications that a revenue-neutral environmental tax reform stimulates growth. If pollution is a function of physical capital and abatement activities there is a *second* growth dividend: a higher pollution tax stimulates growth (first growth dividend), and by using the additional tax revenue for cutting non-environmental taxes an additional positive growth effect arises. This is because all non-environmental taxes

---

[3] Both papers assume not only human capital but also physical capital as an input factor in the studying sector. Additionally, Milesi-Ferretti and Roubini (1994) distinguish between different specifications of leisure, such as raw time – used in this chapter – quality time and home production.

[4] In a modified Barro model where the labor market is distorted by unions, Nielsen et al. (1995) find positive employment effects but no positive growth effects for an environmental tax reform.

reduce growth, so that lowering one of those tax rates yields a positive growth effect. In the last few years an academic debate has emerged on the desirability of environmental taxes. It is suggested that they allow for a double dividend in welfare terms. The first dividend is the reduced environmental damage, and the second dividend is reaped by using the revenue from the pollution tax for cutting existing distortionary taxes, thus reducing the deadweight loss of taxation.[5] The second dividend can be seen in analogy to the second growth dividend since both dividends arise from the use of an additional environmental tax instrument.

The results concerning both growth dividends are driven by endogenous labor supply. This aspect has been neglected so far in the literature of endogenous growth in connection with environmental economics, despite its strong influence on the results. In endogenous growth models with human capital, the growth rate is finally determined in the education sector, which can be regarded as the engine of growth. Via the households' leisure-studying choice, different taxes affect the education sector either positively or negatively, therefore it is important to consider endogenous labor supply.

This chapter is structured as follows. In Section 5.2 the general model is laid out and both market and central planner solutions are derived. Optimal tax rates of all taxes in a first-best setting are analysed in Section 5.3.1. Section 5.3.2 determines the effects of isolated tax and parameter changes on growth, and Section 5.3.3 derives the growth effects of a revenue-neutral tax reform. The discussion is broadened in Section 5.4 by deriving the effects of isolated tax changes on growth for the output-induced pollution specification. Section 5.5 summarizes the results and concludes.

5.2   The Analytical Framework

As in Section 4.2, we assume a two-sector endogenous growth model of a closed economy. The first sector produces one perfectly malleable good, which can be used for consumption, abatement activities and invest-

---

[5] For surveys concerning the possibilties of an environmental tax reform for a double dividend in a static framework, see Bovenberg (1997) and Killinger (2000).

ment in the physical capital stock. The second sector is the education sector where human capital is accumulated. However, we now allow additionally for an elastic labor supply and assume abatement activities to be private. As the present model is similar to that in Section 4.2, we concentrate on explaining the different equations only and replicate the identical equations for convenience.

5.2.1 Technology

The final good production function and the flow resource constraint of the economy are identical to Section 4.2. The final good is produced by using physical capital and effective labor

$$Y_t = A\,K_t^\alpha\,(u_t H_t)^{1-\alpha}, \tag{5.1}$$

and the flow resource constraint of the economy is given by

$$Y_t = C_t + \dot{K}_t + Z_t + \delta_K K_t. \tag{5.2}$$

In the education sector, human capital is still produced with a constant returns-to-scale technology which utilizes human capital whereas physical capital is negligible:

$$\dot{H}_t = (Bs_t - \delta_H)\,H_t, \tag{5.3}$$

where $0 \leqslant s \leqslant 1$. However, now s denotes the fraction of time devoted to production.[6] The maximum growth rate of human capital is given by $B - \delta_H$, for $s = 1$ where the whole unit time budget is devoted to studying.

The first analysed pollution specification is identical to that in Section 4.2 and possesses the functional form

$$P_t = \left(\frac{K_t}{Z_t}\right)^\chi. \tag{5.4}$$

In Section 5.4 we additionally investigate an alternative pollution specification where pollution is a function of output and abatement activities.

---

[6]The new notation is necessary as time is allocated now between work u, study s (in Section 4.2 it was denoted by $1 - u$) and leisure l.

5.2.2   Firms

Firms rent capital and hire effective labor from the households at the interest rate r and the wage rate w. They use these input factors to produce final goods using the technology described by equation (5.1). In contrast to Section 4.2, firms must pay a pollution tax with rate τ_P on their pollution P. The level of pollution and hence the pollution tax liability depends on the effective capital-labor ratio $K/(uH)$ as well as on the abatement level Z. Abatement is assumed to be a private good, which in principle enables firms to increase output without causing more pollution. In a model without abatement activities the capital income tax would serve as an adequate pollution tax, because there would be a direct relation between the physical capital stock and pollution. Profit π in period t is given by

$$\pi_t = Y_t - r_t K_t - w_t (u_t H_t) - Z_t - \tau_P P_t. \tag{5.5}$$

The first-order conditions of the firms' profit maximization problem are given by:

$$w_t = (1-\alpha) A \left(\frac{K_t}{u_t H_t} \right)^{\alpha}, \tag{5.6}$$

$$r_t = \alpha A \left(\frac{K_t}{u_t H_t} \right)^{\alpha-1} - \frac{Z_t}{K_t}, \tag{5.7}$$

$$\frac{\tau_P}{K_t} = \chi^{-1} \left(\frac{Z_t}{K_t} \right)^{1+\chi} \Leftrightarrow 1 = \tau_P \chi \frac{P}{Z}. \tag{5.8}$$

Firms hire effective labor up to the point at which the marginal product equals its marginal costs. They rent physical capital up to the point where its marginal costs equals the private marginal product of capital minus the abatement-capital ratio Z/K, which is determined by the pollution tax in equation (5.8). Equation (5.8) in turn shows that abatement measures are chosen such that its marginal costs correspond to the marginal liability of the pollution tax. Without a pollution tax ($\tau_P = 0$), firms would ignore the negative side product of physical capital in the production process and abatement activities would be zero.

5.2.3 Households

To keep the analysis tractable we simplify the specification and assume in this chapter a logarithmic instantaneous utility function[7]

$$U\left(C_t, l_t, P_t\right) = \ln C_t + \eta_l \ln l_t - \eta_P \ln P_t, \tag{5.9}$$

where $0 \leqslant l \leqslant 1, \eta_l, \eta_P > 0, U_C, U_l > 0, U_{CC}, U_{ll} < 0, U_P < 0$ and $U_{PP} > 0$.[8] The parameters η_l and η_P represent the weights of leisure and pollution in utility. Economic agents allocate their unit time budget in every period between leisure l, production time u and studying time s. Hence the allocation of time is given by: $(1 = l + u + s)$. They rent human and physical capital to firms. Consumption and the allocation of time are chosen in order to maximize lifetime utility, given by the discounted integral of instantaneous utility

$$U_0 = \int_{t=0}^{\infty} \left(\ln C_t + \eta_l \ln l_t - \eta_P \ln P_t\right) e^{-\rho t} dt, \tag{5.10}$$

subject to the human capital accumulation constraint (5.3) and the flow budget constraint

$$\left(1 - \tau_K\right) r_t K_t + \left(1 - \tau_H\right) w_t \left(u_t H_t\right) + T_t = \left(1 + \tau_C\right) C_t + \dot{K}_t + \delta_K K_t. \tag{5.11}$$

The left-hand side of equation (5.11) represents the different sources of income, and the right-hand side the uses of income. Since pollution is assumed to be a public 'bad', consumers regard the level of pollution as fixed and ignore it in their individual maximization problem.

5.2.4 Government

The government is introduced in a minimal fashion; its task is solely to correct the market failure caused by the environmental externality. At

---

[7] A more general utility function would be $U = \left[\left(C l^{\eta_l} P^{\eta_P}\right)^{1-(1/\varepsilon)} - 1\right] / \left[1 - (1/\varepsilon)\right]$ (see Section 2.3.2). As this function does not change the qualitative results but complicates the analysis we use the simplified function (5.9) where the intertemporal substitution elasticity is equal to one.

[8] A more realistic utility function would allow for increasing marginal disutility of pollution $U_{PP} < 0$, but this changes only the optimal allocation of resources between abatement and final good production (5.17). All other first-order conditions of the central planner are unaffected and so are the obtained results.

this stage we assume no real government spending; all revenue is transferred back to households in a lump-sum manner. When we analyse growth effects of a revenue-neutral environmental tax reform in Section 5.3.3, we extend the role of the state and impose an exogenously given government revenue requirement which has to be financed solely by taxing consumption, labor, capital, or pollution.

5.2.5   The Market Solution

Agents maximize lifetime utility, given by the discounted integral of instantaneous utility (5.10), choosing the paths of C, H, K, u and s subject to the human capital accumulation constraint (5.3) and the flow budget constraint (5.11), given the time paths of r and w, and τ_C, τ_H, τ_K and τ_P. The current-value Hamiltonian for this optimization problem takes the form

$$
\max_{C,u,s} \mathcal{H} = \ln C + \eta_l \ln l - \eta_P \ln P
$$
$$
+ \lambda \left[\begin{array}{c} (1 - \tau_K)\, rK + (1 - \tau_H)\, w\,(uH) + T \\ - (1 + \tau_C)\, C - \delta_K K \end{array} \right]
$$
$$
+ \mu\left[(Bs - \delta_H)\, H\right].
$$

After eliminating the shadow prices for physical and human capital and replacing r and w by equations (5.7) and (5.6), the first-order conditions are given by[9]

$$
\frac{C}{K} = \frac{(1 - \tau_H)}{(1 + \tau_C)} \frac{(1 - \alpha)}{\eta_l} \frac{l}{u} \frac{Y}{K}, \tag{5.12}
$$

$$
\hat{C} = (1 - \tau_K)\left(\alpha\frac{Y}{K} - \frac{Z}{K}\right) - \delta_K - \rho, \tag{5.13}
$$

$$
\hat{H} + \hat{l} = B\,(u + s) - \delta_H - \rho, \tag{5.14}
$$

$$
\hat{K} = \frac{Y}{K} - \frac{C}{K} - \frac{Z}{K} - \delta_K, \tag{5.15}
$$

$$
\hat{H} = Bs - \delta_H, \tag{5.16}
$$

[9] In the following, time indices of variables are skipped where no ambiguity arises.

and by equation (5.8) which determines the abatement-capital ratio Z/K. Equation (5.12) equates the marginal rate of substitution between consumption and leisure to the real wage, adjusted for consumption and labor taxes. Equations (5.13) and (5.14) are the Euler conditions determining the optimal accumulation of physical and human capital. Equations (5.15) and (5.16) are the resource constraint of the economy and the human capital accumulation constraint, respectively.

It is obvious that all taxes have effects on the economy. The consumption and labor taxes create a wedge between the marginal rate of substitution of consumption and leisure and the real wage; see equation (5.12). Both the capital and the pollution tax affect the intertemporal incentive to invest in physical capital, described by equation (5.13) in connection with (5.8).

5.2.6   The Central Planner Solution

A central planner maximizes the utility of the representative economic agent but takes into account the negative side-effects of physical capital (pollution) on utility. The central planner maximizes lifetime utility (5.10) by choosing the time paths of C, H, K, Z, u and s subject to the flow resource constraint (5.2) and the human capital accumulation constraint (5.3). The current-value Hamiltonian for this optimization problem takes the form

$$
\max_{C,Z,u,s} \mathcal{H} = \ln C + \eta_l \ln l - \eta_P \ln P
$$
$$
+ \lambda \left[AK^\alpha (uH)^{1-\alpha} - C - Z - \delta_K K \right] + \mu \left[(Bs - \delta_H) H \right].
$$

After eliminating the shadow prices, the first-order conditions of the central planner solution are given by:

$$
\frac{Z}{K} = \eta_P \chi \frac{C}{K}, \tag{5.17}
$$

$$
\frac{C}{K} = \frac{(1-\alpha)}{\eta_l} \frac{l}{u} \frac{Y}{K}, \tag{5.18}
$$

$$
\hat{C} = \alpha \frac{Y}{K} - \frac{Z}{K} - \delta_K - \rho, \tag{5.19}
$$

$$\hat{H} + \hat{i} \;=\; B\,(u+s) - \delta_H - \rho, \qquad (5.20)$$

$$\hat{K} \;=\; \frac{Y}{K} - \frac{C}{K} - \frac{Z}{K} - \delta_K, \qquad (5.21)$$

$$\hat{H} \;=\; Bs - \delta_H. \qquad (5.22)$$

Ignoring the consumption, labor and capital income taxes the central planner solution differs from the market solution only by equation (5.17). It shows that for a social optimum the marginal utility of consumption and abatement must be equalized. The right-hand side of the Keynes–Ramsey rule (5.19) consists of the private marginal product of physical capital, corrected by the term Z/K, the depreciation rate of the physical capital stock δ_K and the rate of time preference ρ. There is a wedge between private and social return to physical capital. The first two terms can be seen as the social return of physical capital, where Z/K reflects the marginal damage of physical capital. Consumption grows, remains constant, or declines if the social return of physical capital is larger than, equal to, or smaller than the sum of the rate of depreciation and the rate of time preference.

In a decentralized economy without government intervention ($\tau_x = 0$) there is too much pollution. Equation (5.8) shows that the abatement-capital ratio Z/K in the market solution is determined solely by the pollution tax. For example, if τ_P were zero, ratio Z/K would be zero as well. In that case the negative externality is totally ignored. The government can in principle correct the market failure and internalize the externality by raising private costs to the level of social costs by means of efficient instruments such as Pigouvian taxes or auctioned permits. In Section 5.3.1 we derive the optimal tax rates of all taxes in a first-best setting.

From comparing the Keynes–Ramsey rules of the market solution (5.13) and the central planner solution (5.19) it is not possible to draw conclusions about the growth effects of the different taxes, as they affect the output-capital ratio differently.

5.3   Results Along a Balanced Growth Path

Along a balanced growth path, the variables C, H, K, Y, Z grow at the same constant rate g, whereas l, u, s are constant over time[10]

$$g \equiv \hat{C} = \hat{H} = \hat{K} = \hat{Y} = \hat{Z}, \quad 0 = \dot{l} = \dot{u} = \dot{s}. \tag{5.23}$$

The ratios $C/K, C/Y, K/H, Y/K$ and Z/K are constant, and therefore pollution P is also constant along a balanced growth path. If one tax rate is greater than zero, the lump-sum transfer T grows with the rate g as well.

5.3.1   Optimal Tax Rates

To assess first-best tax rates, we compare the first-order conditions of the market solution, equations (5.8)–(5.13) with the corresponding first-order conditions of the central planner solution, equations (5.17)–(5.19). By comparing (5.8) with (5.17) we can compute the optimal pollution tax rule:

$$\tau_P^{opt}(t) = \chi^{-1} K_t \left[\left(\frac{Z_t}{K_t} \right)^{cps} \right]^{1+\chi}. \tag{5.24}$$

The Pigouvian tax rate τ_P^{opt} must increase over time in line with the growth rate of the economy. In equation (5.24) the optimal abatement-capital ratio denoted by superscript 'cps' is constant along a balanced growth path and parameter χ is constant but the physical capital stock K increases over time. This result becomes intuitive by remembering that P must be constant along a balanced growth path. To keep the level of P constant, the pollution tax must rise over time, because the physical capital stock, which is responsible for the pollution, accumulates over time. Firms increase their abatement activities over time only if they have the incentive via an increasing pollution tax. Note that this optimal tax rule is identical to that of the linear growth model in the case of private abatement measures (see equation (3.55)). However, the term Z/K is determined differently. For further analysis it is useful to separate the

---

[10]For the interested reader, this formal proof is shown in Section A.3.1 (page 227) in the appendix.

trend and the level of the pollution tax. Therefore we normalize the pollution tax rate by the physical capital stock and define $\bar{\tau}_P \equiv \tau_P/K$, which is constant along a balanced growth path. Thus we assume that the government can adjust the pollution tax in accordance with the evolution of the physical capital stock in order to maintain a certain level of pollution in the presence of economic growth.

Additionally, comparing equation (5.12) with (5.18) and (5.13) with (5.19) we see that for tax rates on consumption, labor and capital equal to zero a first-best solution is attained. Because pollution is the only distortion in the decentralized economy, a first-best solution is reached solely by setting the Pigouvian tax according to the taxation rule (5.24).[11] Note that in the case of private abatement activities – as in this model – non-environmental taxes fail to internalize the environmental externality.

Although every tax affects the allocation of the economy, there is a possibility that the government may receive lump-sum tax revenues: if the tax on consumption is equal to a subsidy on labor ($\tau_C = -\tau_H$), the tax rates cancel out in equation (5.12). Considering the whole time horizon, the consumption tax base equals the tax bases on labor and the returns of the physical capital stock. So basically a consumption tax corresponds to an equivalent labor income tax plus a tax on the initial capital stock. Obviously, the magnitude of the consumption tax base is larger than that of the labor income tax.[12] By taxing consumption and subsidizing labor at the same rate, the government is able to levy a lump-sum tax. This tax-subsidy combination implies a tax on the

---

[11] In Section 5.3.3 we shall expand this analysis by assuming an exogenously given government budget constraint which must be financed by tax revenue.

[12] The following is a formal proof that the consumption tax base C is larger than that of the labor tax base $w\,(uH)$. Rewriting equation (5.15) using (5.6) gives

$$C - w\,(uH) = \left[\alpha A \left(\frac{K}{uH}\right)^{\alpha-1} - \frac{Z}{K} - \delta_K - \hat{K}\right] K.$$

Substituting the first three terms in the square brackets by equation (5.13) and taking into consideration that $\hat{C} = \hat{K} \equiv g$ along a balanced growth path shows that the consumption tax base is larger than that of the labor tax and hence $C - w\,(uH) > 0$:

$$C - w\,(uH) = \frac{\left[\tau_K\left(\hat{C} + \delta_K\right) + \rho\right] K}{(1 - \tau_K)} > 0.$$

initial physical capital endowment which is assumed to be exogenously and inelastically given and therefore constitutes the ideal tax base for a lump-sum tax. In the following we assume no labor subsidy and therefore rule out the possibility of a lump-sum taxation.

5.3.2 The Effects of Isolated Tax and Parameter Changes on Growth

In this section we analyse the long-term consequences of isolated tax changes for economic growth. In addition, we show how parameter variations affect growth. On the balanced growth path, the differential equations of the market solution (5.13)–(5.16) can be rewritten using equation (5.8) and condition (5.23), as:

$$g = (1 - \tau_K) \left[\alpha A \left(\frac{K}{uH} \right)^{\alpha-1} - (\chi \bar{\tau} P)^{\frac{1}{1+x}} \right] - \delta_K - \rho \quad (5.25)$$

$$\equiv R - \rho,$$

$$g = B(u + s) - \delta_H - \rho, \quad (5.26)$$

$$g = A \left(\frac{K}{uH} \right)^{\alpha-1} - \frac{C}{K} - (\chi \bar{\tau} P)^{\frac{1}{1+x}} - \delta_K, \quad (5.27)$$

$$g = Bs - \delta_H, \quad (5.28)$$

whereas equation (5.12) is unchanged. Again R is defined as the real marginal product of capital net of tax. By inserting equation (5.28) in (5.26) we can derive a reduced form for the fraction of time devoted to production u:

$$u = \frac{\rho}{B}. \quad (5.29)$$

It can be seen that the time devoted to production is independent of any tax rates.

To calculate the consequences of fiscal policy and parameter changes for growth we derive two semi-reduced forms in g and l. Rewriting the first-order condition (5.26) by using the time constraint $1 = u + s + l$

and using conditions (5.12), (5.25) and (5.27) gives, respectively:

$$l = \frac{B - \delta_H - \rho - g}{B}, \tag{5.30}$$

$$l = \frac{1 + \tau_C}{1 - \tau_H} \frac{\eta_l \rho}{1 - \alpha} \frac{1}{B} [1 - \alpha (1 - \tau_K) + \Psi_6] \tag{5.31}$$

$$\Psi_6 \equiv \frac{\alpha \left(1 - \tau^K\right) \left(\rho - \tau_K \left(\chi \bar{\tau} P\right)^{\frac{1}{1+x}}\right)}{g + \delta_K + \rho + (1 - \tau_K) \left(\chi \bar{\tau} P\right)^{\frac{1}{1+x}}}.$$

Apart from g and l, equations (5.30) and (5.31) are determined solely by parameters and tax rates. Since leisure time must be between zero and unity, from equation (5.30) it becomes obvious that $B > \delta_H + \rho + g$ is a necessary condition for a balanced growth path. The expression in the square brackets in equation (5.31) is equal to the consumption-output share and hence must be between zero and unity – another necessary condition for the existence of a balanced growth path. Equation (5.30), labelled aa in Figure 5.1, represents the *feasible* whereas equation (5.31), called bb, describes the *desired* leisure/growth combinations. In the left-hand diagram of Figure 5.1, aa shows the technical whereas bb describes the preferred combinations of leisure and growth.

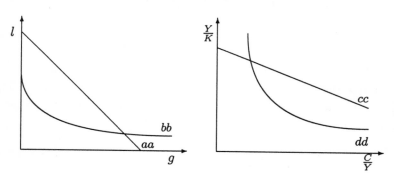

Figure 5.1: Semi-reduced forms of l and g and Y/K and C/K

Curve aa declines at the constant rate B^{-1}, but curve bb declines at a falling rate. To guarantee the negative slope of curve bb, defined by equation (5.31), we must impose the condition that:

$$\rho > \tau_K \left(\chi \bar{\tau}_P \right)^{\frac{1}{1+\chi}} . \qquad (5.32)$$

In principle, both curves can have two points of intersection in the relevant positive quadrant, but in Figure 5.1 only the stable intersection is illustrated. The stable equilibrium requires that the convex curve *bb* is always below the linear curve *aa* for $g = 0$. A small η_l is a sufficient condition for the stable equilibrium.[13] Due to an increase in B, curve *aa* shifts upwards. Due to an increase in $\tau_C, \tau_H, \tau_K, \eta_l$ and ρ, curve *bb* shifts upwards. A higher δ_H and ρ shift curve *aa* downwards, and a higher $\bar{\tau}_P, B$ and δ_K shift curve *bb* downwards. We can use the left-hand diagram of Figure 5.1 to show the effects of tax and parameter changes on growth and leisure. For example: a higher consumption, capital or labor tax shifts curve *bb* upwards whereas curve *aa* remains unchanged. The new intersection of *aa* and *bb* lies north-west of the original one, implying a lower growth rate and increased leisure time. However, a higher pollution tax shifts curve *bb* downwards, whereas curve *aa* is unchanged. The new intersection lies south-east of the original one, implying a higher growth rate and a reduced leisure time. Whereas a higher tax on consumption, labor or capital *reduces* the long-term growth rate, a higher pollution tax *boosts*, *ceteris paribus*, economic growth. In the same way the effects of parameter changes on growth and leisure can be shown. The results are summarized in the second and third lines of Table 5.1.[14]

To analyse through which channels taxes affect economic growth it appears useful to derive the semi-reduced forms of the consumption-output ratio and the output-capital ratio. By using equations (5.12),

---

[13] See Section A.3.2 (page 228) in the appendix for the necessary and sufficient conditions for the stable equilibrium. For the partial derivatives of equation (5.31), see Section A.3.3 (page 229) in the appendix.

[14] Instead of showing the effects of fiscal policy and parameters on growth graphically (via the semi-reduced forms of l and g), one could derive a reduced form of g by setting equation (5.30) equal to (5.31) and calculating the partial derivatives of g by using the implicit function rule. However, the graphical solution seems to be intuitively more appealing and lays the ground for deriving necessary and sufficient conditions for the existence of a balanced growth path.

(5.25), (5.26) and (5.29) we obtain

$$\frac{Y}{K} = \frac{B - \delta_H + \delta_K + (1-\tau_K)(\chi\bar{\tau}_P)^{\frac{1}{1+x}}}{\alpha(1-\tau^K)} - \frac{1+\tau_C}{1-\tau_H}\frac{\eta_l\rho}{1-\alpha}\frac{1}{\alpha(1-\tau_K)}\frac{C}{Y},$$

(5.33)

whereas by using equations (5.25) and (5.27) we get

$$\frac{Y}{K} = \frac{\rho - \tau_K(\chi\bar{\tau}_P)^{\frac{1}{1+x}}}{\frac{C}{Y} - 1 + \alpha(1-\tau_K)}.$$

(5.34)

The ratio Y/K must be positive. Therefore, the first term of equation (5.33) must be larger than the second and because of condition (5.32) the denominator of equation (5.34) is positive.

In the right-hand diagram of Figure 5.1 equations (5.33), labelled *cc*, and (5.34), labelled *dd*, are plotted in a C/Y–Y/K-space. Curve *cc* is linear and negatively sloped and curve *dd* decreases at a falling rate. Again in the right-hand diagram only the stable intersection of *cc* and *dd* is illustrated. To rule out the unstable intersection where the convex curve *dd* cuts the linear curve *cc* from below, curve *cc* must still be above curve *dd* for $C/Y = 1$ (C/Y cannot be larger than unity on the balanced growth path). Again a small η_l is a sufficient condition for a stable equilibrium.[15] Similar to the tax and parameter effects on growth and leisure we can illustrate these effects on C/Y and Y/K by shifting curves *cc* and *dd*. The results are summarized in the fourth and fifth lines of Table 5.1.

Table 5.1: The effects of tax and parameter changes on core variables

	τ_C	τ_H	τ_K	$\bar{\tau}_P$	A	B	η_l	η_P	ρ	δ_H	δ_K
$\frac{\partial g}{\partial x}$ and $\frac{\partial s}{\partial x}$	−	−	−	+	0	+	−	0	−	−	+
$\frac{\partial l}{\partial x}$	+	+	+	−	0	−	+	0	+	+	−
$\frac{\partial(C/Y)}{\partial x}$	+	+	+	−	0	−	+	0	+	+	−
$\frac{\partial(Y/K)}{\partial x}$	−	−	+	+	0	+	−	0	−	−	+

[15] For the necessary and sufficient conditions for a stable equilibrium, see Section A.3.2 (page 228) and for the partial derivatives of equations (5.33) and (5.34), see Section A.3.3 (page 229) in the appendix.

From equation (5.28) and the results of the second line of Table 5.1, we know that taxes and parameters affect the studying time s with the same sign as the growth rate g. Since time devoted to production u is not affected by any tax rates, it is obvious that the sign of $\partial (Y/K)/\partial x$ is equal to the sign of $\partial [K/(uH)]/\partial x$ for all tax-rate changes.

By means of the first-order conditions (5.25) and (5.28), and the results summarized in Table 5.1 it can be shown through which channels taxes affect long-term economic growth:

- Due to a higher labor income tax, final good production becomes more capital intensive and raises the effective capital-labor ratio $K/(uH)$. From equation (5.25) we see that this reduces the net real interest rate of capital R which lowers growth.

- Because a consumption tax basically consists of an income tax and a lump-sum tax (see page 162) it has the same effects as an income tax.

- A higher capital income tax reduces the *net* real interest rate R for a given effective capital-labor ratio $K/(uH)$. From equation (5.25) we know that this single effect reduces growth. But due to the capital tax final good production becomes more human capital-intensive and ratio $K/(uH)$ decreases. Hence *ceteris paribus* the *gross* real interest rate increases. This has a positive effect on growth (see equation (5.25)). The fact that the negative growth effect dominates the positive one can be explained by considering the households' decision: an increased capital income tax raises the consumption share of total output. Households increase leisure l to lower their marginal utility of leisure and reduce their studying time s which lowers output growth (equation (5.28)). In contrast, a reduction of labor time u would reduce output only temporarily and is therefore not appropriate to counteract the increased consumption share of total output permanently.

- A higher pollution tax reduces the effective capital-labor ratio $K/(uH)$, because the dirty input factor K is substituted by the clean input factor H. *Ceteris paribus*, the net real interest rate R increases (see equation (5.25)) and boosts growth. But there is also an effect in the opposite direction: a higher pollution tax $\bar{\tau}_P$

reduces R and lowers growth. In contrast to a capital tax a higher pollution tax *reduces* the households' consumption share of total output. Due to the increased pollution tax, firms increase their abatement activities, which reduces final output net of abatement at the expense of households' consumption. Households increase their marginal utility of leisure by substituting leisure for studying time to counteract reduced consumption. From equation (5.28) it can be seen that a higher s enhances growth. A higher pollution tax $\bar{\tau}_P$ increases ratio Z/K and hence lowers pollution P (see equation (5.8) in connection with (5.4)). The growth-stimulating effect of the pollution tax is the first growth dividend accompanied by a better environmental quality.

The negative growth effects of taxes on capital income, labor income and consumption have already been shown by Devereux and Love (1994). However, they do not consider an environmental externality. In the following it is explained how certain parameter changes affect economic growth.

- A change in A does not affect long-term growth because it does not change the productivity of the final good sector permanently.
- A higher studying efficiency parameter B increases the productivity of the education sector. Increased human capital accumulation leads to a higher growth rate.
- In the case of a higher η_l, individuals' preferences for leisure increase compared to consumption and pollution, therefore they reduce s, while holding u constant (equation (5.29)). A stronger preference for leisure increases leisure time and reduces long-term growth.
- A change in η_P does not affect long-term growth as long as the pollution tax is not adjusted to this change. The reason is that the public 'bad' pollution is ignored in the individual maximization problem. However, the optimal pollution tax is a positive function of η_P.
- When ρ increases, individuals value future utility less and consumption rises at the expense of capital accumulation. As a consequence, both time devoted to production – see equation (5.29) –

and time spent on studying is reduced. Leisure increases which in turn lowers growth.

- A higher depreciation rate of the human capital stock δ_H has the same effects as a reduction in B. It reduces the productivity of human capital accumulation and lowers growth.
- More interestingly, a higher depreciation rate of the physical capital stock δ_K has effects which are similar to a rise in the pollution tax. Because of a higher δ_K, gross investment must rise to maintain the same growth rate of the physical capital stock. This crowds out consumption and makes leisure less scarce, which gives rise to more studying and therefore stimulates growth.

It is important to note that welfare maximization is not equivalent to growth maximization. The relation between welfare and growth is illustrated in Figure 5.2 in a stylized way.[16] As shown in Section 5.3.1,

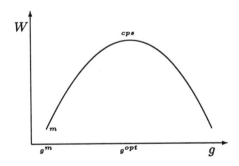

Figure 5.2: Relation between welfare and growth

a Pareto optimum is reached for capital consumption, labor taxes equal to zero, and for the pollution tax scheme described by condition (5.24). In the case of an unregulated market economy – indicated by 'm' – with

---

[16]The actual shape of the graph depends on the parameter specification. However, the graph is always hill-shaped.

all taxes equal to zero and hence with a suboptimally low environmental quality, we are at the beginning of the rising branch of Figure 5.2. Growth in an unregulated market economy g^m is suboptimally low. A tighter environmental policy improves environmental quality and corrects the distorted leisure-studying time decision step by step, thus reducing spare time and boosting economic growth. Both effects lead to higher welfare W as long as the pollution tax is below the Pigouvian level. For the pollution tax equal to the Pigouvian tax, leisure time chosen is optimal and the schedule is maximal with the optimal growth rate g^{opt}. This is equivalent to the central planner solution, indicated by the superscript '*cps*'. If the pollution tax is above the Pigouvian level, a tighter environmental policy would still increase environmental quality and boost growth further but decrease welfare, because growth rises at the expense of leisure, and leisure would be at a suboptimal low level.

Before we proceed to the growth effects of a revenue-neutral environmental tax reform we show how the results of Section 4.2 can be replicated in the present chapter. Inelastic labor supply is a special case of the former setup and can be demonstrated by setting η_l in equation (5.31) equal to zero and hence solving equation (5.30) for $l = 0$. The reduced form of g is then given explicitly by

$$g = B - \rho - \delta_H, \tag{5.35}$$

which corresponds to equation (5.26) with $l = 0$ and $u + s = 1$ (it is identical to equation (4.28)). Using equations (5.28) and (5.35) we get the familiar result that $u = \rho/B$, which is identical to equation (5.29). It can be seen that none of the taxes affect either long-term economic growth, or the fractions of time devoted to production and studying. The studying productivity parameter B influences growth positively, the rate of time preference ρ and the depreciation rate of human capital stock δ_H negatively. Instead of deriving the reduced form (5.35) we can illustrate the effects of tax and parameter changes on growth with the familiar left-hand diagram of Figure 5.1 by setting $\eta_l = 0$. In that case, curve bb coincides with the g-axis for any tax and parameter values and only curve aa shifts due to changes in B, δ_H and ρ. In the right-hand diagram of Figure 5.1, curve cc becomes horizontal.

5.3.3   Growth Effects of a Revenue-neutral Tax Reform

In Section 5.3.2 we analysed the effects of isolated tax changes on growth. In this section we analyse the growth effects of a revenue-neutral environmental tax reform where the pollution tax partly replaces non-environmental taxes. For analysing a revenue-neutral tax reform we now assume that the government's task is to provide a public good which must be supplied in a certain proportion to the physical capital stock. One can think of some kind of infrastructure which is required as a complement to the current stock of physical capital in the economy. Since the physical capital stock grows over time, government revenue G must grow at the same rate to keep the level of the public good $\bar{G}$ constant. Government revenue can be financed by taxes on consumption, capital, labor and pollution. By dividing the government flow budget constraint by K we obtain

$$\frac{G}{K} \equiv \bar{G} = \tau_C \frac{C}{K} + \tau_H \left(\frac{K}{uH} \right)^{-1} w + \tau_K r + \bar{\tau}_P P. \qquad (5.36)$$

The public good has not been modeled in the former setup. Formally this could be done by adding an additive term to the production function (5.1) or the utility function (5.9). This would be the easiest way, since it does not change the first-order conditions of the market solution – apart from the resource constraint of the economy.[17] Therefore, for the following analysis the term $\bar{G}$ must be subtracted from the right-hand side of the resource constraint of the economy (5.27). For simplicity it is assumed that the government automatically supplies a constant amount of the public good, which is not necessarily the optimal amount. Because of the change in the resource constraint, the semi-reduced forms (5.31) and (5.34), and the condition (5.32) are modified as well.[18] However, the qualitative effects of tax-rate changes on growth g, leisure l, and ratios C/Y and Y/K reported in Table 5.1 are unchanged.

---

[17] Certainly, there may be other more realistic modeling possibilities of a public good. However, the target here is on the one hand to analyse a revenue-neutral tax reform by imposing an exogenous budget constraint, but on the other hand to keep the analysis as simple as possible.

[18] See Section A.3.4 (page 231) in the appendix for the modifications.

To analyse the growth effects of a revenue-neutral environmental tax reform where $\bar{G}$ is unchanged we must investigate whether an increase of the pollution tax *ceteris paribus* increases the government revenue or not. In Section A.3.4 it is shown for any tax rate that a higher capital or pollution tax *ceteris paribus* unambiguously raises government revenue $(\partial \bar{G}/\partial \tau_K, \partial \bar{G}/\partial \bar{\tau}_P > 0)$. Certainly, those tax rates are implicitly restricted by the existence of a balanced growth path (see Sections 5.3.2 and A.3.2). However, the influence of a higher consumption or labor tax $(\partial \bar{G}/\partial \tau_C, \partial \bar{G}/\partial \tau_H)$ on government revenue cannot be signed unambiguously. So in principle, in the case of a consumption or labor tax the government could find itself on the falling, that is, inefficient, branch of the Laffer curve.[19] Already a revenue-neutral *non*-environmental tax reform would stimulate growth: the government could reduce the tax rates on consumption and labor jumping from the inefficient negatively sloped branch to the efficient positively sloped branch of the Laffer curve to increase growth by holding the level of $\bar{G}$ constant. Therefore, we rule out tax rates of consumption or labor corresponding to the inefficient branch of the Laffer curve by precluding irrational government behavior. Hence, a revenue-neutral environmental tax reform where non-environmental taxes are partly replaced by a pollution tax would improve environmental quality and stimulate growth for two reasons: (i) an increased pollution tax will boost growth; (ii) due to increased tax revenue from the pollution tax other taxes could be reduced – holding the level of $\bar{G}$ constant – which further enhances growth. Therefore a revenue-neutral environmental tax reform is accompanied by a double growth dividend. But recall that there is a trade-off between growth and leisure. Hence, whether a double dividend in welfare terms can be reaped may depend on the initial tax rates. However, the introduction of a pollution tax increases welfare unambiguously as non-environmental taxes fail to create incentives to conduct abatement activities.

---

[19]The typical course of the Laffer curve looks similar to Figure 5.2, with $\bar{G}$ and τ on the vertical and horizontal axes, respectively.

5.4   Final Output as the Polluting Factor

In this section, pollution is assumed to be a function of total output Y – rather than physical capital K – and abatement activities Z:

$$P = \left(\frac{Y}{Z}\right)^x. \tag{5.37}$$

We shall skip the derivation of the first-order conditions of the firms and the market solution since they are analogous to those in Sections 5.2.2 and 5.2.5. Along a balanced growth path the differential equations of the market solution for this pollution specification corresponding to equations (5.12) and (5.25) are given by

$$\frac{C}{Y} = \frac{(1-\tau_H)}{(1+\tau_C)}\frac{(1-\alpha)}{\eta_l}\frac{l}{u}\left[1-(\chi\tilde{\tau}_P)^{\frac{1}{1+x}}\right], \tag{5.38}$$

$$g = \alpha A(1-\tau_K)\left[1-(\chi\tilde{\tau}^P)^{\frac{1}{1+x}}\right]\left(\frac{K}{uH}\right)^{\alpha-1}-\delta_K-\rho, \tag{5.39}$$

where $\tilde{\tau}_P \equiv (\tau_P/Y) = \chi^{-1}(Z/Y)^{1+x}$. The optimal accumulation of human capital, the resource constraint of the economy, the human capital accumulation constraint and the reduced form of u are identical to equations (5.26)–(5.29).

Rewriting equation (5.26) by using the time constraint $1 = u + s + l$ and using equations (5.38), (5.39) and (5.27) gives the semi-reduced forms of g and l, respectively:

$$l = \frac{B - \delta_H - \rho - g}{B}, \tag{5.40}$$

$$l = \frac{1+\tau_C}{1-\tau_H}\frac{\eta_l\rho}{1-\alpha}\frac{1}{B}\left[1-\alpha(1-\tau_K)+\frac{\alpha(1-\tau_K)\rho}{g+\delta_K+\rho}\right]. \tag{5.41}$$

Again the term in the square brackets of equation (5.41) is equal to the consumption-output share and hence must be between zero and unity on the balanced growth path. Since the semi-reduced forms (5.40) and (5.41) do not depend on $\tilde{\tau}_P$, a pollution tax affects neither the growth rate nor leisure time $(\partial g/\partial\tilde{\tau}_P, \partial l/\partial\tilde{\tau}_P = 0)$. Apart from that, the signs of the partial derivatives in this model variant are identical to those reported in Table 5.1. Furthermore, the discussion concerning the channels through which taxes affect economic growth is analogous to that reported in Section 5.3.2. Although in this model variant a higher pollution tax again indirectly reduces the effective capital-labor ratio, this effect is exactly offset by the direct effect and therefore does not alter the growth rate (see equation (5.39)).

Given a certain level of output, in this specification – different from the one of (5.4) – there is no possibility of reducing pollution by choosing a different input ratio. Only by means of costly abatement activities can this be done. This missing substitution possibility is responsible for the different growth effect of the pollution tax.

At the end of this section we outline briefly the growth effects of a revenue-neutral environmental tax reform for the output-induced pollution specification. We skip the analytical derivation of the result since it is similar to that in Section 5.3.3. By precluding irrational government behavior it can be shown that an environmental tax reform stimulates growth. The increased government revenue of the pollution tax can be used to partly reduce non-environmental taxes. Since growth is not affected by the pollution tax, though negatively affected by all non-environmental taxes, an environmental tax reform boosts growth.

5.5 Summary of the Results

We investigated the interactions between endogenous growth, environmental economics and public finance in a Uzawa–Lucas economy with leisure. We showed that without government intervention the decentralized outcome is inefficient: there is too much pollution, since abatement is too low and final good production is too capital-intensive, and economic growth is too low. The government could in principle reach a first-best solution by setting the optimal pollution tax according to the Pigouvian taxation rule and by setting all other taxes equal to zero. The optimal pollution tax must rise over time because the pollution-causing input factor (physical capital) accumulates over time. Firms are willing to increase their abatement activities, which is necessary to keep the level of pollution constant, by adjusting to an increasing pollution tax.

If we allow for a labor subsidy, it was shown that for a tax on consumption with an equal rate to a subsidy on labor there is a possibility that the government can generate a lump-sum revenue. In our model a consumption tax is equivalent to a labor income tax plus a tax on the initial capital stock. By taxing consumption and subsidizing labor at the same rate, the government effectively taxes the initial physical capital stock which is assumed to be exogenously given. Therefore the tax base is totally inelastic and this tax-subsidy combination represents a lump-sum tax.

If pollution is a function of the physical capital stock and abatement activities it was shown that a higher pollution tax boosts long-term economic growth, whereas taxes on consumption, capital income and labor income reduce it. Concerning the growth-rate effects of taxes on capital income and pollution, there are two effects at work: both taxes reduce the growth rate directly through a drop in the net of tax interest rate; however, the indirect tax effect stimulates growth due to a more labor-intensive final good production. The direct tax effect dominates in the case of a capital income tax while the indirect effect dominates in the case of a pollution tax. A higher pollution tax gives rise to more abatement which crowds out consumption. This makes leisure less scarce which stimulates studying and therefore growth. This stimulating growth effect is the *first* growth dividend of a tighter environmental policy.

However, it is important to note that growth maximization is not equivalent to welfare maximization although it is possible to increase environmental quality and economic growth at the same time. The reason is the distorted leisure-studying time decision: starting from a suboptimal pollution level, a tighter environmental policy improves environmental quality and gradually corrects the distorted leisure-studying time decision and boosts economic growth. Both effects lead to higher welfare as long as the pollution tax is below the Pigouvian level. For the pollution tax equal to the Pigouvian level, leisure time and economic growth are optimal and welfare is maximal. If the pollution tax is above the Pigouvian level, a tighter environmental policy would still increase environmental quality and boost growth, but decrease welfare because growth rises at the expense of leisure. For the special case of a totally inelastic labor supply we replicated the results of Section 4.2 and showed that none of the taxes influence long-term economic growth. In the model variant where pollution is a function of output and abatement activities, the pollution tax does not affect the long-term growth rate whereas non-environmental taxes reduce it. The reason is a missing substitution possibility between production factors to reduce pollution under this specification.

Furthermore, we analysed the growth effects of a revenue-neutral environmental tax reform. It was assumed that the government's task is to provide a public good which must be supplied in a certain proportion to the physical capital stock, implying an exogenously given government budget requirement. If pollution is a function of physical capital and abatement activities we found that a revenue-neutral shift from non-environmental taxes to a pollution tax would boost growth for two reasons: (i) economic growth is stimulated directly by a higher pollution tax; (ii) the additional revenue can be used to reduce non-environmental taxes, which has an additional stimulating growth effect. The latter effect is the *second* growth dividend of a cleaner environment. In the case where pollution is a function of output and abatement activities, a revenue-neutral environmental tax reform stimulates growth: the increased pollution tax does not alter the long-term growth rate directly. However, the additional revenue can be used to reduce a non-environmental tax which stimulates growth.

At the end of the chapter we discuss briefly two other alternative model specifications which could alter the results. In this chapter it was assumed that consumption, leisure and pollution are separable arguments in the utility function. Complementarity between pollution and leisure in the sense that a better environmental quality increases the marginal value of leisure may reverse the growth-stimulating effect of a pollution tax. In that case a higher pollution tax improves environmental quality and increases leisure due to the complementarity, but higher abatement activities as described above crowd out consumption and decrease leisure *ceteris paribus*. If the former leisure effect dominates the latter, the growth effect of a pollution tax in the case of complementarity between pollution and leisure would be negative. In the chapter we investigated the cases where the environmental externality is generated either by the capital stock or by the production of goods. There is a third possibility: the environmental externality could be generated by using human capital in production. A higher pollution tax would then decrease the effective capital-labor ratio and hamper growth, like the discussed tax on labor income. However, a positive relation between human capital and environmental pollution seems to be less reasonable; rather one would assume an inverse relation.

It was shown that the growth effects of a pollution tax depend on the assumptions concerning pollution technology, and utility. However, irrespective of whether pollution is generated by physical capital or by production and without assuming direct positive productivity effects of a cleaner environment, it is shown within an endogenous growth model with standard specifications that a revenue-neutral environmental tax reform stimulates growth.

Chapter 6

Environmental Policy in the Generalized Uzawa–Lucas Model

6.1 Introduction

We have seen in the previous chapters that the effects of a tighter environmental policy on growth crucially depend on the model specification. To test the robustness of the results, again we generalize the closed economy model of Section 4.2. While we extended the model by endogenous leisure in the last chapter we generalize the education sector in the present chapter: the reproducible input factors human capital and physical capital are now used as input factors both in the final good sector *and* in the education sector. The model under consideration is an extension of the generalized Uzawa–Lucas model used by King and Rebelo (1990), which additionally allows for disutility of pollution and public abatement activities that are financed by tax revenues. As before, we investigate two sources of pollution alternatively. Pollution is generated either directly by final good production or by using physical capital in final good production. We investigate the effects and the possibility of environmental policies in both a closed economy and a small open economy setting. The investigation of the small open economy starts out from conventional assumptions in international trade models, thereby simplifying the analysis by an exogenously given world interest rate, but broadening the analysis by assuming perfect international capital mobility.[1]

In the following, the literature on fiscal policy, and international capital mobility in human capital growth models is reviewed. Several authors, King and Rebelo (1990), Rebelo (1991), Devereux and Love (1994) and Milesi-Ferretti and Roubini (1998b) analyse the consequences of tax-rate changes for economic growth with production specifications similar to those in this chapter. However, they do not consider the environment and redistribute the tax revenues lump sum to consumers. In the model under consideration, the tax revenues are used to finance the provision of the public abatement measures. In contrast to the literature, by incorporating the environment we are able to analyse a broader set of tax instruments, namely a tax on pollution in addition to the value-added tax and the taxes on labor and capital income.

King and Rebelo (1990) and Milesi-Ferretti and Roubini (1994) consider the effects of tax rates on growth in small open economies with international capital mobility. In their models, international growth-rate differentials can be explained in a residence-based income capital tax system, but not in a source-based tax system.[2] The production processes are similar to those in this chapter, but these contributions do not consider an environmental externality.

Irrespective of the type of pollution the major conclusions of the present chapter are as follows: factor income taxes and the pollution tax are growth reducing, whereas the consumption tax is a lump-sum tax. The market allocation without government intervention is inefficient due to the presence of the environmental externality: there is too much pollution, too little abatement and excessive economic growth in

---

[1] The model analysed in this chapter is based on Hettich and Svane (1998).

[2] In overlapping generation models of the Uzawa–Lucas type, Buiter and Kletzer (1991, 1993 and 1995) explain persistent growth-rate differentials, independently of the international taxation system. In a variant of the Uzawa–Lucas model augmented with endogenous population Razin and Yuen (1992, 1996) find that the growth-rate effect of taxes depends on the principle of international taxation and the preference bias between child quantity and child quality.

an unregulated market economy. The first-best solution can be achieved by setting the pollution tax equal to the optimal marginal damage of pollution. It turns out that an optimal solution may be reached instead by certain combinations of factor income taxes, if the pollution tax is unavailable as a policy instrument. By considering perfect capital mobility we see that under a residence-based tax system, a small open economy can choose its own fiscal policy and hence determine its long-term growth rate. As long as the environmental problem is national in scope, the government can choose the level of pollution and hence the environmental quality. However, under a source-based tax system, a small open economy is partially restricted in its fiscal policy and can as a consequence conduct only a second-best environmental policy.

The chapter is organized as follows. The model is laid out in Section 6.2 and the first-order conditions of the representative agent problem and central planner problem are derived for the output-induced pollution specification. Section 6.3 determines the optimal tax rates. Furthermore, the balanced growth rate is calculated and the effects of tax and parameter changes on all core variables are determined. Finally, the small open economy version of the model is analysed. Section 6.4 considers environmental policy in a model with physical capital-induced pollution and Section 6.5 concludes this chapter.

6.2   The Analytical Framework

As before, this section presents a two-sector endogenous growth model of a closed economy and derives the first-order conditions of the representative agent problem and the social planner problem. However, in contrast to chapters 4 and 5, physical capital is now necessary to accumulate human capital. Thus, in this model, physical and human capital are devoted to both final good production and human capital accumulation.[3] The production of the final good causes pollution as a negative environmental externality and the government is assumed to engage in public abatement activities.

---

[3] The specification of the two production sectors is similar to those in King and Rebelo (1990) and Rebelo (1991).

6.2.1   Technology

Final goods are produced with a constant returns to scale technology using physical capital and human capital as inputs:

$$Y_t = A \left(v_t K_t\right)^\alpha \left(u_t H_t\right)^{1-\alpha},$$

(6.1)

where variables v and u $(0 < u, v < 1)$ are the shares of the economy's physical and human capital, respectively, that are applied to final goods production. The flow resource constraint of the closed economy reads[4]

$$Y_t = C_t + \dot{K}_t + Z_t.$$

(6.2)

Analogously to final good production (6.1), human capital is accumulated by using human capital representing here education time and knowledge of teachers and parents, and by using physical capital representing here facilities such as school buildings, furnishings, laboratories and so on. The human capital accumulation function is assumed to be a constant returns to scale technology

$$\dot{H}_t = B \left[(1 - v_t) K_t\right]^\beta \left[(1 - u_t) H_t\right]^{1-\beta},$$

(6.3)

where $0 < \beta < 1$ is the exogenous physical capital share in education. The specification of the final goods production function (6.1) and the human capital accumulation function (6.3) ensure that diminishing returns do not arise, when physical and human capital grow at the same rate.

Final good production is assumed to cause pollution, which only harms utility.[5] The public 'bad' pollution can be reduced by means of non-rival abatement activities Z. Pollution is given by the following functional form

$$P_t = \left(\frac{Y_t}{Z_t}\right)^\chi.$$

(6.4)

See section 6.4 for an analysis of a capital-based pollution function.

---

[4] For simplicity, human and physical capital are assumed to depreciate at a zero rate. However, this assumption does not change the qualitative results.

[5] As before, productive spillovers from a better environment to production of goods or human capital accumulation are not analysed analytically but discussed at the end of Section 6.3.2.

6.2.2 Firms

As before, firms rent physical and human capital from households to produce final goods. Firms must pay a pollution tax according to their pollution. Since pollution is complementary to output, the pollution tax is equivalent to a tax on output. Firms are assumed to maximize their profits by choosing uH and vK, given the pollution tax levied on total production. The representative firms' profit condition is given by

$$\pi_t = (1 - \tau_P)\, Y_t - w_t\, (u_t H_t) - r_t\, (v_t K_t). \qquad (6.5)$$

The profits are maximized when the marginal cost of each factor equals its after-tax marginal product:

$$w_t \;=\; (1 - \tau_P)\,(1 - \alpha)\, A \left(\frac{v_t K_t}{u_t H_t} \right)^{\alpha} = (1 - \tau_P)\,(1 - \alpha)\, \frac{Y_t}{u_t H_t}, \quad (6.6)$$

$$r_t \;=\; (1 - \tau_P)\, \alpha A \left(\frac{v_t K_t}{u_t H_t} \right)^{\alpha - 1} = (1 - \tau_P)\, \alpha \frac{Y_t}{v_t K_t}. \qquad (6.7)$$

6.2.3 Households

The preferences of the identical, atomistic agents with perfect foresight over an infinite time horizon are given by

$$U(C_t, P_t) = \ln C_t - \eta_P \ln P_t. \qquad (6.8)$$

For simplicity, we assume a logarithmic instantaneous utility function[6] and do not allow for leisure. Households choose consumption and the allocation of human and physical capital between the two sectors in order to maximize their intertemporal utility subject to the human capital accumulation constraint (6.3) and the flow budget constraint

$$\dot{K}_t = (1 - \tau_K)\, r_t v_t K_t + (1 - \tau_H)\, w_t u_t H_t - (1 + \tau_C)\, C_t. \qquad (6.9)$$

---

[6] A more general utility function is represented by equation (4.8). As this function does not change the qualitative results concerning the growth-rate effects, but complicates the analysis, we use the simplified function (6.8), where the intertemporal elasticity of substitution is equal to one.

Recall that human capital accumulation is a non-market activity, thus it does not give rise to direct income and is not subject to factor income taxation.[7]

6.2.4 Government

The government levies a pollution tax on final good production, a capital income tax, a labor income tax and a consumption tax in order to finance public abatement activities. The government's flow budget constraint is given by

$$\tau_K r_t v_t K_t + \tau_H w_t u_t H_t + \tau_C C_t + \tau_P Y_t = Z_t. \qquad (6.10)$$

6.2.5 The Market Solution

The representative household chooses consumption and the allocation of physical and human capital to final good production and education, respectively, in order to maximize its intertemporal utility subject to the human capital accumulation function (6.3) and the budget constraint (6.9) taking all tax rates and pollution as given. The current-value Hamiltonian for this optimization problem takes the form

$$\begin{aligned}
\max_{C,u,v} \mathcal{H} \; = \; & \ln C - \eta_P \ln P \\
+ \; & \lambda\left[(1-\tau_K)\,rvK + (1-\tau_H)\,wuH - (1+\tau_C)\,C\right] \\
+ \; & \mu\left\{B\left[(1-v)\,K\right]^\beta\left[(1-u)\,H\right]^{1-\beta}\right\}.
\end{aligned}$$

The first-order conditions with respect to C, u, v, K and H become

$$\frac{1}{C} \; = \; \lambda(1+\tau_C) \quad \Rightarrow \quad -\hat{\lambda} = \hat{C}, \qquad (6.11)$$

$$\lambda(1-\tau_H)\,w \; = \; \mu(1-\beta)\,B\left[\frac{(1-v)\,K}{(1-u)\,H}\right]^\beta, \qquad (6.12)$$

$$\lambda(1-\tau_K)\,r \; = \; \mu\lambda\beta B\left[\frac{(1-v)\,K}{(1-u)\,H}\right]^{\beta-1}, \qquad (6.13)$$

---

[7]For human capital as a market good, see Milesi-Ferretti and Roubini (1998b) in a similar model without environment.

$$-\hat{\lambda} = (1 - \tau_K) r - \rho, \tag{6.14}$$

$$-\hat{\mu} = (1 - \beta) B \left[\frac{(1 - v) K}{(1 - u) H} \right]^{\beta} - \rho. \tag{6.15}$$

Equation (6.11) implies that the marginal utility of consumption in every period should equal the after-tax shadow price of physical capital. Equations (6.12) and (6.13) describe the optimal allocation of human and physical capital between the two sectors. The first Euler condition (6.14) shows that the rate of change in the shadow price of physical capital should equal the after-tax marginal product of capital in the final good sector minus the rate of time preference. Finally, the second Euler condition (6.15) requires that the rate of change in the shadow price of human capital must equal the marginal product of human capital in the education sector.

Equations (6.12) and (6.13) yield the sectoral allocation of resources as a function of the tax rates and the parameters of the model:

$$\frac{v}{u} = \left(\frac{\alpha}{1 - \alpha} \frac{1 - \beta}{\beta} \right) \left(\frac{1 - \tau_K}{1 - \tau_H} \right) \frac{1 - v}{1 - u}, \tag{6.16}$$

where equations (6.6) and (6.7) have been used. According to equation (6.16), the after-tax rates of technical substitution between capital and labor must be equalized across sectors in order to achieve an efficient intersectoral allocation of capital and hours. The income taxes on capital and labor affect this allocation in different ways. According to equation (6.16), the capital-labor share in the final good sector v/u increases relative to the capital-labor share in the education sector $(1 - v)/(1 - u)$, whenever the capital income tax declines or the labor income tax increases. In addition, an increase (a decline) in the capital-labor share in final good production (education) leads to an increase in the capital-labor share in final good production relative to the education sector. Note that the sectoral allocation of resources is unaffected by a consumption tax. In addition, the sectoral allocation of factors is unaffected by income taxation, when taxation is comprehensive $\tau_K = \tau_H$, and by a change of the pollution tax, as they affect the return to the two input factors in the same way.

Finally, the Keynes–Ramsey rule for the market economy is derived by using equations (6.11) and (6.14), where r is replaced by equation (6.7):

$$\hat{C} = (1 - \tau_K)(1 - \tau_P)\alpha\frac{Y}{vK} - \rho \quad \equiv \quad R - \rho. \qquad (6.17)$$

It is obvious that the consumption tax is a lump-sum tax, since it is absent in the first-order conditions of the market solution (6.11)–(6.15) and hence does not distort the economy. However, all other taxes change the allocation of the economy. The taxes on capital income and pollution affect the intertemporal incentive to invest in physical capital, described by equation (6.17). In addition, both factor income taxes affect the sectoral allocation of factors, described by equation (6.16).

6.2.6   The Central Planner Solution

A benevolent central planner chooses consumption, the allocation of physical and human capital between the two sectors, and additionally the number of abatement activities, in order to maximize the discounted intertemporal utility of the representative household subject to the human capital accumulation function (6.3) and the resource constraint of the economy (6.2). The current-value Hamiltonian for this optimization problem reads

$$\max_{C,Z,u,v} \mathcal{H} = \ln C - \eta_P \ln P$$
$$+\lambda\left[A\left(v_t K_t\right)^{\alpha}\left(u_t H_t\right)^{1-\alpha} - C - Z\right]$$
$$+\mu\left\{B\left[(1 - v)K\right]^{\beta}\left[(1 - u)H\right]^{1-\beta}\right\}.$$

The first-order conditions with respect to C, Z, u, v, K and H become

$$\lambda = \frac{1}{C} \quad \Rightarrow \quad -\hat{\lambda} = \frac{\dot{C}}{C}, \qquad (6.18)$$

$$\lambda = \chi\eta_P\frac{1}{Z}, \qquad (6.19)$$

$$\lambda\left(1 - \frac{Z}{Y}\right)(1 - \alpha)\frac{Y}{uH} = \mu(1 - \beta)B\left[\frac{(1 - v)K}{(1 - u)H}\right]^{\beta}, \qquad (6.20)$$

$$\lambda\left(1 - \frac{Z}{Y}\right)\alpha\frac{Y}{vK} = \mu\beta B\left[\frac{(1 - v)K}{(1 - u)H}\right]^{\beta-1}, \qquad (6.21)$$

$$-\hat{\lambda} = \left(1 - \frac{Z}{Y}\right)\alpha\frac{Y}{vK} - \rho, \qquad (6.22)$$

$$-\hat{\mu} = (1 - \beta) B \left[\frac{(1 - v) K}{(1 - u) H}\right]^{\beta} - \rho. \quad (6.23)$$

Using equations (6.18) and (6.19) yields

$$\frac{Z}{K} = \eta_P \chi \frac{C}{K}. \qquad (6.24)$$

As in the last chapters, for an optimal solution the marginal utility of consumption and abatement must be equalized (see equation (6.24)). Equations (6.20) and (6.21) describe the optimal allocation of physical and human capital. The first Euler condition (6.22) implies that the rate of change of the shadow price of physical capital should equal the marginal product of capital in the final good sector. The second Euler condition (6.23) is identical to equation (6.15).

After eliminating the shadow prices, equations (6.21) and (6.20) yield the optimal sectoral allocation of resources:

$$\frac{v}{u} = \left(\frac{\alpha}{1-\alpha}\frac{1-\beta}{\beta}\right)\frac{1-v}{1-u}. \qquad (6.25)$$

Finally, the Keynes–Ramsey rule for the socially planned economy is obtained by using equations (6.18) and (6.22):

$$\hat{C} = \left(1 - \frac{Z}{Y}\right)\alpha\frac{Y}{vK} - \rho. \qquad (6.26)$$

As can be seen, the social return equals the private return to capital investment $\alpha(Y/vK)$ corrected by the optimal marginal damage of pollution Z/Y, which is external to firms in the market economy.

6.3   Results Along a Balanced Growth Path

In this section, the optimal tax rates are derived. Furthermore, the reduced forms of the balanced growth rate and all core variables are derived. Finally, the small open economy version of the model is considered.

Along a balanced growth path, the variables C, H, K, Y and Z grow at the same constant rate, whereas u and v are constant over time. Therefore, the balanced growth rate g can be defined as follows

$$g \equiv \hat{C} = \hat{H} = \hat{K} = \hat{Y} = \hat{Z} = -\hat{\mu} = -\hat{\lambda}, \quad 0 = \dot{u} = \dot{v}. \qquad (6.27)$$

According to condition (6.27), the ratios C/K, C/Y, K/H, Z/Y, Z/K and hence P are constant along a balanced growth path.

6.3.1 Optimal Tax Rates

This section derives the optimal tax rates in the model. This can be done by comparing the first-order conditions of the market solution with the corresponding first-order conditions of the central planner solution. Using equations (6.6) and (6.7) and comparing equations (6.12) and (6.14) with (6.20) and (6.22), respectively, reveals the following two conditions for a first-best solution:

$$(1 - \tau_H)(1 - \tau_P) \quad \stackrel{!}{=} \quad (1 - \tau_K)(1 - \tau_P) \quad \stackrel{!}{=} \quad 1 - \left(\frac{Z}{Y}\right)^{cps}.$$

$$(6.28)$$

Note that there are several possibilities for achieving a first-best solution in a market economy. Condition (6.28) can be fulfilled in at least three ways (see Table 6.1).

Table 6.1: Optimal tax rates

Case	τ_H	τ_K	τ_P
1	0	0	$\left(\frac{Z}{Y}\right)^{cps}$
2	$\left(\frac{Z}{Y}\right)^{cps}$	$\left(\frac{Z}{Y}\right)^{cps}$	0
3	$1 - \sqrt{1 - \left(\frac{Z}{Y}\right)^{cps}}$	$1 - \sqrt{1 - \left(\frac{Z}{Y}\right)^{cps}}$	$1 - \sqrt{1 - \left(\frac{Z}{Y}\right)^{cps}}$

Case 1: A first-best solution can be reached by setting tax rates on labor and capital equal to zero and the pollution tax rate equal to the optimal marginal damage of pollution. In this case, the pollution tax corresponds to a Pigouvian tax. *Case 2:* A first-best solution can also be reached by setting both factor income taxes equal to the optimal

marginal damage of pollution and the pollution tax equal to zero. Hence, a comprehensive income tax $(\tau_H = \tau_K)$ equal to the optimal abatement-output ratio mimics a Pigouvian tax. *Case 3:* A first-best solution can be reached in many other ways by combining a comprehensive income tax and a pollution tax in a way which fulfills condition (6.28). One of these possibilities is represented in Table 6.1 for $\tau_H = \tau_K = \tau_P$. In all three cases, the optimal tax structure holds both along and outside the balanced growth path. Outside the balanced growth path, the tax rates change over time since the optimal abatement-output ratio is not constant. However, along the balanced growth path the tax rates are constant, since the abatement-output ratio is constant. In practice the advantage of the pollution tax is given by fewer informational requirements in contrast to the other tax solutions (see page 108).

As in Section 4.2, we can show by inserting the optimal tax rates into the government's budget constraint (6.10) that a first-best solution can be reached without the use of a lump-sum instrument in all three cases. Hence, in case 1, for instance, the pollution tax fulfills two tasks at the same time. It corrects the inefficient input ratio and generates the exact amount of public revenues to provide the optimal level of abatement. However, this result depends on our assumptions.[8] If public abatement measures are not produced with final goods by using a one-to-one technology (see equation (6.2)) a pollution tax is still able to correct the inefficient input ratio in production but additionally a lump-sum instrument is necessary to guarantee sufficient tax revenues for an efficient provision of public abatement measures.

6.3.2 The Effects of Isolated Tax and Parameter Changes on Growth

In the following, we analyse the effects of tax and parameter changes on the reduced forms of all core variables and ratios. At the end of the section, the results are summarized in Table 6.2. Along a balanced growth path, the first-order conditions of the market economy (6.15) and (6.17), the resource constraint of the economy (6.2) and the human capital ac-

---

[8] For a more detailed discussion, see page 107.

cumulation constraint (6.3) can be rewritten by using condition (6.27):

$$g \;=\; (1 - \beta)\, B \left[\frac{(1 - v)\, K}{(1 - u)\, H} \right]^{\beta} - \rho, \tag{6.29}$$

$$g \;=\; (1 - \tau_K)\, (1 - \tau_P)\, \alpha A \left(\frac{vK}{uH} \right)^{\alpha - 1} - \rho \;\equiv\; R - \rho, \tag{6.30}$$

$$g \;=\; A \left(\frac{vK}{uH} \right)^{\alpha - 1} v - \frac{C}{K} - \frac{Z}{K}, \tag{6.31}$$

$$g \;=\; B \left[\frac{(1 - v)\, K}{(1 - u)\, H} \right]^{\beta} (1 - u). \tag{6.32}$$

In order to derive the reduced form of the effective capital-labor ratio in the final good sector $(vK) / (uH)$, we replace the term $(1 - v) / (1 - u)$ in equation (6.29) by (6.16) and set it equal to (6.30):

$$\frac{vK}{uH} = \left\{ \frac{\alpha A}{(1 - \beta)\, B} \left[\frac{\alpha}{1 - \alpha} \frac{1 - \beta}{\beta} \right]^{\beta} \frac{(1 - \tau_P)\, (1 - \tau_K)^{(1 + \beta)}}{(1 - \tau_H)^{\beta}} \right\}^{\frac{1}{1 - \alpha + \beta}}. \tag{6.33}$$

According to equation (6.33), the effective capital-labor ratio $(vK) / (uH)$ depends positively on the tax on labor income and negatively on the taxes on pollution and capital income. It is obvious that a higher labor income tax leads to a more capital-intensive final good production whereas the opposite is true for a higher capital income tax. The effect of a change in the comprehensive income tax on the effective capital-labor ratio is identical to that of a change in the pollution tax. This is the reason behind the equivalence of a comprehensive tax and a pollution tax for internalizing the external effect of pollution. Why do taxes on comprehensive income and pollution affect the effective capital-labor ratio in the final good production negatively, whereas the opposite applies for the studying sector? The intuition behind this is that both taxes reduce the return to physical capital net of tax rate directly, whereas the rate of return to investment in human capital is left unaffected, because education is a non-market activity. Since the return to capital investment should equal the return to human capital investment, final good production must become more human capital-intensive in order to leave the return to capital investment net of tax unaffected.

The reduced forms of the return to capital investment net of tax and the growth rate can now be obtained by substituting equation (6.33) in (6.30):

$$R = \left[\Psi_1 (1 - \tau_H)^{(1-\alpha)\beta} (1 - \tau_P)^\beta (1 - \tau_K)^{\alpha\beta} \right]^{\frac{1}{1-\alpha+\beta}}, \qquad (6.34)$$

$$g = \left[\Psi_1 (1 - \tau_H)^{(1-\alpha)\beta} (1 - \tau_P)^\beta (1 - \tau_K)^{\alpha\beta} \right]^{\frac{1}{1-\alpha+\beta}} - \rho \quad (6.35)$$

$$\Psi_1 \equiv (\alpha A)^\beta \left[(1 - \beta) B \right]^{(1-\alpha)} \left(\frac{1-\alpha}{\alpha} \frac{\beta}{1-\beta} \right)^{(1-\alpha)\beta}.$$

According to equation (6.35), the balanced growth rate in the market economy depends positively on the levels of the technology in the final good sector A and the education sector B, while it depends negatively on the capital income tax, the labor income tax, the comprehensive income tax $\tau_H = \tau_K$, the pollution tax and the rate of time preference.[9] It can be seen that a tax on consumption does not affect the long-term growth rate. Furthermore, the value-added tax is a lump-sum tax, since it does not distort the economy. The result that non-environmental taxes reduce growth has already been shown by Milesi-Ferretti and Roubini (1998b) in a similar model without pollution. Furthermore, they state that growth and welfare are maximized, when factor income is taxed at a zero rate. Hence, in their model the outcome of the unregulated market economy is a first-best solution. However, we consider the environment in addition and show that the long-term growth rate and pollution in an unregulated market economy is too high from a welfare perspective, when pollution harms utility.

In the following, the reduced forms of the fractions of human and physical capital that are devoted to final good production are determined. The fraction of human capital allocated to final goods production

---

[9] In the case where the more general multiplicative separable utility function (4.8) is used, the right-hand side of equation (6.35) is additionally multiplied by the intertemporal elasticity of substitution ε. Obviously, an intertemporal elasticity of substitution ε unequal to unity does not alter the qualitative growth-rate effects of parameter and tax-rate changes.

is derived from equations (6.29), (6.32) and (6.35):

$$u = \beta + (1 - \beta)\rho \left[\Psi_1 (1 - \tau_H)^{(1-\alpha)\beta} (1 - \tau_P)^\beta (1 - \tau_K)^{\alpha\beta} \right]^{-\frac{1}{1-\alpha+\beta}}.$$

(6.36)

It can be seen immediately that the fraction of human capital allocated to final good production depends positively on both factor income taxes, the comprehensive income tax and the pollution tax. It seems counterintuitive that an increase in the labor income tax induces agents to spend more time at work. However, the capital-labor share v/u and not the absolute value of u is relevant for the allocation of physical and human capital between the two production sectors. As we shall see below, a labor income tax also increases the fraction of physical capital allocated to final good production. However, v rises more than u, since a labor income tax increases the capital-labor share in the final good sector v/u relative to the capital-labor share in the education sector $(1 - v)/(1 - u)$ (see equation (6.16)).

Now, the fraction of physical capital allocated to final good production is derived from equations (6.16) and (6.36) and by introducing (6.35):

$$v = \left[1 + \frac{1-\alpha}{\alpha} \frac{1-\tau_H}{1-\tau_K} \frac{1}{1 + \frac{\rho}{\beta\left\{ \left[\frac{\Psi_1(1-\tau_H)^{(1-\alpha)\beta}(1-\tau_P)^\beta}{(1-\tau_K)^{-\alpha\beta}} \right]^{\frac{1}{1-\alpha+\beta}} - \rho \right\}}} \right]^{-1}.$$

(6.37)

It depends positively on the labor income tax, the comprehensive income tax and the pollution tax, while the effect of the capital income tax is presumed to be negative, but cannot be signed unambiguously.

In the following, the reduced form of the abatement-output ratio is derived. Therefore, the budget constraint of the government (6.10) is rewritten by using equations (6.6) and (6.7):

$$(1 - \tau_P)\left[\tau_K \alpha + \tau_H (1 - \alpha)\right] + \tau_P + \tau_C \frac{C}{Y} = \frac{Z}{Y}.$$

(6.38)

Substituting the resource constraint of the economy (6.31) in equation (6.38) yields either

$$\frac{Z}{Y} = \frac{(1 - \tau_P)\left[\tau_K \alpha + \tau_H (1 - \alpha)\right] + \tau_P + \tau_C \left[1 - \frac{g}{Av}\left(\frac{vK}{uH}\right)^{1-\alpha}\right]}{1 + \tau_C},$$

(6.39)

or

$$\frac{C}{Y} = \frac{\left[1 - \frac{g}{Av}\left(\frac{vK}{uH}\right)^{1-\alpha}\right] - (1 - \tau_P)\left[\tau_K \alpha + \tau_H (1 - \alpha)\right] - \tau_P}{1 + \tau_C}.$$

(6.40)

It can be seen that a consumption tax increases the abatement-output ratio. However, the exclusive use of the consumption tax cannot yield a first-best solution, as it does not correct the sectoral allocation of factors. For the derivation of the other effects we have to set the lump-sum consumption tax equal to zero, otherwise the effects cannot be signed. Due to tax interaction effects, a higher pollution tax erodes the tax bases of the non-environmental taxes, which finally could lead to a lower abatement-output ratio and thereby to higher pollution: an increase in the pollution tax raises tax revenue directly, but lowers the factor income tax revenue indirectly through a drop in the returns to capital and labor. However, an increase in the pollution tax increases the abatement-output ratio and hence reduces pollution as long as the taxes on capital and labor are between zero and one. The effects of a comprehensive income tax are equivalent to a pollution tax. Isolated increases in either the labor income tax or the capital income tax raise the abatement-output ratio without eroding any other tax bases.

Even though a consumption tax is a lump-sum tax, it has a negative effect on the consumption-output ratio, since its revenues are used for the provision of the public abatement activities, which changes the economy's allocation (see equation (6.40)).[10] However, the effects of all other taxes and parameters on the consumption-output ratio cannot be signed unambiguously. The effects of changes in the tax rates and the parameters on the core variables and ratios are summarized in Table 6.2.

By means of the Keynes–Ramsey rule (6.30) and the results in Table 6.2 (second and fifth rows), the channels through which taxes affect long-term economic growth can be shown:

---

[10] For further explanation, see Section 4.2.2 (page 111).

Table 6.2: Effects of tax and parameter changes on core variables

	τ_C	τ_H	τ_K	$\tau_H = \tau_K$	τ_P	A	B	ρ
$\frac{\partial g}{\partial x}$	0	−	−	−	−	+	+	−
$\frac{\partial u}{\partial x}$	0	+	+	+	+	−	−	+
$\frac{\partial v}{\partial x}$	0	+	−*	+	+	+	+	−
$\frac{\partial[(vK)/(uH)]}{\partial x}$	0	+	−	−	−	+	−	0
$\frac{\partial(Z/Y)}{\partial x}$	+	+°	+°	+°	+°	0°	0°	0°

° Signs are obtained by setting the lump-sum tax $\tau_C = 0$.

* Cannot be signed unambiguously, but is expected to be negative.

- The direct effect of higher taxes on capital and pollution reduces the net interest rate R for a given effective capital-labor ratio. From equation (6.30), we know that this single effect reduces growth. Due to the indirect effect of these taxes, final good production becomes more labor-intensive, which *ceteris paribus* stimulates growth due to a higher marginal product of physical capital. Equation (6.35) shows that the direct effect dominates the indirect effect.
- A higher labor income tax has no direct effect on growth but leads to a more capital-intensive final good production, which lowers growth indirectly (see equation (6.30)).

In the preceding analyses, productive spillovers of a better environmental quality have not been taken into account. However, an improvement in the quality of the environment may increase the productivity in the final good production or in the education sector. Formally, these cases could have been analysed in the present setup by adding a multiplicative term $P^{-\epsilon}$ on the right-hand side of the production function (6.1) or the human capital accumulation function (6.3). As before we discuss productive spillovers of a better environment without a formal analysis. Along a balanced growth path, a better environmental quality is equivalent to higher levels of the technology A or B, because the level of pollution is constant along a balanced growth path. From Table 6.2, an increase in productivity is seen to increase economic growth. Hence, environmental improvements stimulate economic growth, *ceteris paribus.* Whether this positive growth-rate effect dominates the above-mentioned negative growth-rate effect depends on the strength of the productive spillover and remains an empirical question.

6.3.3 The Small Open Economy

So far we have analysed the effects of environmental policy in a closed economy setting. In this section, we complement the analysis by investigating the possibilities of a small open economy conducting an independent environmental policy. Throughout, the conventional assumptions of international trade models are made: domestic capital goods and foreign assets F are perfect substitutes, there is international borrowing and lending, and international trade in capital and consumption goods, but international immobility of labor, that is, human capital. The latter assumption ensures that the small open economy will not specialize over time in either final good production or education. Furthermore, the world interest rate $\bar{r}_F$ cannot be influenced by a small open economy and is therefore exogenous. Given these assumptions, the flow resource constraint of the small open economy becomes

$$Y + \bar{r}_F F = C + \dot{K} + \dot{F} + Z, \qquad (6.41)$$

where $\bar{r}_F F$ is the interest payment earned on foreign assets and $\dot{F}$ is investment in foreign assets. In the small open market economy, the first-order conditions of the representative agent's maximization problem are still given by equations (6.11)–(6.15), but depending on the tax system an additional requirement is necessary. By assuming a *residence-based* (worldwide) tax system[11] the after-tax return to domestic capital must equal the after-tax return to investment in foreign assets:

$$R \;=\; (1 - \tau_K)r \;=\; (1 - \tau_F)\bar{r}_F. \qquad (6.42)$$

If the small country discriminates between taxes on foreign and domestic capital income it can still determine the domestic interest rate

---

[11] This is the prevailing taxation system (see, for example, OECD 1991). Agents pay taxes in their home country on capital income from foreign investments, but receive a tax credit for any taxes paid abroad on this income.

net of tax R by its own tax policy.[12] But the arbitrage equilibrium requires that the domestic interest rate net of tax must equal the net of tax world interest rate. As a consequence, the only difference between the closed economy and the small open economy is that the government must accommodate the tax on foreign capital income in order to fulfill equation (6.42). Thus, the tax on foreign capital income $\bar{r}_F$ is not a real decision variable of the government. In the case where the after-tax return is higher on foreign assets, there will be a permanent outflow of capital from the domestic economy. In the case where the after-tax return is lower on foreign assets, there will be a permanent inflow of capital. Obviously, both cases are unstable. The endogenous determination of the tax on foreign capital income is derived by introducing the after-tax interest rate (6.34) in equation (6.42):

$$\tau_F \quad = \quad 1 - \frac{R}{\bar{r}_F} \tag{6.43}$$

$$= \quad 1 - \frac{1}{\bar{r}_F} \left[\Psi_1 \left(1 - \tau_H\right)^{(1-\alpha)\beta} \left(1 - \tau_P\right)^{\beta} \left(1 - \tau_K\right)^{\alpha\beta} \right]^{\frac{1}{1-\alpha+\beta}}.$$

It can be seen that for given taxes on labor income, capital income and pollution, there exists a unique feasible value of the tax on foreign assets that equalizes the returns to domestic and foreign investment. Since the equilibrium interest rate net of tax R (6.34) is a negative function of the taxes on capital, labor and pollution, the tax on foreign assets is a positive function of these taxes. This result is similar to that obtained by Milesi-Ferretti and Roubini (1994), except for the effect of the pollution tax.

The key insight from the above analysis is that a small open economy under a residence-based tax system can determine the after-tax return earned by domestic residents as long as the tax rate on foreign capital income is set according to condition (6.43).[13] Thus, the after-tax returns on domestic capital equal the world interest rate net of the tax on foreign capital income levied on domestic residents. Hence, a small

---

[12]Note that in a pure residence-based taxation system, domestic and foreign capital income would be taxed at the same rate.

[13]The papers by King and Rebelo (1990) and Rebelo (1992) also show that a residence-based taxation system allows for a wedge between both domestic and world interest rates, and growth rates.

open economy can decide its own growth rate through taxation of factor income and pollution which is necessary for an efficient environmental policy (see Section 6.3.2). In fact, the balanced growth rate is the same in the small open economy and in the closed economy (6.35). However, to guarantee an independent environmental policy we furthermore must assume that the environmental externality is national in scope since by definition a small country has no significant influence on global environmental degradation.[14]

Because of the similarities between the closed and the small open economies, the optimal taxation results of Section 6.3.1 are still valid. However, the government in the small open economy obtains an additional revenue from the tax on foreign assets. This tax revenue must be redistributed in a lump-sum manner to guarantee a first-best solution. The main difference between the closed and the open economy is that the latter will exhibit no transitional dynamics as long as there are no adjustment costs for capital accumulation. The domestic capital stock can be changed immediately by borrowing or lending in the international capital markets.

If, in contrast, capital income is taxed according to the *source* principle, the government becomes partially restricted in its tax policy. Under such a system the net of tax interest rate in the small open economy must equal the world interest rate

$$R = (1 - \tau_K)r = \bar{r}_F. \qquad (6.44)$$

Thus, the growth rate of the small open economy is determined solely by the world interest rate. If on the one hand, the technology of the production processes are identical at home and abroad, the government of the small open economy cannot levy positive taxes on labor, capital and pollution, since this would violate condition (6.44) which ensures a stable solution. However, the small open economy is not fully restricted in its environmental policy: public abatement activities can still be financed by the revenues of the (lump-sum) consumption tax or of certain tax-subsidy combinations which do not alter the return to capital net of

---

[14]In the case of global environmental problems such as the anthropogenic greenhouse effect or the destruction of the ozone layer, a small open economy has no influence on the pollution level at all.

tax R and thereby lower pollution. But note that this is a second-best environmental policy. An optimal environmental policy requires a more labor-intensive final good production and a reduced growth rate.

If on the other hand, the technologies are different at home and abroad, the government must use at least one of the above-mentioned tax instruments to fulfill condition (6.44). If the gross interest rate of the small open economy r is larger than the world interest rate $\bar{r}_F$, there is a slight change for a first-best environmental policy. A first-best solution applies if and only if the optimal net of tax interest rate in the small open economy coincides with the world interest rate by accident. However, if the gross interest rate is smaller than the world interest rate, the small open economy must subsidize the interest rate and finance it with a lump-sum tax. In this case again only a second-best environmental policy is possible.

6.4   Physical Capital as the Polluting Factor

We now turn back to a closed economy setting but assume pollution to be a function of physical capital used in the final good production and public abatement activities.[15] The alternative specification of the pollution function is

$$P = \left(\frac{vK}{Z}\right)^{\chi}, \tag{6.45}$$

where pollution is seen to be increasing in the use of physical capital in final good production and decreasing in public abatement. Hence only the share of physical capital used in production and its complement used in human capital accumulation causes pollution. For example, driving an automobile causes pollution but dismantling it into its component parts in order to demonstrate and to study its mode of operation does not harm the environment. In contrast to the pollution function (6.4), this specification allows for a reduction in pollution without lowering output,

---

[15]The transitional dynamics of this version of the model are simulated numerically by Svane and Hettich (1998). We shall skip the results since they are similar to those in Section 4.3 where we analysed the adaptation process of a Uzawa–Lucas economy.

through a substitution of physical by human capital in production. This would lead to a cleaner and a more labor-intensive final good production.

In the following, we derive the growth-rate effects of changes in the tax rates and the parameters and compute the optimal tax rates for this pollution specification given that all other things are equal to Section 6.2.1. In contrast to the setup above, the pollution tax is now levied on the use of physical capital in the final good production. Therefore, the after-tax marginal products of labor and capital change as follows:

$$w \; = \; (1-\alpha)\frac{Y}{uH}, \tag{6.46}$$

$$r \; = \; \alpha\frac{Y}{vK} - \tau_P. \tag{6.47}$$

The wage rate is seen to be unaffected by a pollution tax, while the interest rate is a negative function of the pollution tax.

The first-order conditions of the market solution (6.11)–(6.12) are unchanged. But due to the changes in the wage and interest rate, the sectoral allocation of factors is no longer unaffected by a pollution tax:

$$\frac{v}{u} = \frac{\alpha}{1-\alpha}\frac{1-\beta}{\beta}\frac{1-\tau_K}{1-\tau_H}\frac{\alpha\frac{Y}{vK} - \tau_P}{\alpha\frac{Y}{vK}}\frac{1-v}{1-u}, \tag{6.48}$$

where equations (6.13), (6.12), (6.46) and (6.47) have been used.

The alternative pollution specification changes the differential equations, which govern the balanced growth path. Thus, along the balanced growth path equations (6.29)–(6.31) still hold, while the Keynes–Ramsey rule (6.30) of the market economy changes to:

$$g = (1-\tau_K)\left(\alpha\frac{Y}{vK} - \tau_P\right) - \rho. \tag{6.49}$$

In order to determine the growth-rate effects of changes in the tax rates and the parameters, we derive the reduced form of the growth rate by using equations (6.29), (6.48) and (6.49). The implicit function of the reduced form is called Ψ_2:

$$\Psi_2 \; \equiv \; 0 = (1-\beta)B\left(\frac{1-\beta}{\beta}\frac{\alpha}{1-\alpha}\frac{1-\tau_K}{1-\tau_H}\right)^{-\beta} \tag{6.50}$$

$$\left\{\frac{1}{\alpha A}\left[\frac{1}{\alpha A}\left(\frac{g+\rho}{1-\tau_K}+\tau_P\right)\right]^{\frac{\alpha}{1-\alpha}}\left(\frac{g+\rho}{1-\tau_K}\right)\right\}^{-\beta}-\rho-g$$

The effects of parameter and tax rate changes can be derived by using the implicit function rule.[16] The growth rate is negatively affected by taxes on labor income, capital income and pollution, and by the rate of time preference.[17] In this specification again, a consumption tax is a lump-sum tax and therefore does not affect economic growth. Growth is stimulated by increases in the levels of technology in both sectors, A and B. These results are similar to the second row of Table 6.2 in Section 6.3.2.

In the following, the optimal tax rates are found by a comparison of the first-order conditions of the representative agent problem (6.11)–(6.12) and the social planner problem (A.43)–(A.48).[18] This comparison yields the following two equations that must be fulfilled in order to achieve the first-best optimum:

$$(1-\tau_K)\left(\alpha\frac{Y}{vK}-\tau_P\right)\quad\stackrel{!}{=}\quad\alpha\left(\frac{Y}{vK}\right)^{cps}-\left(\frac{Z}{vK}\right)^{cps},\quad(6.51)$$

$$(1-\tau_H)(1-\alpha)\frac{Y}{uH}\quad\stackrel{!}{=}\quad(1-\alpha)\left(\frac{Y}{uH}\right)^{cps}.\quad(6.52)$$

Equation (6.51) can be fulfilled in at least two ways (see Table 6.3). And inspection of equation (6.52) immediately reveals that the optimal labor income tax is zero.

Table 6.3: Optimal tax rates

	τ_H	τ_K	τ_P
Case 1	0	0	$\left(\frac{Z}{vK}\right)^{cps}$
Case 2	0	$\left(\frac{Z}{vK}\right)^{cps}\left[\alpha\left(\frac{Y}{vK}\right)^{cps}\right]^{-1}$	0

---

[16] See Section A.4.1 (page 232) in the appendix for the partial derivatives of Ψ_2.

[17] We cannot sign the growth-rate effect of the capital income tax, but we expect it to be negative.

[18] See Section A.4.2 in the appendix for the first-order conditions of the social planner solution with this pollution specification.

Case 1: A first-best solution can be reached by setting taxes on labor and capital income equal to zero and the pollution tax equal to the optimal marginal damage of pollution. Such a pollution tax corresponds to a Pigouvian tax. *Case 2:* Another way to achieve a first-best solution is to set the labor and pollution tax equal to zero and the capital tax equal to the optimal marginal damage of pollution divided by the optimal marginal product of capital. Since the use of physical capital in final good production is the dirty input factor, the effects of a capital income tax are similar to the effects of a tax on pollution. However the tax-base is different.[19] Therefore, it is necessary to correct the optimal marginal damage of pollution by $[\alpha Y/(vK)]^{-1}$ in order to equate the tax-base differences of the two taxes, when a capital income tax is used. Note that both the pollution and the capital income tax lead to a more labor-intensive and thereby a cleaner final good production. Furthermore, there is a rationale for capital income taxation, when capital is the dirty input factor and the pollution tax instrument is not available.

Comparison of Table 6.1 and Table 6.3 reveals that the optimal labor income tax becomes zero, once human capital becomes a clean input factor in production. The discussion of the small open economy version for the alternative pollution specification is similar to the one in Section 6.3.3 and is therefore ignored.

6.5   Summary of the Results

This chapter has examined the effects of fiscal policy in the generalized Uzawa–Lucas model with pollution, where the tax revenues are used to finance public abatement activities. Again, we investigated two pollution specifications: pollution is generated either by final good production or by using physical capital in final good production. In both cases, the decentralized outcome is inefficient without government intervention. From a welfare perspective there is too much pollution and economic growth is too high in an unregulated market economy, since economic agents

---

[19] A tax on capital is levied on the capital income which consists of the marginal product of capital times the use of physical capital in production $[\alpha Y/(vK)]\, vK$, whereas the tax on pollution is levied solely on the use of physical capital in production vK.

do not take the environmental externality into account. Both factor income taxes and the pollution tax reduce economic growth, whereas a consumption tax is a lump-sum tax.[20] If productive spillovers of a better environmental quality are considered additionally, there may be a stimulating growth effect of a tighter environmental policy depending on the strength of these spillovers. At least productive environmental spillovers partially offset the negative growth effect of providing a better environmental quality.

The results are similar to those of the one-sector linear growth model analysed in Section 3.4: a tighter environmental policy reduces growth and as long as the pollution tax is below the Pigouvian level it increases welfare. So what are the new insights from the present complex model? Concerning the growth-rate effects of taxes on capital income and pollution, in the present model there are two effects at work: both taxes reduce the growth rate directly through a drop in the net of tax interest rate, but stimulate growth indirectly through an increase in the interest rate, because final good production becomes more labor-intensive. However, the direct effect dominates the indirect effect. The linear model on the other hand possesses no indirect tax effects which could soften the direct effect. For that reason the linear model overdraws the tax effects on growth. To give an impression of the indirect tax effect, Svane and Hettich (1998) quantify the growth effect of a pollution tax in both the linear model and the generalized Uzawa–Lucas model. They found that doubling the abatement-output share from 1.6 per cent to 3.2 per cent lowers the output growth rate from 2 per cent to 0.31 per cent in the linear model and from 2 per cent to 1.98 per cent in the generalized Uzawa–Lucas model.[21] Thus the indirect tax effect compensates the direct effect by more than 98 per cent. Hence although the qualitative effects of both models are identical, the quantitative results differ substantially.

If pollution is induced by final good production, it was shown that

---

[20] In a model with identical production processes but augmented by leisure, a consumption tax is growth reducing as well (see Milesi-Ferretti and Roubini 1998b).

[21] The parameters are chosen and the models are calibrated so as to capture stylized empirical facts of industrialized countries, similar to Section 4.3. For both models it is assumed that pollution is generated using physical capital in production.

the government can reach a first-best solution either by setting the pollution tax equal to the optimal marginal damage of pollution or by setting a comprehensive income tax at the same level. Furthermore, a combination of the comprehensive income tax and the pollution tax can be used to reach a first-best solution. Thus a comprehensive income tax is well-founded, when output is responsible for pollution. However, the informational requirements for the government in the case of a comprehensive income tax solution may be much higher in practice. For both tax solutions the government needs estimates of marginal environmental damages. For a comprehensive factor income tax the government additionally needs to know the elasticities of factor inputs with respect to prices, and the elasticity of final output with respect to factor input quantities. Although the pollution tax is equivalent to a tax on output, it does affect the effective capital-labor ratio in final goods production, since education is assumed to be a non-market activity. Furthermore, we have shown that a higher pollution tax erodes the tax bases of both factor income taxes. Nevertheless it increases the government revenue and thereby the abatement-output ratio, which is accompanied by a better environmental quality.

When pollution is caused by the use of physical capital in production, the first-best solution once more can be reached by setting the pollution tax equal to the optimal marginal damage of pollution. However, the negative externality can also be internalized by a capital income tax that equals the optimal marginal damage of pollution divided by the optimal marginal product of capital. The latter correction is necessary to equate the tax-base differences between the capital income tax and the pollution tax. Thus, capital income taxation is well-founded, when capital is a dirty input factor, because it induces firms to use more of the clean input factor in production. However, note that, compared with a pollution tax, the informational requirements for the government are higher in the case of a capital income tax.

By assuming a one-to-one transformation technology between tax revenues and abatement activities, the optimal tax analysis of our model implies that non-lump-sum taxes may be efficient as well when the tax revenue is spent on public abatement activities. However, this result depends on our assumptions. If public abatement measures are not produced with final goods by using a one-to-one technology, income taxes are still able to correct the inefficient input ratio in production but additionally a lump-sum instrument is necessary to guarantee sufficient tax revenues for an efficient provision of public abatement measures. Obviously the same applies for a pollution tax.

In addition to the closed economy, we investigated a small open economy version of the model with international borrowing and lending, and international trade in capital and consumption goods. We found that under a residence-based income tax system that discriminates between domestic and foreign income, a small open economy can conduct an independent first-best environmental policy, where it chooses its own fiscal policy and thereby determines its own growth rate. However, this applies only to national environmental problems, as a small open country by definition has an insignificant influence on global environmental pollution. Furthermore, in order to rule out a permanent inflow or outflow of capital and hence the unstable solution, the tax on foreign capital income is no longer a decision variable of the government. Instead, the government must accommodate any domestic tax-rate change by changing the foreign income tax such that the domestic after-tax interest rate equals the after-tax world interest rate.

Under a source-based tax system, the government is restricted in its tax policy since the latter must be constrained in such a way that the after-tax interest rate equals the world interest rate. However, in order to conduct a first-best environmental policy, the government must be able to determine its interest rate. But there is still room for an independent second-best environmental policy. By means of a lump-sum tax such as the consumption tax or other non-distorting tax-subsidy combinations, the level of the abatement activities and hence the level of pollution can be varied to a certain extent without changing the interest rate. However, an optimal environmental policy requires a more labor-intensive final good production and a reduced growth rate. Hence, should the EU decide to move towards a source-based income tax system, as, for instance, proposed by the Commission of the European Communities (1998), Genser et al. (2000) and Eggert (1999), then a common

EU environmental policy might be necessary, since individual member states can no longer conduct an effective environmental policy.

Chapter 7

Summary and Outlook

The aim of this study was to investigate the interactions between growth, environmental quality and fiscal policy. The neoclassical growth theory is not suited to analysing these interactions as the long-term growth rate is determined exogenously. Starting from recent literature we therefore systematically extended the modern theory of economic growth by embedding the environmental sector, international trade and international spillovers within a coherent modeling framework. In contrast to neoclassical growth models, in all models employed by this study the real rate of capital return does not decline towards zero as the capital stock increases without having to assume an exogenous labor-augmenting technical progress. We analysed different models with increasing complexity but restricted the analysis to endogenous growth models driven by human capital accumulation.[1] This restriction can be justified by the importance of human capital in explaining growth, as many econometric studies show (see Section 2.3.1). Pollution was generated either as a direct side product of economic output or by physical capital used in production, and could be reduced by either private or public abatement activities. We furthermore extended the usual long-term focus by explicitly investigating the short and medium terms by means of a numerical

---

[1] We assumed economies consisting of a large number of identical and competitive firms, and identical, atomistic agents with perfect foresight over an infinite time horizon. Furthermore, human capital was assumed to be a non-market activity and thus not subject to taxation.

207

simulation.

In the following we summarize the results of the respective analyses. While we structured the study mainly according to the increasing complexity of the production technologies, we now proceed by subject: the optimal tax instrument; the growth effects of isolated tax changes; the growth effects of a revenue-neutral environmental tax reform; the small open economy; the effects of cooperation in the presence of international spillovers; and the transitional dynamics. In the outlook we then describe possible routes for further research. Finally we try to answer the questions raised in the introduction and derive policy recommendations.

7.1   Results of the Study

7.1.1   The Optimal Tax Instrument

We found not surprisingly that the decentralized outcome without government intervention is inefficient since there is too much pollution. The government could in principle reach a first-best solution by setting an optimal pollution tax according to the derived tax rules and by setting all other taxes equal to zero. In the case of *private* abatement measures we found that the optimal pollution tax is rising over time because the pollution-causing factor accumulates over time (see Sections 3.4.2 and 5.3.1). Firms increase abatement activities over time only if they have the incentive via an increasing pollution tax. In the case of *public* abatement measures, not only a constant pollution tax but also certain non-environmental tax combinations may yield a first-best solution since there is a degree of freedom which might be attractive. The tax combinations depend on the pollution-causing factor. When pollution is caused directly by final good production, the environmental externality can also be internalized by using a comprehensive income tax (see Section 6.3). On the other hand, when pollution is caused indirectly using physical capital in production, the negative externality can also be internalized by a capital income tax because it induces firms to use more of the clean input factor labor and thus to lower pollution (see Sections 3.4.3, 4.2.2, and 6.4). Thus a comprehensive income tax or a capital income tax are well-founded when output or physical capital is responsible for pollution, respectively.

7.1.2 The Effects of Isolated Tax Changes on Growth

The tax implications on long-term growth for the analysed models are summarized in Table 7.1. The first and the second columns describe the respective chapters and models. The third column represents the effects of taxes on growth in the case where the environment possesses only an amenity value. The fourth column shows how the environmental tax affects growth, *ceteris paribus*, in the case of productive spillovers of a better environment.

We now summarize the effects of isolated tax changes in the different models and start by assuming that the environmental quality affects the well-being of people only through beautiful landscapes or as an essential ingredient of recreational activity and so on (see column 3). We found that taxes affect the long-term economic growth if they affect the real rate of return to physical capital net of tax. Furthermore, it is important to distinguish between their direct and indirect tax effects. The *direct* tax effect always reduces the real return of physical capital net of tax. Hence it is negative and reduces economic growth. The *indirect* tax effect works through factor substitution, and depending on the tax it can be either positive or negative. Due to higher taxes on labor or consumption, final good production may become more capital-intensive, which lowers the real return of physical capital net of tax. Thus for those taxes the indirect tax effect – if existent – is always negative and reduces growth. However, higher taxes on capital income or pollution decrease the capital-labor ratio in production and thus increase the real return of physical capital net of tax. Hence for those taxes the indirect tax effect is positive and works exactly in the opposite direction to the direct effect. Recall that only taxes on capital income and pollution possess a direct effect. Furthermore, the appearance and strength of the indirect effect depend on the specifications of the production technologies and preferences. For instance, due to the absence of factor substitution possibilities, taxes in the linear model cannot possess an indirect effect (see Chapter 3). However, we have seen that the indirect tax effect, effective in more complex models, may alter the result of the direct tax

Table 7.1: Growth effects of fiscal policy – a survey

Ch.	Model	Amenity	Prod. spillover
3	Linear	$\frac{\partial g}{\partial \tau^C} = 0$ (ls) $\frac{\partial g}{\partial \tau^K} < 0$ $\frac{\partial g}{\partial \tau^P} < 0$	$\overset{+}{\frac{\partial g}{\partial A}} \overset{-}{\frac{\partial A}{\partial P}} \overset{-}{\frac{\partial P}{\partial \tau^P}} > 0$ $\frac{\partial g}{\partial \delta} \frac{\partial \delta}{\partial P} \frac{\partial P}{\partial \tau^P} > 0$
4	Uzawa–Lucas	$\frac{\partial g}{\partial \tau^C} = 0$ (ls) $\frac{\partial g}{\partial \tau^H} = 0$ (ls) $\frac{\partial g}{\partial \tau^K} = 0$ $\frac{\partial g}{\partial \tau^P} = 0$	$\frac{\partial g}{\partial A} \frac{\partial A}{\partial P} \frac{\partial P}{\partial \tau^P} = 0$ $\frac{\partial g}{\partial B} \frac{\partial B}{\partial P} \frac{\partial P}{\partial \tau^P} > 0$ $\frac{\partial g}{\partial \delta_K} \frac{\partial \delta_K}{\partial P} \frac{\partial P}{\partial \tau^P} = 0$ $\frac{\partial g}{\partial \delta_H} \frac{\partial \delta_H}{\partial P} \frac{\partial P}{\partial \tau^P} > 0$
5.3	Uzawa–Lucas with l, when $P = f(K/Z)$	$\frac{\partial g}{\partial \tau^C} < 0$ $\frac{\partial g}{\partial \tau^H} < 0$ $\frac{\partial g}{\partial \tau^K} < 0$ $\frac{\partial g}{\partial \tau^P} > 0$	$\frac{\partial g}{\partial A} \frac{\partial A}{\partial P} \frac{\partial P}{\partial \tau^P} = 0$ $\frac{\partial g}{\partial \delta_K} \frac{\partial \delta_K}{\partial P} \frac{\partial P}{\partial \tau^P} < 0$ $\frac{\partial g}{\partial B} \frac{\partial B}{\partial P} \frac{\partial P}{\partial \tau^P} > 0$ $\frac{\partial g}{\partial \delta_H} \frac{\partial \delta_H}{\partial P} \frac{\partial P}{\partial \tau^P} > 0$
5.4	Uzawa–Lucas with l, when $P = f(Y/Z)$	$\frac{\partial g}{\partial \tau^C} < 0$ $\frac{\partial g}{\partial \tau^H} < 0$ $\frac{\partial g}{\partial \tau^K} < 0$ $\frac{\partial g}{\partial \tau^P} = 0$	$\frac{\partial g}{\partial A} \frac{\partial A}{\partial P} \frac{\partial P}{\partial \tau^P} = 0$ $\frac{\partial g}{\partial \delta_K} \frac{\partial \delta_K}{\partial P} \frac{\partial P}{\partial \tau^P} < 0$ $\frac{\partial g}{\partial B} \frac{\partial B}{\partial P} \frac{\partial P}{\partial \tau^P} > 0$ $\frac{\partial g}{\partial \delta_H} \frac{\partial \delta_H}{\partial P} \frac{\partial P}{\partial \tau^P} > 0$
6	gen. Uzawa–Lucas: closed economy smopec (residence)	$\frac{\partial g}{\partial \tau^C} = 0$ (ls) $\frac{\partial g}{\partial \tau^H} < 0$ $\frac{\partial g}{\partial \tau^K} < 0$ $\frac{\partial g}{\partial \tau^P} < 0$	$\frac{\partial g}{\partial A} \frac{\partial A}{\partial P} \frac{\partial P}{\partial \tau^P} > 0$ $\frac{\partial g}{\partial B} \frac{\partial B}{\partial P} \frac{\partial P}{\partial \tau^P} > 0$
6	gen. Uzawa–Lucas smopec (sourced)	$\frac{\partial g}{\partial \tau^C} = 0$ (ls) $\frac{\partial g}{\partial \tau^H} = 0$ $\frac{\partial g}{\partial \tau^K} = 0$ $\frac{\partial g}{\partial \tau^P} = 0$	$\frac{\partial g}{\partial A} \frac{\partial A}{\partial P} \frac{\partial P}{\partial \tau^P} = 0$ $\frac{\partial g}{\partial B} \frac{\partial B}{\partial P} \frac{\partial P}{\partial \tau^P} = 0$

effect.

A *consumption tax* does not affect economic growth and even possesses the properties of a lump-sum tax – indicated by '(ls)' in Table 7.1 – as long as the leisure-work decision is not taken into account. If it is taken into account, a consumption tax lowers growth through its indirect effect. Similarly, a *labor income tax* reduces growth solely by its indirect effect. An exception is the Uzawa–Lucas model (see Chapter 4 row 3 in Table 7.1) where it is a lump-sum tax.

A *capital income tax* always reduces growth *ceteris paribus* through its direct effect. However, the indirect effect works in the opposite direction. In the linear model the overall effect is identical to the direct effect because of missing factor substitution possibilities (see Chapter 3). In the Uzawa–Lucas model with leisure (see Chapter 5) and the generalized Uzawa–Lucas model (see Chapter 6) the direct effect dominates the indirect effect. An exception is again the Uzawa–Lucas model (see Chapter 4) where the direct tax effect is exactly offset by its indirect effect.

A *pollution tax* – as a capital income tax – reduces growth *ceteris paribus* through its direct effect but increases growth by its indirect effect. The strength of the indirect effect depends not only on the production function or preferences, but also on the pollution specification. The overall growth effect is negative in the linear model (see Chapter 3). Independent of the pollution-causing factor in the Uzawa–Lucas model (see Chapter 4), the direct tax effect of the pollution tax is exactly offset by its indirect effect. The same applies to the Uzawa–Lucas model with leisure if pollution is generated by final good production (see Section 5.4). However, in the Uzawa–Lucas model with leisure the pollution tax stimulates growth if pollution is generated by physical capital (see Section 5.3). Thus the indirect tax effect even overcompensates the direct tax effect, and hence boosts growth. The reason is that due to the increased pollution tax firms increase their abatement activities, which reduces final output net of abatement at the expense of households' consumption. Households increase their marginal utility of leisure by substituting leisure through studying time to counteract reduced consumption which finally stimulates growth. As in the linear model the pollution tax reduces growth in the generalized Uzawa–Lucas model (see Chapter 6) independent of the pollution specification. However, quantitative results for the generalized Uzawa–Lucas model show that for plausible parameter values the indirect effect compensates the direct effect by 98 per cent. Hence, the linear model exaggerates the effects of fiscal policy by assuming a fixed ratio of physical to human capital.

In addition to the amenity effect it is sometimes argued that the environment affects the production processes. Improvements in the environmental quality may increase the productivity of the final good sector and/or the studying sector (see column 4 of Table 7.1). In both cases a better environment may increase productivity directly or indirectly via the depreciation rates. The direct productivity effect can be mimicked by increased technology levels of the production and the studying sector (A, B). For example, in the linear model a higher pollution tax reduces pollution $\partial P/\partial \tau^P < 0$, reduced pollution in turn increases the productivity of production $\partial A/\partial P < 0$ which finally stimulates growth $\partial g/\partial A > 0$. The indirect productivity effect can be mimicked analogously by higher human capital and physical capital depreciation rates (δ_H, δ_K). Depending on the model, productive spillovers from a better environment are either growth neutral or growth stimulating.[2]

Whether the growth effect of the environmental tax reported in column 3 dominates the one reported in column 4 – if signs are different – depends on the existence and the strength of the productive environmental spillover. However, the influence of productive spillovers of a better environment is questionable. Positive productivity effects of a better environmental quality are certainly conceivable in specific sectors like agriculture or tourism. Moreover they may become significant in other sectors if pollution exceeds a certain threshold level. However, as long as pollution does not exceed a certain level, there is doubt whether these

---

[2] However, there is one exception: in the Uzawa–Lucas model with leisure a higher physical capital depreciation rate stimulates growth. Due to a higher δ_K, gross investment must rise to maintain the same growth rate for the physical capital stock. This crowds out consumption and makes leisure less scarce, which gives rise to more studying and therefore stimulates growth. Hence, if the physical capital depreciation is a negative function of the level of pollution, a better environmental quality reduces growth via the productive environmental spillover.

have effects on the whole economy.

7.1.3 Growth Effects of a Revenue-neutral Environmental Tax Reform

In Chapter 5 we analysed the growth effects of a revenue-neutral environmental tax reform. It was assumed that the government's task is to provide a public good which must be supplied in a certain proportion to the physical capital stock, implying an exogenously given government budget requirement. If pollution is a function of physical capital and private abatement activities, we found that a revenue-neutral shift from non-environmental taxes to a pollution tax might reap a *double growth dividend*: a higher pollution tax stimulates growth directly (first growth dividend), and by using its revenues for cutting non-environmental taxes an additional positive growth effect arises (second growth dividend). This is because all non-environmental taxes reduce growth, so that lowering any of them yields a positive growth effect (see Table 7.1, rows 4 and 5). If, on the other hand, pollution is a function of output and private abatement activities, the first growth dividend disappears since the pollution tax does not affect growth. Nevertheless, a revenue-neutral environmental tax reform still stimulates growth via the second growth dividend. Thus, irrespective of the initial tax rates and the chosen pollution specification a revenue-neutral environmental tax reform stimulates growth and increases environmental quality but reduces leisure. Hence, whether a double dividend in welfare terms can be reaped depends on the initial tax rates. However, the introduction of a pollution tax increases welfare unambiguously as non-environmental taxes fail to create incentives to conduct private abatement activities.

7.1.4 The Small Open Economy with International Capital Mobility

We found that the growth effects of taxes and the possibilities of conducting an independent environmental policy do not change if we assume a small open economy with perfect international capital mobility rather than a closed economy. However, this is only true under a residence-based income tax system that discriminates between domestic and foreign capital income (see row 6 of Table 7.1). By contrast, under a source-based tax system the after-tax interest rate is determined by the world interest rate and growth is not affected by tax-rate changes (see row 7 of Table 7.1). However, for an efficient environmental policy the interest rate and hence the growth rate must be controllable by the government.

7.1.5 International Knowledge and Pollution Spillovers

In Sections 3.5 and 4.4 we considered international knowledge spillover and international environmental externalities, and analysed the strategic interactions between two identical countries within the framework of a differential game. Starting from the noncooperative open-loop Cournot–Nash equilibrium we investigated the effects of environmental cooperation, knowledge cooperation and full cooperation. In the open economy model with a linear production function the welfare effects of partial cooperations are ambiguous due to the model's inherent trade-off between pollution and growth (see Section 3.5). Our developed model, based on the Uzawa–Lucas production technology, allows a more positive appraisal concerning welfare effects of partial cooperations and environmental protection (see Section 4.4). This is due to the more precisely specified final good production where physical and human capital are used in a substitutive relation.

We showed that *environmental cooperation* improves welfare unambiguously since pollution reduction is possible without harming growth. However, the effects of *knowledge cooperation* depend on the chosen pollution function, that is, whether pollution is a side product of physical capital or of final good production. (i) If output is responsible for pollution we confirm the results of the linear model: knowledge cooperation increases growth at the expense of environmental quality, hence the effects on welfare are ambiguous. (ii) However, if pollution is assumed to be a function of physical capital the pessimistic result changes to a positive one: under this specification knowledge cooperation not only boosts growth but also lowers pollution and increases welfare. With this pollution specification it is possible to reduce pollution for a given level of output and abatement. This additional substitution possibility is responsible for the more optimistic results.

Finally we compare the effects of *full cooperation* for both pollution specifications. The Uzawa–Lucas framework suggests (unlike the linear growth model) that full cooperation increases growth unambiguously independent of the pollution specification. However, whereas environmental quality increases if pollution is generated by physical capital, the effect becomes ambiguous and depends on the relative strength of both spillovers if pollution is generated by output.

7.1.6 Transitional Dynamics

In Section 4.3 we focused on the transitional dynamics of the Uzawa–Lucas model after a change in environmental policy. For that purpose we simulated numerically the adaptation process of the calibrated model. Since the quantitative results depend on the chosen parameter values, we selected the parameters and calibrated the model so as to capture some stylized empirical facts of industrialized countries. We simulated the transitional dynamics for a market economy triggered by an unexpected, or an announced, or a gradual increase of the pollution tax. For all simulations we assumed that the share of abatement activities must double in the long term from 1.6 per cent to 3.2 per cent of GDP, which implies that pollution reduces by 46 per cent. In the market economy this can be reached by increasing the pollution tax from 0.62 per cent to 1.33 per cent. For all scenarios we have seen that welfare is higher in *every* period compared to the business-as-usual scenario.

7.2 Research Agenda

Despite the increasing number of endogenous growth models with environment there are still interesting and important issues that have to be investigated. This is true not only for theoretical but even more for empirical models. There is hardly any econometric study based on an endogenous growth model with environment. Furthermore, as regards the results of this study we can state that for founded policy recommendations – from both a qualitative and a quantitative point of view – there is a need for empirical investigations: for the qualitative results it is important to know which pollution specification describes best the real world in our models (see Section 4.4 and Chapter 5). Furthermore, we should know whether a tighter environmental policy affects the productivity of an aggregate production function (see column 4 of Table 7.1). Finally, for more realistic quantitative results from numerical simulations we should know the size of investment costs, frictions concerning the allocation of time between production and studying, and the share of physical capital in final good production (see Section 4.3).

Starting from our study it would be interesting from a theoretical point of view to model an endogenous leisure-work decision within the generalized Uzawa–Lucas model in order to test the robustness of the results obtained in Chapter 5 with the Uzawa–Lucas model. However, a formal analysis is likely to become intractable, hence a numerical analysis might be necessary. Furthermore, to be more realistic it would be interesting to model both public and private abatement measures at the same time and to derive the optimal tax structure. In general, economic policy institutions or realistic public finance aspects are rarely incorporated into models of endogenous growth. Exceptions are Nielsen et al. (1995), who investigate the interactions between environmental policy and unemployment induced by union monopoly power, and Bovenberg and de Mooij (1997) and Hettich (1998), who explore the impacts of a revenue-neutral environmental tax reform.

Furthermore, the usual long-term focus should be complemented by investigating the transitional dynamics for assessing short- and medium-term effects of policy measures. Note, however, that certain model simplifications which are admissible for the long-run analysis change the adaptation process and hence should be taken into account for realistic reasons. (i) Following the literature we assumed perfect mobility between the education and the final good sector and ignored additional adjustment costs. However, we suppose that the introduction of mobility or investment costs will create welfare losses during the transition periods, and that intergenerational problems in turn may arise. (ii) With respect to several environmental problems (for instance, the ozone shield depletion, global warming, or acidification of the soil) the effects of accumulated pollution rather than flow effects of pollution are important for ecological systems, production and welfare. For example, the ozone-layer depletion will not stop when chlorofluorocarbon emissions and other direct causes[3] are curbed, but only after the stock of accumulated pollution is reduced. As mentioned in Section 2.1, the results along a balanced growth path in our models do not depend on whether pollution is modeled as a flow or as a stock, however, the transitional dynamics do. The introduction of an environmental stock into the framework of the linear model creates transitional dynamics. In more complex models the transitional dynamics of the environmental stock would interfere with the inherent transitional dynamics and would create non-trivial adaptation processes. Furthermore, the transitional dynamics would depend on the initial pollution stock.

So far the literature on endogenous growth and environment has restricted the analysis mainly to closed economies. This seems to be an inadmissible simplification as economic growth and the state of the environment are both influenced by the economic relations and spillovers between countries. Thus one should check the results of the closed economies by assuming open economies and allowing for international spillovers and international trade.

7.3 Policy Recommendations

In this study we have shown that a growing economy can in principle produce a growing number of abatement activities to stabilize environmental pollution. Hence, permanent growth may be compatible with a sustainable natural environment. However, this result hinges on the assumptions on the pollution function and the production of abatement activities: if the latter grow at the same rate as the pollution-generating factor, only a pollution function homogeneous of degree zero or homogeneous with a negative degree guarantees a sustainable development. However, without abatement activities sustainable growth implies a sta-

---

[3] Other main ozone-depleting substances are halons, methyl chloroform, carbon tetrachloride, hydrochlorofluorocarbon and methyl bromide (see OECD 1998, p. 19).

tionary economy. Although the functional form of the pollution function
is exogenously determined in this study, this must not be the case in reality. Giving the right incentives to economic agents, governments may
alter the functional pollution relation indirectly to guarantee a function
homogeneous of degree zero.

In this study we assumed either private or public abatement activities. In reality certainly both types occur. Thus a necessary condition
to achieve sustainable development is to tax pollution, which creates an
incentive to develop and implement private abatement activities. In addition, with rational agents relying on free-riding instead of developing
or purchasing non-rival goods, only the government can provide an efficient level of public abatement technologies, such as, for instance, basic
research.

For public abatement activities we found that not only a pollution
tax but also certain combinations of non-environmental taxes may yield a
first-best solution since there is a degree of freedom. However, using non-
environmental taxes for the internalization of environmental externalities
can be problematic since informational requirements for the pollution tax
versus non-environmental taxes may be asymmetric in practice. Furthermore, conditional on a given abatement effort, pollution was assumed to
be proportional to output or the physical capital stock. In a more disag-
gregated model considering intermediate inputs this proportionality may
not hold and the equivalence would disappear. In a world with perfect
information and no administrative costs, every negative environmental
externality should be taxed. However, because of administrative costs it
might be inefficient to tax every single emission and aggregate tax bases
may be resorted to as second-best instruments.

We found that a tighter environmental policy or a revenue-neutral environmental tax reform does not inevitably reduce economic growth. As
shown in Table 7.1, we found that the effects of environmental policy on
long-term growth depend on the assumptions concerning (i) the factor-
substitution possibilities in production, (ii) the existence of productive
spillovers of a better environment and (iii) the leisure-work decision. In
general all taxes, including the environmental tax, tend to reduce growth.
In the case of taxes on capital income and pollution, additional factor-

substitution possibilities in production mitigate these negative growth effects, whereas productive spillovers of a better environment increase growth, *ceteris paribus*. Depending on its relative strength the latter may even overcompensate the former. Furthermore, under an endogenous leisure-work decision a pollution tax tends to stimulate growth. The last two arguments in particular distinguish a pollution tax from non-environmental taxes.

We can state that there exists a positive relation between the real return to physical capital net of tax and economic growth. Thus governments should be aware that every fiscal policy measure which affects the real return to physical capital net of tax reduces economic growth. It is often argued that effective environmental taxes are bad from a fiscal point of view as they erode their own tax bases. However, we can state that environmental taxes are not only efficient instruments for internalizing environmental externalities but also provide a permanent source of revenue for government expenditure.

The analysis of a small open economy with international trade in capital and consumption goods showed that the prevailing income tax system is responsible for conducting an independent environmental policy. Only under a residence-based income tax system that discriminates between domestic and foreign capital income can a small open economy conduct an independent environmental policy. Hence, should the EU decide to move towards a source-based income tax system, then a common EU environmental policy might be necessary, since individual member states no longer have instruments for an effective national environmental policy.

Environmental protection has not been included as a Community objective in the Treaty of Rome (1957). Despite this absence of an explicit constitutional obligation, the European Commission decided to engage in supranational environmental activities and prepared its first Environmental Action Programme in 1973, which was followed by another four programmes, the last covering the period 1993–2000. Environmental protection became an explicit EU objective through the Single European Act (1987) and the Maastricht Treaty (1992). Article 130r of the amended EC Treaty states the Community's responsibility to preserve and protect the environment and to improve its quality, to protect human health, to ensure prudent and rational utilization of natural resources and to promote measures which help to resolve regional and global environmental problems. Although well over 150 different legally binding acts relating to the protection of the environment had been adopted before 1992, none of them made use of the efficient internalization instrument, the Pigouvian tax. The superiority of such an efficient instrument in comparison with command and control measures is well known in the literature. This study suggests that an efficient instrument like the Pigouvian tax influences economic growth. It seems a likely supposition that this applies much more to command and control measures. Following this line of thought, the EU could grow faster for a given pollution level by imposing pollution taxes instead of using command and control instruments.

National authorities are presently not willing to install a supranational authority vested with the competencies required to internalize global environmental externalities. Therefore we adopted the framework of two economies (for instance Europe and the rest of world) and analysed their strategic interactions in the presence of international knowledge spillovers and international environmental externalities – both are empirically significant. Starting from noncooperation we investigated the effects of environmental cooperation, knowledge cooperation and full cooperation. We argued that because of international patent markets, knowledge spillovers are already internalized to a huge extent. For the output-induced pollution specification we found that among other things the existence of international patent markets is partly responsible for the present environmental degradation. Therefore it is uncertain whether the creation of patent markets in the past – though stimulating growth – increased welfare. However, for the capital-induced pollution specification, internalizing the knowledge spillovers goes hand in hand with a better environmental quality. Hence, whether the creation of international patent markets tends to improve or tends to reduce environmental quality depends on the pollution specification.

By investigating the transitional dynamics triggered by a tighter environmental policy, we found that welfare is higher in every period compared to the business-as-usual scenario as long as the pollution tax is below its Pigouvian level. During the transition process individuals do not suffer from the structural change because the material utility losses arising from the decline in consumption and output are more than offset by the immaterial utility gains from decreased pollution. Hence, from a welfare point of view, not only in the long run but also in the short run there is no reason to refrain from environmental policy making. Although from a welfare point of view it is optimal to increase the pollution tax unexpectedly, we nevertheless recommended a gradual implementation of this tax. This was done as we expect investment costs and other frictions that are not considered in the model to prevail in practice.

Although in public eyes GDP growth is *the* performance indicator of an economy, it is well known that it is an unsatisfactory welfare indicator. Following the results of this study, governments should not strive to maximize economic growth if they are interested in welfare maximization. Feasible growth is determined solely by technology; optimal growth, however, is determined additionally by preferences. In all models, previously analysed optimal growth was not identical to maximal growth. This is obvious if a tighter environmental policy reduces growth. But this is also true if a tighter environmental policy stimulates growth, as in Section 5.3. Although an increase of the pollution tax above its Pigouvian level would still boost growth, it would reduce welfare as leisure would become suboptimally low. Finally, we can state that a tighter environmental policy improves welfare irrespective of whether it affects growth negatively or positively as long as the externality is not fully internalized.

This study has shown that by providing the right incentives for individuals and nations, a sustainable protection of the environment is in accordance with permanent economic growth. Indeed, most EU countries have witnessed in the last twenty years substantial reductions of environmentally harmful emissions such as ozone-depleting substances, sulphur oxide emissions or carbon dioxide emissions (see OECD 1998, part II) without significantly hampering economic growth. Nevertheless developed countries like the United States are still reluctant to reduce carbon dioxide emissions as they are perceived to jeopardize their economic development. The world distribution of energy-related carbon dioxide emissions is unequal, with industrialized countries like the United States, EU countries, Japan and Australia together having 12.48 per cent of the world population, but being responsible for 45.75 per cent of the world CO_2 emissions.[4] Furthermore, many developing countries argue that economic development is possible only with increasing CO_2 emissions as they are currently at a low level. However, in the case of transboundary environmental pollution, sustainable environmental protection requires worldwide actions rather than stabilization or reduction of certain emissions by individual countries. Thus designs of international agreements that guarantee broad participation – possibly including compensation payments and knowledge transfers – are needed to curb environmental degradations.

---

[4] Own calculations; data taken from United Nations (1996, Tables 2, 8 and 20).

Appendix A

Technical Appendix

A.1 The Linear Model with Home Production

In this section we outline the linear model with home production. The production function is given by

$$Y = A(1-l)K, \tag{A.1}$$

where $(1-l)$ is the share of capital devoted to production and l is the share of capital devoted to home production L. The flow resource constraint of the economy (3.2) and the first-order condition of the firm's maximization problem (3.3) are unchanged. The instantaneous utility function now reads

$$U(C,L) = \frac{(CL^{\eta_L})^{1-1/\varepsilon} - 1}{1 - 1/\varepsilon}, \quad \text{for} \quad \varepsilon > 0, \ \varepsilon \neq 1, \tag{A.2}$$

where $L = AlK$ and η_L denotes the weight factor of home production in utility.

Along a balanced growth path the variables C, K and Y grow at the same rate g, whereas l is constant. For simplicity we assume in the following the logarithmic utility function, that is, an intertemporal elasticity of substitution equal to unity. The reduced forms of the growth rate g, the share of capital devoted to home production l and the consumption-capital ratio C/K are then given by

$$g \;=\; (1 - \tau_K)\, A - \delta - \rho, \tag{A.3}$$

$$l \;=\; \frac{\eta_L \left(1 + \tau_C\right) \left(A\tau_K + \rho\right)}{A \left[\eta_L \left(1 + \tau_C\right) + \left(1 - \tau_K\right)\right]}, \tag{A.4}$$

$$\frac{C}{K} \;=\; \frac{\left(1 - \tau_K\right) \left(A\tau_K + \rho\right)}{\eta_L \left(1 + \tau_C\right) + \left(1 - \tau_K\right)}. \tag{A.5}$$

It is seen that the consumption tax affects the share of capital devoted to home production and the consumption-capital ratio but not growth.

A.2 The Uzawa–Lucas Model

A.2.1 Growth Rates Along a Balanced Growth Path

A balanced growth path is characterized as a state where all variables grow at a constant, possibly zero, rate. Therefore, derivatives of growth rates with respect to time are zero along a balanced growth path. From the human capital accumulation constraint (4.3) we see that the growth rate of human capital can only be constant over time for

$$0 = \dot{u}. \tag{A.6}$$

Substituting λ of equation (4.18) into equation (4.19), taking logs and differentiating with respect to time yields

$$\hat{C} = \hat{Z}. \tag{A.7}$$

Rearranging the flow resource constraint of the economy (4.2) gives

$$\hat{K} = \frac{Y}{K} - \frac{C}{K} - \frac{Z}{K} - \delta_K. \tag{A.8}$$

Substituting C/K of equation (4.23) into equation (A.8) gives

$$\hat{K} = \frac{Y}{K} - \left(\frac{1}{\eta_P \chi} + 1\right) \frac{Z}{K} - \delta_K. \tag{A.9}$$

Substituting ratio Z/K and ratio Y/K of equation (A.9) into equation (4.21) and differentiating with respect to time gives, respectively,

$$\hat{K} \;=\; \hat{Y}, \tag{A.10}$$

$$\hat{Z} = \hat{K}. \tag{A.11}$$

Taking logs and differentiating the production function (4.1) and taking conditions (A.6) and (A.10) into consideration yields

$$\hat{H} = \hat{Y}. \tag{A.12}$$

Taking logs and differentiating equations (4.18) and (4.20) and taking conditions (A.6), (A.11) and (A.12) into consideration gives, respectively

$$\hat{C} = -\lambda \varepsilon, \tag{A.13}$$

$$\hat{\lambda} = \hat{\mu}. \tag{A.14}$$

Together, conditions (A.6), (A.7) and (A.10)–(A.14) yield (4.25) in the text.

A.2.2 The First-order Conditions – Discrete

For the purpose of the numerical simulations with the software GAMS-MINOS 5 we reformulate the model analysed in Section 4.2 to a discrete version. The discrete maximization problem for the market solution is given by

$$\max_{C_t, u_t} U_0 = \sum_{t=0}^{T} \left[U\left(C_t, P_t\right)\left(1+\rho\right)^{-1} \right],$$

$$\text{s.t. } K_{t+t} - K_t = (1-\tau_K)\, r_t K_t + T_t - (1+\tau_C)\, C_t - \delta K_t,$$

$$\text{s.t } H_{t+1} - H_t = H_t\left[B\left(1-u_t\right) - \delta_H\right],$$

$$C_t, H_t, K_t \geqslant 0\ \forall t,\ H_0, K_0 \text{ given.}$$

The system of difference equations for the market solution in the case of an additive separable utility function ($\varepsilon = 1$) is given by

$$\frac{C_{t+1}}{C_t} - 1 = \frac{(1-\tau_K)\left[\alpha\left(Y_{t+1}/K_{t+1}\right) - \tau_P\right] - \delta_K - \rho}{1+\rho}, \tag{A.15}$$

$$\frac{C_{t+1}}{C_t} = \frac{1+B-\delta_H}{1+\rho}\left(\frac{K_{t+1}}{K_t}\right)^{\alpha}\left(\frac{H_{t+1}}{H_t}\frac{u_{t+1}}{u_t}\right)^{-\alpha}, \tag{A.16}$$

$$\frac{Z}{K} = \frac{\tau_C C}{K} + [\alpha \tau_K + (1-\alpha)\tau_H]\frac{Y}{K} + (1-\tau_K)\tau_P \quad (\text{A.17})$$

$$\frac{K_{t+1}}{K_t} - 1 = \frac{Y_t}{K_t} - \frac{C_t}{K_t} - \frac{Z_t}{K_t} - \delta_K, \quad\quad (\text{A.18})$$

$$\frac{H_{t+1}}{H_t} - 1 = B(1-u_t) - \delta_H. \quad\quad (\text{A.19})$$

Equation (A.15) represents the Keynes–Ramsey rule for the market solution; it corresponds to the differential equation (4.17). Equation (A.16) is the second Euler equation; it corresponds to the differential equation (4.22) after eliminating the shadow prices by using equations (4.18) and (4.20). Equations (A.17), (A.18) and (A.19) are the discrete versions of the government budget constraint, the resource constraint of the economy and the human capital accumulation constraint, respectively.

The difference equations of the central planner solution in the case of $\varepsilon = 1$ differ from the market solution by

$$\frac{C_{t+1}}{C_t} - 1 = \frac{\alpha(Y_{t+1}/K_{t+1}) - (Z_{t+1}/K_{t+1}) - \delta_K - \rho}{1+\rho}, \quad (\text{A.20})$$

$$Z_t = \eta_P \chi C_t, \quad\quad (\text{A.21})$$

where equations (A.16), (A.18) and (A.19) are unchanged. Equation (A.20) represents the Keynes–Ramsey rule for the central planner solution and equation (A.20) is identical to equation (4.23) and shows that for an optimal solution the marginal utility of consumption and abatement must be equalized.

The reduced forms of the growth rate and the production time for both the market solution and the central planner solution given by, respectively,

$$g = \frac{B - \delta_H - \rho}{1+\rho}, \quad\quad (\text{A.22})$$

$$u = \frac{\rho(1 + B - \delta_H)}{B(1+\rho)}. \quad\quad (\text{A.23})$$

A.3 The Uzawa–Lucas Model with Leisure

A.3.1 Growth Rates Along a Balanced Growth Path

A balanced growth path is characterized as a state where all variables grow at a constant, possibly zero, rate. Therefore, derivatives of growth rates with respect to time are zero along a balanced growth path. From differentiating equations (5.20) and (5.22) with respect to time and taking into account that $(1 = l + u + v)$, it follows that

$$\dot{l} = \dot{u} = \dot{v} = 0. \tag{A.24}$$

Taking logs and derivatives with respect to time from equation (5.17) yields

$$(1 + \chi)\,\hat{Z} - \chi\hat{K} = \hat{C}. \tag{A.25}$$

Inserting C/K from equation (5.17) into equations (5.19) and (5.21) yields, respectively,

$$\hat{C} = \alpha\frac{Y}{K} - \left(\eta_P\chi\frac{C}{K}\right)^{\frac{1}{1+\chi}} - \delta_K - \rho, \tag{A.26}$$

$$\hat{K} = \frac{Y}{K} - \frac{C}{K} - \left(\eta_P\chi\frac{C}{K}\right)^{\frac{1}{1+\chi}} - \delta_K. \tag{A.27}$$

Inserting C/K and Y/K from equation (A.26) into (A.27) and differentiating with respect to time gives, respectively,

$$\hat{K} = \hat{Y}, \tag{A.28}$$

$$\hat{C} = \hat{K}. \tag{A.29}$$

Taking logs and differentiating equation (5.1) and taking equation (A.28) into consideration yields

$$\hat{H} = \hat{Y}. \tag{A.30}$$

Inserting condition (A.29) into (A.25) leads to:

$$\hat{C} = \hat{Z}. \tag{A.31}$$

Together, conditions (A.24) and (A.28)–(A.31) yield (5.23) in the text.

A.3.2   Necessary and Sufficient Conditions for a Balanced Growth Path

This section contains no formal stability analysis. Caballé and Santos (1993) show the stability of a similar model without environment. In the following, we show some necessary and sufficient conditions for a balanced growth path.

The equations (5.25)–(5.27) contain necessary conditions for a balanced growth path since one requirement for its existence is that $g \geqslant 0$. Therefore, for example, it is obvious from equation (5.26) that B must be larger than $\rho + \delta_H$, because total available time is normalized to unity.

In principle, the left-hand diagram of Figure 5.1 can have two points of intersection in the positive quadrant. We rule out the unstable equilibrium where bb cuts aa from above: starting from this point of intersection it pays to reduce growth. Households want higher leisure than feasible and choose the corner solution. To guarantee that there is just one intersection in the positive quadrant where the bb curve cuts the aa curve from below, the right-hand side of equation (5.30) must be larger than the right-hand side of equation (5.31) for $g = 0$. Formally this is the case if the following inequality is fulfilled:

$$B - \delta_H - \rho - \frac{1 + \tau_C}{1 - \tau_H} \frac{\eta_l \rho}{1 - \alpha} \, . \tag{A.32}$$

$$\frac{[1 - \alpha (1 - \tau_K)] \delta_K + \rho + (1 - \alpha)(1 - \tau_K)(\chi \bar{\tau} P)^{\frac{1}{1+x}}}{\delta_K + \rho + (1 - \tau^K)(\chi \bar{\tau} P)^{\frac{1}{1+x}}} \overset{!}{>} 0.$$

Since $B - \delta_H - \rho$ is positive (see equation (5.30)), a sufficiently small η_l is a sufficient condition that inequality (A.32) is fulfilled. The possibility that this inequality is violated increases *ceteris paribus* as $\tau_C, \tau_H, \tau_K, \delta_H, \delta_K$, η_l and ρ become large. On the other hand, a larger B secures the inequality.

In principle, the right-hand diagram of Figure 5.1 can possess two intersections as well. To rule out the unstable intersection where the convex dd cuts the linear cc curve from below, the right-hand side of equation (5.33) must be larger than that of equation (5.34) for $C/Y = 1$. This is the case when the following inequality is fulfilled:

$$\left[B - \delta_H - \rho + \delta_K + (\chi \bar{\tau} P)^{\frac{1}{1+x}} \right] - \frac{1 + \tau_C}{1 - \tau_H} \frac{\eta_l \rho}{1 - \alpha} \overset{!}{>} 0. \tag{A.33}$$

Again since $B > \delta_H + \rho$ (see equation (5.30)), a sufficiently small η_l is a sufficient condition that inequality (A.33) is fulfilled.

A.3.3 Partial Derivatives of the Semi-reduced Forms

The partial derivatives of equation (5.31) are given by[1]

$$\frac{\partial l}{\partial g} = -\frac{\alpha\left(1-\tau_K\right)\left(\rho-\tau_K\Phi_3\right)\Phi_1}{B\Phi_2^2} < 0,$$

$$\frac{\partial^2 l}{\partial g^2} = \frac{\alpha\left(1-\tau^K\right)\left(\rho-\tau_K\Phi_3\right)\Phi_1}{B\Phi_2^3} > 0,$$

$$\frac{\partial l}{\partial \tau_C} = \frac{\Phi_1}{\left(1+\tau_C\right)B}\frac{C}{Y} > 0,$$

$$\frac{\partial l}{\partial \tau_H} = \frac{\Phi_1}{\left(1-\tau_H\right)B}\frac{C}{Y} > 0,$$

$$\frac{\partial l}{\partial \tau_K} = \frac{\alpha\Phi_1\left[\left(g+\delta_K+\Phi_3\right)\left(g+\delta_K+\rho\right)\right]}{B\Phi_2^2} > 0,$$

$$\frac{\partial l}{\partial \bar{\tau}_P} = -\frac{\alpha\left(1-\tau_K\right)\chi\left[\tau_K\left(g+\delta_K\right)+\rho\right]\Phi_1}{\left(1+\chi\right)B\Phi_2^2\Phi_3} < 0,$$

$$\frac{\partial l}{\partial B} = -\frac{\Phi_1}{B^2}\frac{C}{Y} < 0,$$

$$\frac{\partial l}{\partial \eta_l} = \frac{\Phi_1}{\eta_l B}\frac{C}{Y} > 0,$$

$$\frac{\partial l}{\partial \rho} = \left[\frac{1}{\rho}\frac{C}{Y} + \frac{\alpha\left(1-\tau^K\right)\left(g+\delta_K+\Phi_3\right)}{B\Phi_2^2}\right]\frac{B}{B} > 0$$

$$\frac{\partial l}{\partial \delta_K} = -\frac{\alpha\left(1-\tau_K\right)\left(\rho-\tau_K\Phi_3\right)\Phi_1}{B\Phi_2^2} < 0.$$

where the following definitions are used:

$$\frac{C}{Y} = 1-\alpha\left(1-\tau_K\right) + \frac{\alpha\left(1-\tau_K\right)\left(\rho-\tau_K\Phi_3\right)}{\Phi_2} > 0,$$

---

[1]$\rho - \tau_K\Phi_3$ must be positive, see (5.32).

$$\Phi_1 \equiv \frac{1+\tau_C}{1-\tau_H}\frac{\eta_l \rho}{1-\alpha} > 0,$$

$$\Phi_2 \equiv g + \delta_K + \rho + (1-\tau_K)\Phi_3 > 0,$$

$$\Phi_3 \equiv (\chi\bar{\tau}_P)^{1/(1+x)} > 0.$$

The partial derivatives of equation (5.33) are given by

$$\frac{\partial(Y/K)}{\partial(C/Y)} = -\frac{\Phi_1}{\alpha(1-\tau_K)} < 0,$$

$$\frac{\partial(Y/K)}{\partial\tau_C} = \frac{-\Phi_1}{\alpha(1+\tau_C)(1-\tau_K)}\frac{C}{Y} < 0,$$

$$\frac{\partial(Y/K)}{\partial\tau_H} = \frac{-\Phi_1}{\alpha(1-\tau_H)(1-\tau_K)}\frac{C}{Y} < 0,$$

$$\frac{\partial(Y/K)}{\partial\tau_K} = \frac{B-\delta_H+\delta_K-\Phi_1\frac{C}{Y}}{\alpha(1-\tau_K)^2} > 0,$$

$$\frac{\partial(Y/K)}{\partial\bar{\tau}_P} = \frac{\chi}{1+\chi}\frac{1}{\alpha\Phi_3} > 0$$

$$\frac{\partial(Y/K)}{\partial B} = \frac{1}{\alpha(1-\tau_K)} > 0,$$

$$\frac{\partial(Y/K)}{\partial\eta_l} = -\frac{\Phi_1}{\alpha(1-\tau_K)\eta_l}\frac{C}{Y} < 0,$$

$$\frac{\partial(Y/K)}{\partial\rho} = -\frac{\Phi_1}{\alpha(1-\tau_K)\rho}\frac{C}{Y} < 0,$$

$$\frac{\partial(Y/K)}{\partial\delta_H} = -\frac{1}{\alpha(1-\tau_K)} < 0,$$

$$\frac{\partial(Y/K)}{\partial\delta_K} = \frac{1}{\alpha(1-\tau_K)} > 0.$$

The partial derivatives of equation (5.34) are given by (see footnote 1)

$$\frac{\partial(Y/K)}{\partial(C/Y)} = -\frac{\rho-\tau_K\Phi_3}{\left(\frac{C}{Y}\right)^2} < 0,$$

$$\frac{\partial^2 (Y/K)}{\partial (C/Y)^2} = \frac{\rho - \tau_K \Phi_3}{\left(\frac{C}{Y}\right)^3} > 0,$$

$$\frac{\partial (Y/K)}{\partial \tau_K} = \frac{\Phi_3 \left(1 - \frac{C}{Y}\right) + \alpha (\rho - \Phi_3)}{\left[\frac{C}{Y} - 1 + \alpha (1 - \tau_K)\right]^2} > 0,$$

$$\frac{\partial (Y/K)}{\partial \bar{\tau}_P} = \frac{-\tau_K \frac{x}{1+x} \Phi_3^{-1}}{\frac{C}{Y} - 1 + \alpha (1 - \tau_K)} < 0,$$

$$\frac{\partial (Y/K)}{\partial \rho} = \frac{1}{\frac{C}{Y} - 1 + \alpha (1 - \tau_K)} > 0.$$

A.3.4 A Revenue-neutral Tax Reform

The corresponding semi-reduced forms (5.31), (5.34) and the condition (5.32) in the case of the public good are, respectively, given by

$$l = \frac{\Phi_1}{B} \left\{ 1 - \alpha (1 - \tau_K) + \frac{\alpha (1 - \tau_K) \left[\rho - \tau_K \left(\chi \bar{\tau}^P\right)^{\frac{1}{1+x}} - \bar{G}\right]}{g + \delta_K + \rho + (1 - \tau_K) (\chi \bar{\tau}_P)^{\frac{1}{1+x}}} \right\},$$
(A.34)

$$\frac{Y}{K} = \frac{\rho - \tau_K (\chi \bar{\tau}_P)^{\frac{1}{1+x}} - \bar{G}}{(C/Y) - 1 + \alpha (1 - \tau_K)},$$
(A.35)

$$\rho > \tau_K (\chi \bar{\tau}_P)^{1/(1+x)} + \bar{G},$$
(A.36)

where the semi-reduced forms (5.30) and (5.33) are unchanged.

To analyse whether an increase of a certain tax rate *ceteris paribus* increases the government revenue, in (5.36) we replace w, r and $\bar{\tau}_P$ by equations (5.6), (5.7) and (5.8), respectively, to get:

$$\bar{G} = \tau_C \frac{C}{K} + (1 - \alpha) \tau_H \frac{Y}{K} + \tau_K \left[\alpha \frac{Y}{K} - (\chi \bar{\tau}_P)^{\frac{1}{1+x}}\right] + \chi^{-1} (\chi \bar{\tau}_P)^{\frac{x}{1+x}}.$$
(A.37)

The partial derivative $\partial \bar{G}/\partial \tau_K$ is given by

$$\frac{\partial \bar{G}}{\partial \tau_K} = \tau_C \left(\frac{C}{Y} \frac{\partial (Y/K)}{\partial \tau_K} + \frac{\partial (C/Y)}{\partial \tau_K} \frac{Y}{K}\right)$$
(A.38)

$$+ \quad [(1-\alpha)\,\tau_H + \alpha\tau_K]\,\frac{\partial \frac{Y}{K}}{\partial \tau_K} + \alpha\frac{Y}{K} - (\chi\bar{\tau}_P)^{\frac{\chi}{1+\chi}} > 0$$

Using the results of Table 5.1, it can be shown that $\partial\bar{G}/\partial\tau_K > 0$. To show that $\partial\bar{G}/\partial\bar{\tau}_P > 0$ we replace ratio C/K and Y/K by using the resource constraint (5.27) and equation (5.25) to get:

$$\bar{G} = \frac{[1-\alpha\,(1-\tau_K)]\,\tau_C + (1-\alpha)\,\tau_H + \alpha\tau_K}{\alpha\,(1+\tau_C)\,(1-\tau_K)}\,(g + \delta_K)$$
$$+ \frac{[\tau_C + (1-\alpha)\,\tau_H + \alpha\tau_K]}{\alpha\,(1+\tau_C)\,(1-\tau_K)}\,\rho$$
$$+ \left[\frac{(1-\alpha)\,(\tau_C + \tau_H) + \alpha\chi^{-1}}{\alpha\,(1+\tau_C)}\right]\,\Phi_3. \qquad \text{(A.39)}$$

The partial derivative of $\partial\bar{G}/\partial\bar{\tau}_P$ is given by

$$\frac{\partial\bar{G}}{\partial\bar{\tau}_P} = \frac{[1-\alpha\,(1-\tau_K)]\,\tau_C + (1-\alpha)\,\tau^H + \alpha\tau_K}{\alpha\,(1+\tau_C)\,(1-\tau_K)}\,\frac{\partial g}{\partial\bar{\tau}_P}$$
$$+ \frac{(1-\alpha)\,(\tau_C + \tau_H) + \alpha\chi^{-1}}{\alpha\,(1+\tau_C)\,(1+\chi)\,\Phi_3}\chi > 0. \qquad \text{(A.40)}$$

Using the results of Table 5.1, it can be shown that $\partial\bar{G}/\partial\bar{\tau}_P > 0$.

A.4 The Generalized Uzawa–Lucas Model

A.4.1 Partial Derivatives of Ψ

Partial derivatives of the reduced form of the growth rate Ψ:

$$\frac{\partial\Psi}{\partial\tau_H} = -\beta\,(1-\beta)\,B\frac{\left[\frac{1-\beta}{\beta}\frac{\alpha}{(1-\alpha)}\,(1-\tau_K)\right]^{-\beta}}{(1-\tau_H)^{1-\beta}\,\Omega_2^{\beta}} < 0,$$

$$\frac{\partial\Psi}{\partial\tau_P} = -\beta\Omega_1\Omega_2^{-\beta-1}\frac{\alpha}{1-\alpha}\frac{1}{\alpha A}\Omega_3^{\frac{\alpha}{1-\alpha}}\left(1 - \frac{1}{\alpha A}\tau_P\Omega_3^{-1}\right) < 0,$$

$$\frac{\partial\Psi}{\partial A} = \frac{1}{A}\beta\Omega_1\Omega_2^{-\beta-1}\frac{1}{1-\alpha}\Omega_3^{\frac{1}{1-\alpha}}\left(1 - \frac{1}{\alpha A}\tau_P\Omega_3^{-1}\right) > 0, \qquad \text{(A.41)}$$

$$\frac{\partial\Psi}{\partial B} = \frac{1}{B}\Omega_1\Omega_2^{-\beta} > 0,$$

$$\frac{\partial \Psi}{\partial \rho} = \frac{-\beta \Omega_1}{\Omega_2^{1+\beta}} \frac{1}{\alpha A} \frac{1}{1-\tau_K} \frac{1}{1-\alpha} \Omega_3^{\frac{\alpha}{1-\alpha}} \left(1 - \frac{1}{A}\tau_P\Omega_3^{-1}\right) - 1 < 0,$$

$$\frac{\partial \Psi}{\partial g} = \frac{-\beta \Omega_1}{\Omega_2^{1+\beta}} \frac{1}{\alpha A} \frac{1}{1-\tau_K} \frac{1}{1-\alpha} \Omega_3^{\frac{\alpha}{1-\alpha}} \left(1 - \frac{1}{A}\tau_P\Omega_3^{-1}\right) - 1 < 0,$$

where the following definitions are used:

$$\Omega_1 \equiv (1-\beta) B \left[\frac{1-\beta}{\beta} \frac{\alpha}{(1-\alpha)} \frac{(1-\tau_K)}{(1-\tau_H)}\right]^{-\beta} > 0,$$

$$\Omega_2 \equiv \frac{1}{\alpha A} \left[\frac{1}{\alpha A}\left(\frac{g+\rho}{1-\tau_K} + \tau_P\right)\right]^{\frac{\alpha}{1-\alpha}} \left(\frac{g+\rho}{1-\tau_K}\right) > 0, \quad \text{(A.42)}$$

$$\Omega_3 \equiv \frac{1}{\alpha A}\left(\frac{g+\rho}{1-\tau_K} + \tau_P\right) > 0.$$

To show that the term in the brackets of the second and third lines of equation (A.41) is positive we replace Ω_3 by $[(vK)/(uH)]^{\alpha-1}$ (see equation (6.47)). Therefore

$$1 - \frac{1}{\alpha A}\tau_P\Omega_3^{-1} = \frac{1}{\alpha A}\left(\frac{vK}{uH}\right)^{1-\alpha}\left[\alpha A\left(\frac{vK}{uH}\right)^{\alpha-1} - \tau_P\right]$$

$$= \frac{1}{\alpha A}\left(\frac{vK}{uH}\right)^{1-\alpha} r > 0,$$

where a positive interest rate is a necessary condition for the existence of a balanced growth path. Then it is straightforward to see that the term in the brackets in the fifth and sixth lines of equation (A.41) is positive as well:

$$1 - \frac{1}{A}\tau_P\Omega_3^{-1} = \frac{1}{A}\left(\frac{vK}{uH}\right)^{1-\alpha}\left[A\left(\frac{vK}{uH}\right)^{\alpha-1} - \tau_p\right] > 0.$$

A.4.2 First-order Conditions of the Social Planner Solution

When pollution is caused by the use of physical capital in final good production, the first-order conditions of the social planner problem with respect to C, Z, u, v, K and H become:

$$\lambda = \frac{1}{C}, \quad \text{(A.43)}$$

$$\lambda = \chi\eta_P \frac{1}{Z}, \tag{A.44}$$

$$\lambda(1-\alpha)\frac{Y}{uH} = \mu(1-\beta)B\left[\frac{(1-v)K}{(1-u)H}\right]^{\beta}, \tag{A.45}$$

$$\lambda\left(\alpha\frac{Y}{vK} - \frac{Z}{vK}\right) = \mu\beta B\left[\frac{(1-v)K}{(1-u)H}\right]^{\beta-1}, \tag{A.46}$$

$$-\hat{\lambda} = \left(\alpha\frac{Y}{vK} - \frac{Z}{vK}\right) - \rho, \tag{A.47}$$

$$-\hat{\mu} = (1-\beta)B\left[\frac{(1-v)K}{(1-u)H}\right]^{\beta} - \rho. \tag{A.48}$$

It can be see that equations (A.43), (A.44) and (A.48) are identical to equations (6.18), (6.19) and (6.23) and hence independent of the pollution specification.

Bibliography

Aghion, Philippe and Peter Howitt (1998), *Endogenous Growth Theory*, MIT Press, Cambridge, MA.

Alesina, Alberto and Dani Rodrick (1994), 'Distributive politics and economic growth', *Quarterly Journal of Economics* 109, 465–90.

Allais, Maurice (1947), *Economie et intérêt*, Imprimerie Nationale, Paris.

Anderson, Kent P. (1972), 'Optimal growth when the stock of resources is finite and depletable', *Journal of Economic Theory* 4(2), 256–67.

Arrow, Kenneth. J. (1962), 'The economic implications of learning by doing', *Review of Economic Studies* 29, 155–73.

Arrow, Kenneth J. and Mordecai Kurz (1970), *Public Investment, the Rate of Return, and Optimal Fiscal Policy*, Johns Hopkins Press, Baltimore, MD.

Azariadis, Costas (1995), *Intertemporal Macroeconomics*, Blackwell, Oxford, UK et al.

Azariadis, Costas and Allan Drazen (1990), 'Threshold externalities in economic development', *Quarterly Journal of Economics* 105(2), 501–26.

Ballard, Charles L. and Steven G. Medema (1993), 'The marginal efficiency effects of taxes and subsidies in the presence of externalities: a computational general equilibrium approach', *Journal of Public Economics* 52(2), 199–216.

Barrett, Scott (1994), 'Self-enforcing international environmental agreements', *Oxford Economic Papers* 46, 878–94.

Barro, Robert J. (1974), 'Are government bonds net wealth?', *Journal of Political Economy* 82(6), 1095–117.

Barro, Robert J. (1990), 'Government spending in a simple model of endogenous growth', *Journal of Political Economy* 98(5), S103–S125.

Barro, Robert J. (1991), 'Economic growth in a cross section of countries', *Quarterly Journal of Economics* 106(2), 407–43.

Barro, Robert J. and Gary S. Becker (1989), 'Fertility choice in a model of economic growth', *Economica* 57(2), 481–501.

Barro, Robert J. and Jong-Wha Lee (1993), 'International comparisons of educational attainment', *Journal of Monetary Economics* 32(3), 373–410.

Barro, Robert J. and Xavier Sala-i-Martin (1992), 'Public finance in models of economic growth', *Review of Economic Studies* 59(4), 645–61.

Barro, Robert J. and Xavier Sala-i-Martin (1995), *Economic Growth*, Advanced Series in Economics, McGraw-Hill, New York et al.

Baumol, William J. and Edward N. Wolf (1988), 'Productivity growth, convergence, and welfare: reply', *American Economic Review* 78(5), 1155–59.

Beavis, Brian and Ian M. Dobbs (1990), *Optimization and Stability Theory for Economic Analysis*, Cambridge University Press, Cambridge et al.

Becker, Gary S. (1964), *Human Capital*, National Bureau of Economic Research, New York.

Becker, Gary S. (1965), 'A theory of the allocation of time', *Economic Journal* 75, 493–517.

Becker, Gary S. (1993), *Human Capital – A Theoretical and Empirical Analysis with Special Reference to Education*, University of Chicago Press, Chicago.

Becker, Gary S., Kevin M. Murphy and Robert F. Tamura (1990), 'Human capital, fertility, and economic growth', *Journal of Political Economy* 98(5), S12–S37.

Behrman, Jere R. and Mark R. Rosenzweig (1994), 'Caveat emptor: cross-country data on education and the labor force', *Journal of Development Economics* 44(1), 147–71.

Benhabib, Jess and Roberto Perli (1994), 'Uniqueness and indeterminacy: in the dynamics of endogenous growth', *Journal of Economic Theory* 63(1), 113–42.

Benveniste, Lawrence M. (1976), 'Two notes on the Malinvaud condition for efficiency of infinite horizon programs', *Journal of Economic Theory* 12(2), 338–46.

Bergström, Villy (1997), *Government and Growth*, Clarendon, Oxford.

Blanchard, Oliver Jean and Stanley Fischer (1989), *Lectures on Macroeconomics*, MIT Press, Cambridge, MA.

Bovenberg, A. Lans (1997), 'Environmental policy, distortionary labor taxation and employment: pollution taxes and the double dividend', in Carlo Carraro and Domenico Siniscalco, eds, *New Directions in the Economic Theory of the Environment*, Cambridge University Press, Cambridge, chapter 4, pp. 69–104.

Bovenberg, A. Lans and Casper van Ewijk (1997), 'Progressive taxes, equity, and human capital accumulation in an endogenous growth model with overlapping generations', *Journal of Public Economics* 64, 153–79.

Bovenberg, A. Lans and Ruud A. de Mooij (1997), 'Environmental tax reform and endogenous growth', *Journal of Public Economics* 63, 207–37.

Bovenberg, A. Lans and Sjak A. Smulders (1995), 'Environmental quality and pollution-augmenting technical change in a two-sector endogenous growth model', *Journal of Public Economics* 57, 369–91.

Bovenberg, A. Lans and Sjak A. Smulders (1996), 'Transitional impacts of environmental policy in an endogenous growth model', *International Economic Review* 37(4), 861–91.

Brendemoen, Anne and Haakon Vennemo (1994), 'A climate treaty and the Norwegian economy: a CGE assessment', *Energy Journal* 15(1), 77–93.

Bretschger, Lucas (1993), *Neue Wachstumstheorie*, Vol. 3 of *Wf-Dokumentation Wirtschaftskunde*, Gesellschaft zur Förderung der schweizerischen Wirtschaft, Zürich.

Bretschger, Lucas (1998a), 'Nachhaltige Entwicklung der Weltwirtschaft: Ein Nord–Süd Ansatz', *Schweizerische Zeitschrift für Volkswirtschaft und Statistik* 3, 369–90.

Bretschger, Lucas (1998b), 'The sustainability paradigma: a macroeconomic perspective', *Revue Region et Developpement* 7, 1–31.

Bretschger, Lucas and Hannes Egli (2000), 'Sustainability, growth, and the environment in open economies', in Günther Schulze and Heinrich Ursprung, eds, *Globalization and the Environment: a Survey of the Issues*, Oxford University Press, Oxford, chapter 8. Forthcoming.

Brooke, Anthony, David Kendrick and Alexander Meeraus (1992), *GAMS: A User's Guide – Release 2.25*, Scientific Press, San Francisco.

Buiter, Willem H. and Kenneth M. Kletzer (1991), 'Persistent differences in national productivity growth rates with a common technology and free capital mobility: the roles of public debt, capital taxation and policy towards human capital formation', *Journal of the Japanese and International Economy* 5(4), 325–53.

Buiter, Willem H. and Kenneth M. Kletzer (1993), 'Permanent international productivity growth differentials in an integrated global economy', *Scandinavian Journal of Economics* 95(4), 467–93.

Buiter, Willem H. and Kenneth M. Kletzer (1995), 'Capital mobility, fiscal policy, and growth under self-financing of human capital formation', *Canadian Journal of Economics* 18, S163–S194.

Burmeister, Edwin (1980), *Capital Theory and Dynamics*, Cambridge Surveys of Economic Literature, Cambridge University Press, Cambridge et al.

Burmeister, Edwin and A. Rodney Dobell (1970), *Mathematical Theories of Economic Growth*, Macmillan, London.

Caballé, Jordi and Manuel S. Santos (1993), 'On endogenous growth with physical and human capital', *Journal of Political Economy* 101, 1042–67.

Carraro, Carlo and Domenico Siniscalco (1993), 'Strategies for the international protection of the environment', *Journal of Public Economics* 52(3), 309–28.

Cass, David (1965), 'Optimum growth in an aggregative model of capital accumulation', *Review of Economic Studies* 32, 233–40.

Chamley, Christophe (1986), 'Optimal taxation of capital income in general equilibrium with infinite lives', *Econometrica* 54(3), 607–22.

Chamley, Christophe (1993), 'Externalities and dynamics in models of learning by doing', *International Economic Review* 34(3), 583.

Chang, Roberto (1998), 'Political party negotiations, income distribution, and endogenous growth', *Journal of Monetary Economics* 41(2), 227–55.

Chatterjee, Satyajit (1994), 'Transitional dynamics and the distribution of wealth in a neoclassical model', *Journal of Public Economics* 54(1), 97–119.

Chiang, Alpha C. (1992), *Elements of Dynamic Optimization*, McGraw-Hill, New York et al.

Coe, David T. and Elhanan Helpman (1995), 'International R&D spillover', *European Economic Review* 39(5), 859–87.

Commission of the European Communities (1998), *Proposal for a Council Directive to ensure a minimum of effective taxation of savings income in the form of interest payments within the Community*, COM(1998) 295.

Corsetti, Ginacarlo and Nouriel Roubini (1996), *Optimal Government Spending and Taxation in Endogenous Growth Models*, Vol. 5851 of *NBER Working Paper*, National Bureau of Economic Research, Cambridge, MA.

Cukierman, Alex, Zvi Hercowitz and Leonardo Leiderman (1992), *Political Economy, Growth, and Business Cycles*, MIT Press, Cambridge, MA.

d'Arge, Ralph C. (1971), 'Essays on economic growth and environmental quality', *Swedish Journal of Economics* 73(1), 25–41.

Dasgupta, Partha S. and Geoffrey M. Heal (1974), 'The optimal depletion of exhaustible resources', *Review of Economic Studies* (Symposium 1974), 3–28.

Dasgupta, Partha. S. and Geoffrey M. Heal (1979), *Economic Theory and Exhaustible Resources*, Cambridge Economic Handbooks, Nisbet, Welwyn.

Dasgupta, Patha S. and Joseph E. Stiglitz (1981), 'Resource depletion under technological uncertainty', *Economica* 49(1), 85–104.

Davies, James and John Whalley (1991), 'Taxes and capital formation: how important is human capital?', in Douglas B. Bernheim and John B. Shoven, eds, *National Saving and Economic Performance*, A National Bureau of Economic Research Project Report, University of Chicago Press, Chicago and London, pp. 163–97.

De Long, Bradford D. (1988), 'Productivity growth, convergence, and welfare: comment', *American Economic Review* 78(5), 1138–54.

Devereux, Michael B. and David R. Love (1994), 'The effects of factor income taxation in a two sector model of endogenous growth', *Canadian Journal of Economics* 27, 509–36.

Diamond, Peter A. (1965), 'National debt in a neoclassical growth model', *American Economic Review* 55, 1126–50.

Domar, Evsey D. (1946), 'Capital expansion, rate of growth, and employment', *Econometrica* 14(2), 137–47.

Easterly, William and Sergio Rebelo (1993), 'Fiscal policy and economic growth: an empirical investigation', *Journal of Monetary Economics* 32(3), 417–58.

Eggert, Wolfgang (1999), *Nationale Besteuerung und wirtschaftliche Integration*, Dissertation, Universtät Konstanz.

Elbasha, Elamin H. and Terry L. Roe (1996), 'On endogenous growth: the implications of environmental externalities', *Journal of Environmental Economics and Management* 31, 240–68.

Engelbrecht, Hans-Jürgen (1997), 'International R&D spillover, human capital and productivity in OECD countries: an empirical investigation', *European Economic Review* 41(8), 1479–88.

Engen, Eric M. and Jonathan Skinner (1992), *Fiscal Policy and Economic Growth*, Vol. 4223 of *NBER Working Paper*, National Bureau of Economic Research, Cambridge, MA.

Fagerberg, Jan (1994), 'Technology and international differences in growth rates', *Journal of Economic Literature* 32, 1147–75.

Faig, Miguel (1995), 'A simple economy with human capital: transitional dynamics, technology shocks, and fiscal policies', *Journal of Macroeconomics* 17, 421–46.

Feichtinger, Gustav and Richard F. Hartl (1986), *Optimale Kontrolle ökonomischer Prozesse – Anwendungen des Maximumprinzips in den Wirtschaftswissenschaften*, Walter de Gruyter, Berlin et al.

Fischer, Stanley (1991), *Growth, Macroeconomics and Development*, Vol. 3702 of *NBER Working Paper*, National Bureau of Economic Research, Cambridge, MA.

Forster, Bruce A. (1973), 'Optimal capital accumulation in a polluted environment', *Southern Economic Journal* 39, 544–47.

Frenkel, Jacob A. and Assaf Razin (1996), *Fiscal Policies and Growth in the World Economy*, MIT Press, Cambridge, MA.

Frenkel, Jakob A., Assaf Razin and Efraim Sadka (1991), *International Taxation in an Integrated World*, MIT Press, Cambridge, MA.

Gale, David and W.R. Sutherland (1968), 'Analysis of a one good model of economic development', in Georg B. Dantzig and Arthur F. Veinott, eds, *Mathematics of the Decision Sciences*, Vol. 12, American Mathematical Society, Providence, RI, chapter 7, pp. 120–36.

Genser, Bernd, Andreas Haufler, Frank Hettich and Carsten Schmidt (2000), 'International taxation and pollution control: how should priorities be chosen in the European Union's policy agenda', in Hans-Jürgen Vosgerau, ed., *Institutional Arrangements for Global Economic Integration*, Macmillan, London. Forthcoming.

Gradus, Raymond and Sjak A. Smulders (1993), 'The trade-off between environmental care and long-term growth – pollution in three prototype growth models', *Journal of Economics / Zeitschrift für Nationalökonomie* 58(1), 25–51.

Greenwood, Jeremy and Zwi Hercowitz (1991), 'The allocation of capital and time over the business cycle', *Journal of Political Economy* 99, 1188–214.

Grossman, Gene M. and Elhanan Helpman (1991), *Innovation and Growth in the Global Economy*, MIT Press, Cambridge, MA.

Grove, Richard H. (1992), 'Origins of western environmentalism', *Scientific American* 267, 42–7.

Grüner, Hans Peter and Burkhard Heer (1994), 'Taxation of income and wealth in a model of endogenous growth', *Public Finance* 49(3), 359–72.

Gruver, Gene (1976), 'Optimal investment and pollution control in a neoclassical growth context', *Journal of Environmental Economics and Management* 5, 165–77.

Hagen, Everett E. (1942), 'Capital theory in a system with no agents fixed in quantities', *Journal of Political Economy* 50, 837–59.

Hammond, Peter J. and Andrés Rodriguez-Clare (1993), 'On endogenizing long–run growth', *Scandinavian Journal of Economics* 95(4), 391–425.

Harrod, Roy F. (1939), 'An essay in dynamic theory', *Economic Journal* 49(193), 14–33.

Hartwick, John M. and Nancy D. Olewiler (1986), *The Economics of Natural Resource Use*, Harper & Row, New York.

Heckman, James (1976), 'A life-cycle model of earnings, learning, and consumption', *Journal of Political Economy* 84, S11–S44.

Helpman, Elhanan (1992), 'Endogenous macroeconomic growth theory', *European Economic Review* 36(2–3), 237–67.

Hettich, Frank (1995), *The Consequences of Environmental Policy for Economic Growth: A Numerical Simulation of the Transition Path*, Vol. 266 of *Diskussionsbeiträge, Serie II*, Sonderforschungsbereich 178, Universität Konstanz.

Hettich, Frank (1998), 'Growth effects of a revenue-neutral environmental tax reform', *Journal of Economics / Zeitschrift für Nationalökonomie* 67(3), 287–316.

Hettich, Frank and Minna Selene Svane (1998), *Environmental Policy in a Two Sector Endogenous Growth Model*, Vol. 1998-04 of *EPRU Working Paper*, Economic Policy Research Unit, Copenhagen.

Hirshleifer, Jack (1987), 'Disaster and recovery: an historical survey', in Jack Hirshleifer, ed., *Economic Behaviour in Adversity*, Wheatsheaf Books, Brighton, UK, chapter 1, pp. 5–94.

Hoel, Michael (1993), 'Cost-effective and efficient international environmental agreements', *International Challenges* 13(2), 36–46.

Höfert, Andreas (1993), *Neue Wachstumstheorien – Eine Systematik der Hauptströmungen*, Vol. 70, Forschungsgemeinschaft für Nationalökonomie an der Hochschule St. Gallen, St. Gallen.

Huang, Chung-Huang and Deqin Cai (1994), 'Constant-returns endogenous growth with pollution control', *Environmental and Resource Economics* 4, 383–400.

Inada, Ken-Ichi (1963), 'On a two sector model of economic growth: comments and a generalization', *Review of Economic Studies* 30, 119–27.

Jaffe, Adam B, Steven R. Peterson, Paul A. Portney and Robert N. Stavins (1995), 'Environmental regulation and the competitiveness of U.S. manufacturing: what does the evidence tell us?', *Journal of Economic Literature* 33, 132–63.

Jones, Larry E. and Rodolfo E. Manuelli (1990), 'A convex model of equilibrium growth', *Journal of Political Economy* 98(5), 1008–38.

Jones, Larry E. and Rodolfo E. Manuelli (1995), *A Positive Model of Growth and Pollution Controls*, Vol. 5205 of *NBER Working Paper*, National Bureau of Economic Research, Cambridge, MA.

Jones, Larry E. and Rodolfo E. Manuelli (1997), 'The sources of growth', *Journal of Economic Dynamics and Control* 21, 75–114.

Jones, Larry E., Rodolfo E. Manuelli and Peter E. Rossi (1993), 'Optimal taxation in models of endogenous growth', *Journal of Political Economy* 101, 485–517.

Jones, Larry E., Rodolfo E. Manuelli and Peter E. Rossi (1996), 'On the optimal taxation of capital income', *Journal of Economic Theory* 73(1), 93–117.

Jorgenson, Dale W. and Peter J. Wilcoxen (1990), 'Environmental regulation and U.S. economic growth', *RAND Journal of Economics* 21(2), 314–40.

Kaldor, Nicholas (1961), 'Capital accumulation and economic growth', in Friedrich A. Lutz and Douglas C. Hague, eds, *The Theory of Capital*, St. Martin's, New York.

Kaldor, Nicholas and James A. Mirrlees (1962), 'A new model of economic growth', *Review of Economic Studies* 29(3), 174–92.

Keeler, Emmett, Michael Spence and Richard Zeckhauser (1971), 'The optimal control of pollution', *Journal of Economic Theory* 4(1), 19–34.

Kendrick, John W. (1976), *The Formation of Stocks and Total Capital*, Columbia University, New York.

Killinger, Sebastian (2000), *International Environmental Externalities and the Double Dividend*, New Horizons in Environmental Economics, Edward Elgar, Cheltenham. Forthcoming.

King, Robert G., Charles I. Plossner and Sergio T. Rebelo (1988), 'Production, growth and business cycles: I. The basic neoclassical model', *Journal of Monetary Economics* 21, 195–232.

King, Robert G. and Sergio Rebelo (1990), 'Public policy and economic growth: developing neoclassical implications', *Journal of Political Economy* 98(5), S126–S150.

King, Robert G. and Sergio Rebelo (1993), 'Transitional dynamics and economic growth in the neoclassical model', *American Economic Review* 83(4), 908–31.

Klundert, Theo van de and Sjak A. Smulders (1992), 'Reconstructing growth theory: a survey', *De Economist* 144(2), 177–203.

Knight, Frank H. (1935), 'The Ricardian theory of production and distribution', *Canadian Journal of Economics and Political Science* 1, 3–25.

Knight, Frank H. (1944), 'Diminishing return from investment', *Journal of Political Economy* 52, 26–47.

Koopmans, Tjalling C. (1965), 'On the concept of optimal economic growth', in *The Economic Approach to Development Planning*, North-Holland, Amsterdam.

Kormendi, Roger C. and Philip G. Meguire (1985), 'Macroeconomic determinants of growth: cross-country evidence', *Journal of Monetary Economics* 16, 141–63.

Krautkrämer, Jeffrey A. (1985), 'Optimal growth, resource amenities and the preservation of natural environments', *Review of Economic Studies* 52(1), 153–70.

Krelle, Wilhelm (1985), *Theorie des wirtschaftlichen Wachstums*, Springer, Berlin et al.

Kroch, Eugene and Kriss Sjoblom (1986), 'Education and the national wealth of the United States', *Review of Income and Wealth* 32(1), 87–106.

Kverndokk, Snorre (1993), 'Global CO_2 agreements: a cost-effective approach', *Energy Journal* 14(2), 91–112.

Kydland, Finn E. and Edward C. Prescott (1977), 'Rules rather than discretion: the inconsistency of optimal plans', *Journal of Political Economy* 85, 473–91.

Ladrón-de Guevara, Antonio, Salvador Ortigueira and Manuel S. Santos (1997), 'Equilibrium dynamics in two-sector models of endogenous growth', *Journal of Economic Dynamics and Control* 21, 115–43.

Lessat, Vera (1994), *Endogenes Wirtschaftswachstum: Theoretische Modelle und wirtschaftspolitische Implikationen*, Vol. 618, Peter Lang, Frankfurt am Main et al.

Levine, Ross and David Renelt (1992), 'A sensitivity analysis of cross-country growth regressions', *American Economic Review* 82(4), 942–63.

Ligthart, Jenny E. and Frederick van der Ploeg (1994), 'Pollution, the cost of public funds and endogenous growth', *Economics Letters* 46, 339–48.

Lipsey, Richard G. and Kelvin J. Lancaster (1956), 'The general theory of second best', *Review of Economic Studies* 24, 11–32.

Lucas, Robert E. (1988), 'On the mechanics of economic development', *Journal of Monetary Economics* 22, 3–42.

Lucas, Robert E. (1990), 'Supply side economics: an analytical review', *Oxford Economic Papers* 42, 293–316.

Mäler, Karl-Göran (1990), 'International environmental problems', *Oxford Review of Economic Policy* 6(1), 80–108.

Mankiw, N. Gregory, David Romer and David N. Weil (1992), 'A contribution to the empirics of economic growth', *Quarterly Journal of Economics* 107, 407–37.

Margulis, Sergio (1992), *Back-of-the-Envelope Estimates of Environmental Damage Costs in Mexico*, Policy Research Working Paper, World Bank, Washington, DC.

Marsden, Keith (1986), 'Links between taxes and economic growth: some empirical evidence', *Journal of Economic Growth* 4, 3–16.

Meadows, Donellea H., Dennis L. Meadows, Jørgen Randers and William W. Behrens III (1972), *The Limits to Growth – A Report for the Club of Rome's Project on the Predicament of Mankind*, Universe Books, New York.

Mendoza, Enrique G., Gian Maria Milesi-Ferretti and Patrick K. Asea (1997), 'On the ineffectiveness of tax policy in altering long-run growth: Harberger's superneutrality conjecture', *Journal of Public Economics* 66(1), 99–126.

Milesi-Ferretti, Gian Maria and Nouriel Roubini (1994), *Taxation and Endogenous Growth in Open Economies*, Vol. 94/77 of *IMF Working Paper*, International Monetary Fund, Washington, DC.

248   *Economic Growth and Environmental Policy*

Milesi-Ferretti, Gian Maria and Nouriel Roubini (1998a), 'On the taxation of human and physical capital in models of endogeous growth', *Journal of Public Economics* 70(2), 237–54.

Milesi-Ferretti, Gian Maria and Nouriel Roubini (1998b), 'Growth effects of income and consumption taxes', *Journal of Money, Credit and Banking* 30(4), 721–44.

Mulligan, Casey B. and Xavier Sala-i-Martin (1993), 'Transitional dynamics in two-sector models of endogenous growth', *Quarterly Journal of Economics* 108(3), 739–73.

Mulligan, Casey B. and Xavier Sala-i-Martin (1995), *Measuring Aggregate Human Capital*, Vol. 5016 of *NBER Working Paper*, National Bureau of Economic Research, Cambridge, MA.

Mulligan, Casey B. and Xavier Sala-i-Martin (1997), 'A labor-income-based measure of the value of human capital: an application to the states of the United States', *Japan and the World Economy* 9(2), 159–91.

Musu, Ignazio (1990), 'A note on optimal accumulation and the control of environmental quality', *Revista Internationale di Scienze Economiche e Commerciali* 37(3), 193–202.

Nelson, Richard R. (1995), 'Recent evolutionary theorizing about economic change', *Journal of Economic Literature* 33, 48–90.

Neumann, John von (1937), 'Über ein ökonomisches Gleichungssystem und eine Verallgemeinerung des Brouwerschen Fixpunktsatzes', *Ergebnisse eines mathematischen Kolloquiums* 8.

Nielsen, Søren Bo, Lars Haagen Pedersen and Peter Birch Sørensen (1995), 'Environmental policy, pollution, unemployment, and endogenous growth', *International Tax and Public Finance* 2, 185–205.

Organisation for Economic Cooperation and Development (1991), *Taxing Profits in a Global Economy: Domestic and International Issues*, OECD, Paris.

Organisation for Economic Cooperation and Development (1993), *OECD Environmental Data – Compendium 1993*, OECD, Paris.

Organisation for Economic Cooperation and Development (1998), *Environmental Indicators: Towards Sustainable Development*, OECD, Paris.

Osang, Thomas and Alfredo Pereira (1996), 'Import tariffs and growth in a small open economy', *Journal of Public Economics* 60(1), 45–71.

Pearce, David W. and Jeremy J. Warford (1993), *World Without End: Economics, Environment, and Sustainable Development*, Oxford University Press, Oxford et al.

Pecorino, Paul (1993), 'Tax structure and growth in a model with human capital', *Journal of Public Economics* 52, 252–71.

Perotti, Roberto (1992), 'Income distribution, politics, and growth', *American Economic Review* 82(2), 311–16.

Perotti, Roberto (1996), 'Growth, income distribution, and democracy: what the data say', *Journal of Economic Growth* 1(2), 149–87.

Perroni, Carlo (1994), *Endogenous Growth and Tax Reform*, University of Warwick, Warwick, UK.

Perroni, Carlo (1995), *Income Taxation, Environmental Emissions, and Technical Progress*, Vol. 436 of *Warwick Economic Research Paper*, University of Warwick, Warwick, UK.

Persson, Torsten and Guido Tabellini (1992), 'Growth, distribution and politics', *European Economic Review* 36, 593–602.

Persson, Torsten and Guido Tabellini (1994), 'Is inequality harmful for growth?', *American Economic Review* 84(3), 600–21.

Petrakis, Emmanuel and Anastasios Xepapadeas (1996), 'Environmental consciousness and moral hazard in international agreements to protect the environment', *Journal of Public Economics* 60(1), 95–110.

250   *Economic Growth and Environmental Policy*

Pezzey, John (1989), *Economic Analysis of Sustainable Growth and Sustainable Development*, Vol. 15 of *Environmental Department Working Paper*, World Bank, Washington, DC.

Phelps, Edmund S. (1966), 'Models of technical progress and the golden rule of research', *Review of Economic Studies* 33(2), 133–45.

Plosser, Charles I. (1992), 'The search for growth', in Federal Reserve Bank of Kansas City, ed., *Policies for Long-run Economic Growth: A Symposium Sponsored by the Federal Reserve Bank of Kansas City*, Symposium, Federal Reserve Bank of Kansas City, Kansas City, pp. 57–86.

Ramser, Hans Jürgen (1993), 'Grundlagen der 'neuen' Wachstumstheorie', *WiSt – Wirtschaftswissenschaftliches Studium* 3, 17–123.

Ramsey, Frank P. (1928), 'A mathematical theory of saving', *Economic Journal* 38, 543–59.

Razin, Assaf (1972), 'Investment in human capital and economic growth', *Metroeconomica* 24, 1010–116.

Razin, Assaf and Chi-Wa Yuen (1992), *Convergence in Growth Rates: The Role of Capital Mobility and International Taxation*, Vol. 4214 of *NBER Working Paper*, National Bureau of Economic Research, Cambridge, MA.

Razin, Assaf and Chi-Wa Yuen (1996), 'Capital income taxation and long-run growth: new perspectives', *Journal of Public Economics* 59(2), 239–63.

Rebelo, Sergio (1991), 'Long-run policy analysis and long-run growth', *Journal of Political Economy* 99(3), 500–21.

Rebelo, Sergio (1992), 'Growth in open economies', *Carnegie–Rochester Conference Series on Public Policy* 36, 5–46.

Romer, Paul M. (1986), 'Increasing returns and long-run growth', *Journal of Political Economy* 94(5), 1002–37.

Romer, Paul M. (1989), 'Capital accumulation in the theory of long-run growth', in Robert E. Barro, ed., *Modern Business Cycle*, Harvard University Press, Cambridge, MA, chapter 2, pp. 51–127.

Romer, Paul M. (1990), 'Endogenous technical change', *Journal of Political Economy* 98(5), S71–S102.

Rustichini, Aldo and James A. Schmitz (1991), 'Research and imitation in long run growth', *Journal of Monetary Economics* 27, 271–92.

Sala-i-Martin, Xavier (1990a), *Lecture Notes on Economic Growth (I): Introduction to the Literature and Neoclassical Models*, Vol. 3563 of *NBER Working Paper*, National Bureau of Economic Research, Cambridge, MA.

Sala-i-Martin, Xavier (1990b), *Lecture Notes on Economic Growth (II): Five Prototype Models of Endogenous Growth*, Vol. 3564 of *NBER Working Paper*, National Bureau of Economic Research, Cambridge, MA.

Samuelson, Paul (1958), 'An exact consumption-loan model of interest with or without the social contrivance of money', *Journal of Political Economy* 66, 467–82.

Sandler, Todd (1997), *Global Challenges: An Approach to Environmental, Political, and Economic Problems*, Cambridge University Press, Cambridge, UK.

Schmidt, Carsten (1997), *Enforcement and Cost-effectiveness of International Environmental Agreements – The Role of Side Payments*, Vol. 350 of *Diskussionsbeiträge des Sonderforschungsbereich 178, Serie II*, Universität Konstanz.

Schmidt, Carsten (2000), *Designing International Environmental Agreements: Incentive Compatible Strategies for Cost-Effective Cooperation*, New Horizons in Environmental Economics, Edward Elgar, Cheltenham. Forthcoming.

Seierstad, Atle and Knut Sydsæter (1987), *Optimal Control Theory with Economic Applications*, Advanced Textbooks in Economics, North-Holland, Amsterdam.

Shell, Karl (1967), 'A model of incentive activity and capital accumulation', in Karl Shell, ed., *Essays on the Theory of Optimal Economic Growth*, MIT Press, Cambridge, MA, pp. 67–85.

Siebert, Horst, J. Eichberger, R. Gronych and R. Pethig (1980), *Trade and Environment: A Theoretical Enquiry*, Vol. 6 of *Studies in Environmental Science*, North-Holland, Amsterdam et al.

Smulders, Sjak A. (1995), 'Entropy, environment, and endogenous economic growth', *International Tax and Public Finance* 2(2), 319–40.

Smulders, Sjak A. and Raymond Gradus (1996), 'Pollution abatement and long-term growth', *European Journal of Political Economy* 12, 505–32.

Solow, Robert M. (1956), 'A contribution to the theory of economic growth', *Quarterly Journal of Economics* 70(1), 65–94.

Solow, Robert M. (1974), 'Intergenerational equity and exhaustible resources', *Review of Economic Studies* 41, 29–45. Symposium 1974.

Solow, Robert M. (1991), 'New directions in growth theory', in Bernhard Gahlen, Helmut Hesse and Hans Jürgen Ramser, eds, *Wachstumstheorie und Wachstumspolitik: Ein neuer Anlauf*, Vol. 20 of *Schriftenreihe des wirtschaftlichen Seminars Ottobeuren*, J.C.B. Mohr (Paul Siebeck), Tübingen, chapter 1, pp. 3–16.

Solow, Robert M. (1994), 'Perspectives on growth theory', *Journal of Economic Perspectives* 8(1), 45–54.

Solow, Robert M. and Frederic Y. Wan (1976), 'Extraction costs in the theory of exhaustible resources', *Bell Journal of Economics* 7(2), 359–70.

Stiglitz, Joseph E. (1974), 'Growth with exhaustible natural resources: efficient and optimal growth paths', *Review of Economic Studies* 0(Symposium), 123–37.

Stokey, Nancy L. (1991), 'Credible public policy', *Journal of Economic Dynamics and Control* 15, 627–56.

Stokey, Nancy L. and Robert E. Lucas Jr. (1993), *Recursive Methods in Economic Dynamics*, third edn, Harvard University Press, Cambridge, MA et al.

Stokey, Nancy L. and Sergio Rebelo (1995), 'Growth effects of flate-rate taxes', *Journal of Political Economy* 103(3), 519–50.

Summers, Robert and Alan Heston (1991), 'The Penn world table (mark 5): an expanded set of international comparisons, 1950-1988', *Quarterly Journal of Economics* 106(2), 327–68.

Svane, Minna Selene and Frank Hettich (1998), 'Transitional dynamics of environmental policy – a numerical simulation of a two sector endogenous growth model'. October, mimeo Universität Konstanz.

Swan, Trevor W. (1956), 'Economic growth and capital accumulation', *Economic Record* 32, 334–61.

Tahvonen, Olli and Jari Kuuluvainen (1991), 'Optimal growth with renewable resources and pollution', *European Economic Review* 35(2–3), 650–61.

Tahvonen, Olli and Jari Kuuluvainen (1993), 'Economic growth, pollution, and renewable resources', *Journal of Environmental Economics and Management* 24(2), 101–18.

Trostel, Phillip (1993), 'The effect of taxation on human capital', *Journal of Political Economy* 101(2), 327–50.

Turnovsky, Stephen J. (1996), 'Optimal tax, debt, and expenditure policies in a growing economy', *Journal of Public Economics* 60(1), 21–44.

United Nations (1996), *Statistical Yearbook – Forty-first issue*, United Nations, New York.

Uzawa, Hirofumi (1965), 'Optimal technical change in an aggregative model of economic growth', *International Economic Review* 6(1), 18–31.

van der Ploeg, Frederick and Cees Withagen (1991), 'Pollution control and the Ramsey problem', *Environmental and Resource Economics* 1, 215–30.

van der Ploeg, Frederick and Jenny E. Ligthart (1994), 'Sustainable growth and renewable resources in the global economy', in Carlo Carraro, ed., *Trade, Innovation, Environment*, Vol. 2 of *Fondazione Eni Enrico Mattei (FEEM) Series on Economics, Energy and Environment*, Kluwer Academic, Dordrecht, Netherlands, chapter 2.5, pp. 259–80.

van Ewijk, Caspar and Sweder van Wijnbergen (1995), 'Can abatement overcome the conflict between environment and economic growth?', *De Economist* 143(2), 197–216.

van Marrewijk, Charles, Federick van der Ploeg and Jos Verbeek (1993), *Is Growth Bad for the Environment? – Pollution Abatement and Endogenous Growth*, Vol. WPS 1151 of *Policy Research Working Papers Environment*, International Economics Department, World Bank, Washington, DC.

Verspagen, Bart (1992), 'Endogenous innovation in neo-classical growth models: a survey', *Journal of Macroeconomics* 14(4), 631–62.

Weitzman, Martin L. (1994), 'On the environmental discount rate', *Journal of Environmental Economics and Management* 26, 200–209.

World Bank (1992), *World Development Report*, Oxford University Press, Oxford.

World Commission on Environment and Development (WCED) (1987), *Our Common Future*, Oxford University Press, Oxford et al. Brundtland Report.

Xu, Bin (1994), *Tax Policy Implications in Endogenous Growth Models*, Vol. 94/38 of *IMF Working Paper*, International Monetary Fund, Washington, DC.

Zee, Howell H. (1997), 'Endogenous time preference and endogenous growth', *International Economic Journal* 1(2), 1–20.

Index

255

DATE DUE

~~FEB 1 0 2009~~			
			Printed in USA

HIGHSMITH #45230